SECURING AN URBAN RENAISSANCE

Crime, community, and British urban policy

Edited by Rowland Atkinson and Gesa Helms

Books are to b

First published in Great Britain in 2007 by

The Policy Press
University of Bristol
Fourth Floor
Beacon House
Queen's Road
Bristol BS8 1QU
UK

Tel +44 (0)117 331 4054
Fax +44 (0)117 331 4093
e-mail tpp-info@bristol.ac.uk
www.policypress.org.uk

British Library Cataloguing in Publication Data
A catalogue record for this book is available from the British Library.

Library of Congress Cataloging-in-Publication Data
A catalog record for this book has been requested.

ISBN 978 1 86134 814 2 paperback
ISBN 978 1 86134 815 9 hardcover

Cover design by Qube Design Associates, Bristol
Front cover: image kindly supplied by www.alamy.com
Printed and bound in Great Britain by Cromwell Press, Trowbridge

Contents

List of tables and figures

Tables

Figures

Acknowledgements

This edited collection is based on a conference organised by the Department of Urban Studies, University of Glasgow, held in June 2005. The quality of the conference presentations and ensuing discussions formed the backdrop for this book project and we would like to thank all participants and contributors for this. Elizabeth Nicholson, the department's events administrator ensured the professional and smooth running of the event – thank you so much, Elizabeth. The financial contributions from both the *Urban Studies* journal and the Centre for Neighbourhood Research have been much appreciated. Many thanks are also due to Richard Lever for copy-editing the manuscript. Throughout the whole editorial process, Philip de Bary, Laura Greaves and the team at The Policy Press with their professionalism, eye to detail and excellent communication have been a pleasure to work with.

Notes on contributors

Rowland Atkinson (rowland.atkinson@utas.edu.au) is a senior researcher and Director of the Housing and Community Research Unit at the School of Sociology, University of Tasmania. His work has focused on issues of neighbourhood change and patterns of social exclusion and privilege in cities including research on gentrification, gated communities, and defensive homeownership.

Rosie Campbell (rosie.campbell@armistead.nwest.nhs.uk) was a founding member, and is now chair, of the UK Network of Sex Work Projects and works with sex work projects throughout the UK. Rosie has carried out applied policy research and consultation on sex work since 1995. She was part of the research team who carried out the Joseph Rowntree Foundation-funded study *Living and working in areas of street sex work: From conflict to co-existence* (The Policy Press, 2006). She has been involved in the development of good practice guidance for service interventions for sex workers and policy advice to authorities developing policies related to sex work at a local, regional, and national level. With Maggie O'Neill she is co-editor of the book *Sex work now* (Willan Publishing, 2006).

Jon Coaffee (jon.coaffee@manchester.ac.uk) is Lecturer in Spatial Planning at the University of Manchester's School of Environment and Development. In addition to research into urban development and management, notably in relation to regeneration, Jon is also involved in research around defensive and resilient cities and regions in response to urban insecurity.

John Flint (j.f.flint@shu.ac.uk) is a principal research fellow at the Centre for Regional Economic and Social Research, Sheffield Hallam University. Experienced in conducting research in the areas of housing, regeneration, anti-social behaviour, and urban governance, his research interests include housing policy, housing management, crime and anti-social behaviour, neighbourhood renewal, and community cohesion.

Lynn Hancock (l.hancock@liverpool.ac.uk), Lecturer in Sociology at Liverpool University's School of Sociology and Social Policy, has researched widely on the interconnections between criminology, sociology, and urban studies, most notably in relation to urban regeneration, housing and community responses to crime and disorder.

Gesa Helms (g.helms@lbss.gla.ac.uk) is a research fellow at the Department of Urban Studies, University of Glasgow. Her research interests lie in the political economies of urban restructuring, in particular urban governance, economic regeneration, labour markets and social inclusion policies in old-industrial regions, as well as in social regulation, policing, and surveillance.

Joe Hermer is Assistant Professor at the Department of Sociology, University of Toronto.

Phil Hubbard (p.j.hubbard@lboro.ac.uk) is a professor in urban social geography at the Geography Department of Loughborough University. His recent publication, *City: Key ideas in geography* (Routledge, 2006) exemplifies his interest on the socio-spatial transitions in western cities, and more specifically questions of urban governance and politics, consumption, and sexuality.

Charlie Johnston (charles.johnston@paisley.ac.uk) is Lecturer in Sociology in the School of Social Sciences, University of Paisley. He has written widely in the areas of urban policy and the sociology of the city.

Craig Johnstone (r.c.johnstone@brighton.ac.uk) is a senior lecturer in criminology at the University of Brighton. His research interests include public policy and the city, especially the intersection of urban and criminal justice policies as well as strategies to secure liveability and improve 'quality of life' in deprived communities.

David MacGregor (mcgregor@uwo.ca) is chair at the Department of Sociology, King's University College at the University of Western Ontario.

Gordon MacLeod (gordon.macleod@durham.ac.uk) is Reader in the Department of Geography, University of Durham. Besides his interests in the new regionalism and changing forms of urban governance in a devolved UK, Gordon's work focuses on struggles over public space and geographies of exclusion.

Andrew Millie (a.e.millie@lboro.ac.uk) is a lecturer in criminology and social policy in the Department of Social Sciences, Loughborough University. His research interests include anti-social behaviour, crime and the city, policing, crime prevention, and sentencing.

Gerry Mooney (g.c.mooney@open.ac.uk) is Senior Lecturer in Social Policy and Staff Tutor, Faculty of Social Sciences, The Open University. He is co-editor of *Exploring social policy in the 'new' Scotland* (The Policy Press, 2005), co-editor of *New Labour/hard labour? Restructuring and resistance inside the welfare industry* (The Policy Press, 2007), and has published widely on different aspects of New Labour's urban and social policies.

David Murakami Wood (d.f.j.wood@ncl.ac.uk) is a lecturer in the School of Architecture, Planning and Landscape at Newcastle University of with research interests in studies of surveillance in urban spaces. He is also the co-founder and Managing Editor of *Surveillance & Society*, a major new international e-journal of surveillance studies.

Maggie O'Neill (m.oneill@lboro.ac.uk) is Senior Lecturer in Criminology and Social Policy in the Department of Social Sciences at Loughborough University. Experienced in ethnography, participatory action research, and visual methodologies, she has published extensively on street sex work, communities affected by prostitution, feminisms and prostitution, forced migration, and cultural criminology.

Caroline Paskell (c.a.paskell@lse.ac.uk) is an associate of the Centre for Analysis of Social Exclusion at the London School of Economics and Political Science, where she has recently completed a large-scale longitudinal study on social deprivation in British urban neighbourhoods.

Jane Pitcher (jepitcher@btinternet.com) is an independent social researcher, affiliated to Staffordshire and Aston Universities and other research organisations. She has been undertaking research for the past 20 years into social exclusion, including research concerning regeneration programmes, disadvantaged young people, and women sex workers.

Mike Raco (mike.raco@kcl.ac.uk) is a senior lecturer in human geography at King's College London. His research centres on the nature of urban governance, processes of community formation and on the sustainable communities agenda, with his recent publication on *Building sustainable communities: Spatial policy and labour mobility in post-war Britain* (The Policy Press, 2006).

Jane Scoular (jane.scoular@strath.ac.uk) is a senior lecturer at the Law School, University of Strathclyde. Her research is concerned with the intersection of theories of gender and law. Recent publications and empirical studies focus on the subjects of informal justice, domestic violence, and prostitution.

Gavin J.D. Smith (g.j.d.smith@abdn.ac.uk) is currently finishing his ESRC-funded PhD at the School of Social Sciences, University of Aberdeen. His ethnographic study delves into the working practices of CCTV operators in an extensive array of monitoring facilities, detailing how such agents are located within wider socio-cultural surveillance networks and political economies of spatial control.

Hannah Smithson (h.smithson@hud.ac.uk) is a senior research fellow at the Applied Criminology Centre, University of Huddersfield. Her main research interests are developmental criminology, early intervention programmes, youth offending, youth justice, and young people and anti-social behaviour.

Kevin Stenson (k.stenson@mdx.ac.uk) is Professor of Criminology at Middlesex University and also Co-Director of the Crime and Conflict Research Centre. He has widely researched and published on the politics and governance of crime, community safety, crime prevention, and policing.

ONE

Introduction

Rowland Atkinson and Gesa Helms

> Over the past few decades many of our urban areas
> have suffered neglect and decline with an exodus from
> inner cities, driven by a lack of confidence in schools,
> fear of crime, an unhealthy environment, and poor
> housing.... One of the key political challenges of the
> new Century is to make Britain's towns and cities not
> just fit to live in, but thriving centres of human activity.
> (John Prescott, Foreword, in Urban Task Force, 1999)

For many commentators concerned with the future of British cities,
the period since New Labour's victory in the 1997 General Election
has been a dynamic one (Amin, Massey, & Thrift, 2000; Imrie & Raco,
2003). The new administration set about addressing the continuing
problems of urban Britain: pockets of high unemployment, poor and
obsolete housing, low educational achievement, and the ongoing
task of urban regeneration, under the banner of urban renewal, or,
in its visionary form, an *urban renaissance* (Urban Task Force, 1999).
Throughout this agenda there has been a particular focus on Britain's
older and de-industrialised city-regions, with significant energy
devoted to commitments to social justice and achieving greater social
inclusion (Levitas, 1998; SEU, 2000a). Nevertheless, social policy
commentators (eg, Fooks & Pantazis, 1999) have identified what they
see as the 'criminalisation' of social policy initiatives, in the sense that
policies devoted to social problems have come to operate in punitive
ways that criminalise targeted recipients, such as the street homeless,
beggars, and the unemployed.

One of our core contentions in this volume is that criminal justice
and policing systems have extended their remit and relevance to
urban policy and regeneration initiatives through what Coleman,
Tombs, and Whyte (2005) and Simon (1997) have called a process
of 'governing through crime'. In other words, urban regeneration
programmes operating in British cities have come to resemble a broader

criminalisation running through social and other policy interventions. By this we mean that the agenda of urban renewal has come not only to be expressed through the physical and social revitalisation of our towns and cities but also via strongly linked attempts to reduce disorder and combat crime. Delivering community safety, to take one key example, now appears to have as much in common with efforts to sustain and rebuild communities and urban economies as it does as an end of policing in its own right. On the one hand this has demonstrated the expansion and interconnection of policy agendas under New Labour, yet it is also suggestive of a tension within these interventions. The places and communities singled out for the promotion of self-help under these initiatives are, perhaps as often, seen as problem areas containing intractable forms of criminality and apathy – these communities are curiously both the potential saviour and problem under the kind of policy diagnosis revealed in the urban renewal and policing agendas. It is to this particular tension and to the meshing of criminal and urban policy agendas that this volume is devoted.

The interlinking of 'crime' and the 'city' is not a new concern, yet a renewed emphasis on the connections between these fields of public administration and governance has developed to the point where commonsense understandings of how to deal with the renewal of deprived areas, the security of iconic spaces, and broader city economies have become almost synonymous with an agenda of law and order, anti-social behaviour, and incivility. Such an agenda has been moulded by New Labour's concerns to produce a society with a strong moral basis and social cohesion wherein individual and communal responsibilities are emphasised (Raco & Imrie, 2000; Matthews & Pitts, 2001). There is little doubt that this has been a broad and ambitious agenda and it is therefore surprising that little work has tackled the specific interconnections of criminal justice, policing, and urban social and physical change to date (initial work in this area can be found in Hancock, 2001; Coleman, 2004a; Helms, forthcoming). Nevertheless, there has been a tendency for researchers to examine policy specific to urban areas, neighbourhoods, social policy transformations, employability, and to crime, yet rarely to see these domains as intrinsically linked. In short, urban policy has been deeply inflected by a need to engage with confidence-boosting techniques that require the management of crime and disorder, as an essential prerequisite to securing an urban renaissance. Focusing on this crossroads of complex policy development, civic renewal, and British urbanism provides this volume's distinctive contribution to ongoing debates and critiques of the broader New Labour project. The central purpose of this volume, then, has been to gather contributions that help us to understand how it is that this integration of the criminal justice agenda into a vision of British urbanism has come about under the banner of an urban renaissance and what its effects have been – in theory, policy and practice.

New Labour's urban agenda has generated a newfound dynamism in the debate about the future of British cities. However, this enthusiasm has also delivered a bewildering array of initiatives, programmes, pathfinders, and policies devoted to such regeneration and which included a broadened set of key actors and institutions at state, local authority, and regional levels (Whitehead & Johnstone, 2001; Imrie & Raco, 2003). Indeed, and with similarities to other policy fields, this proliferation has made it difficult for analysts to track and evaluate the quality, impact, and substance of initiatives – even more so because a considerable number of initiatives end up being wound down or restructured before they are completed. To this end it has also become, perhaps, more difficult to track responsibility for policy failure. In the communitarian agenda of the New Labour administration, the extending renewal agenda has also brought resident citizens more firmly into the policy frame through, for example, multiagency partnerships focused on policing, community safety, regeneration, and political participation. On one level this has empowered residents looking to tackle local problems themselves, but it has also obligated them to become a part of strategies that have no place in more affluent and untroubled neighbourhoods. Such 'responsibilisation' strategies have generated significant concern for writers like Flint (2006) and Crawford (2006), in particular since the crime and disorder agenda is both targeting deprived contexts as well as writing in residents as the authors of their own problems and solutions.

The contributions to this volume represent a broadened and bold academic engagement with the contemporary British policy context of urban renewal, crime, disorder, and policing. Our reason for organising the meeting that led to this book was that, in our observations of how criminal, legal, social, economic, and urban policies were developing, these could no longer be seen as discrete fields for analysis. The blending of these agendas became more particularly evident as the rubric of Blairite social and political renewal turned to the question of how to tackle anti-social behaviour and disorder. It was at this time that the spaces where such problems were seen to proliferate became conflated with impressions of concentrated deprivation and social renting. When combined, these two programmes generated a political project that sought authority and political legitimacy generated by a familiar turn to matters of crime and disorder in second and third-term government, itself amplified by wider international events. As the contributions to this volume illustrate, these issues deserve multidisciplinary analysis and interrogation about the terms on which this kind of urban revitalisation in the UK is taking place. Commentators speaking from criminological, sociological, geographical, urban policy, and social policy backgrounds examine here the diverse ways in which this brand of policy is impacting on communities and cities, where a commitment to social justice – as defined through the social inclusion agenda – has increasingly become expressed as being tough (and tougher still) on crime.

The 'rebirth' of British cities

The improvement of the urban fabric, public health, and housing has been a significant concern of central government at least since the late 19th century, with these efforts becoming more systematic after the Second World War (Hall, 1992). Since that time the planning and delivery of better housing and improved living conditions more generally formed significant strands of government policy, reflecting the often abysmally poor conditions in which large parts of the urban population lived. Privatisation and other neoliberal initiatives sought to 'roll back' the existing postwar welfare state (Jessop, 1995; Peck & Tickell, 2002). More widely, throughout the 1980s and 1990s the Thatcher and Major governments delivered new modalities for, and models of, public policy delivery through their emphasis on entrepreneurialism and partnership working and set against a social and economic background dominated by deindustrialisation. With the paring-back of the welfare state, the full brunt of these changes were generally borne by working-class communities where people not only lost their jobs but also became reliant on a social welfare net to support them, which was itself being rationalised. To force through the restructuring of the country's economic base, the Conservative Party embarked on a series of initiatives to promote inward investment and with it an urban renewal, such as through Urban Development Corporations (UDCs). With this curtailing of local state power the central state expanded notably through the establishment of a criminal justice system dominated by a concern for law and order and for property investment as the hallmark of broader urban transformation, rather than for a deeper boost to the social and economic lives of city residents. For analysts of Thatcherism (eg, Gamble, 1988), urban regeneration in particular was one area that appeared to contradict the ideological war cry of 'rolling back the state'. Here, in fact, state expenditure and intervention increased significantly, along with rising incarceration rates and more punitive interventions against minorities and young people, to say nothing of the break-up of the Miners' Strike in 1984.

Urban policy, in a more narrow sense, also started to take up concerns over security and safety, notably through attempts to prevent crime through architectural alterations aimed at 'designing out' crime and through Home Office initiatives (Clarke & Mayhew, 1980), but also later on through the implementation of the Single Regeneration Budget (SRB), introduced in 1994. Yet, the larger problem of Britain's inner cities stayed throughout the Conservative administration, largely because any ameliorative actions to tackle poverty and unemployment were dramatically undermined by policies in other areas of welfare and economic restructuring that saw massive unemployment and heightened fatalism in many places already suffering from the effects of deindustrialisation then compounded by deregulation laws enacted by the Thatcher government. An era of urban unrest, particularly in cities like Bristol and London, generated concerns about the links between poverty and the exclusion of minority groups from the burgeoning, yet socially highly selective, opportunities that accrued during the financial deregulation of the late 1980s.

Criticism in enquiries, like that of Scarman (1981), considered these explanations as well as the heavy-handedness of policing in areas of social and economic disadvantage, and became instrumental in the establishment of community policing. Yet, twenty years, on in 2001, English cities saw another round of inner-city rioting as primarily young urban Asian males rioted under similar circumstances. Here, as in many earlier urban 'riots', the cause for the disturbance was found in a 'parallel culture', a lack of inter-ethnic community cohesion, and a little publicised neo-fascist element that had issued racialised threats to minority ethnic groups. And as with earlier urban 'riots', the policing and punishment of the rioters – many young and first-time offenders – was harsh (Allan, 2003). These more recent events cast doubt not only over the extent to which community policing had achieved its aims (see Herbert, 2006), but also over the extent to which the current urban regeneration agenda was able to address these issues.

In the beginning of New Labour's urban policy an early move of the new government had been the formation of the largely independent fact-finding group, the Urban Task Force, headed by the architect Lord Rogers, as well as of the Social Exclusion Unit, located within the Prime Minister's Strategy Unit. The foundation of these key groups led to the subsequent urban White Paper (OPDM, 2000) while innovation in various areas like education, health, and employment were connected to strongly spatialised understandings of social problems in order to deliver what became known as 'joined-up' thinking and solutions, and centred on the conditions of British towns and cities. Such reorganisation of government, in partnership with other statutory and voluntary organisation as well as the much-coveted private sector, set out to achieve the prospect that "urban neighbourhoods should be attractive places to live" (Urban Task Force, 1999, p 3). This was to be achieved by improving design quality, with a focus on relatively high-density development so as to limit further urban sprawl, and with mixed-use developments and better transport and services. These aspirations were also seen as potential contributors to a strong sense of community and public safety, a concern we will return to shortly.

With the formulation of the urban White Paper, Labour established not only a vision for the future of urban Britain, but also a way forward for how this was to be achieved. A stronger market orientation and lower community engagement strategy would be adopted as a key means for its delivery. Following this, housing market renewal (HMR) areas in the North of England were declared as part of the broader 'sustainable communities' plan (ODPM, 2005a; also see Raco, Chapter Three, this volume). These plans represented attempts to deliver housing supply in line with regional demand structures, but they could also be read as heavily top-down approaches to planning, without the participation of local residents or local authorities. This new paternalism in regeneration plans aroused earlier fears that the original plans for renaissance were more a revised version of gentrification than a recipe for socially inclusive renewal (Lees, 2003a). These outcomes were also suggestive of a facilitation of insulated living for affluent households in city cores (Atkinson, 2006), as well as of continuing suburbanisation (Champion & Fisher, 2004), both of which undermined publicly espoused visions for socially diverse and 'included' communities, to say nothing of broader attempts to prevent urban sprawl.

It is also in this fully-fledged formulation of the renaissance agenda that we see the emergence of a stronger emphasis on crime and disorder. As part of the government's attempts to 'join up' previously discrete policy fields there was a gathering together of different policies as urban policy became more visible and vied with education and health as a key area for policy initiative and Treasury funding. Not only that but urban policy was seen as delivering on some of the preconditions that might themselves improve outcomes in those other policy domains. New Labour's promotion and front-lining of concerns over social inclusion marked a gear change in contrast to the previous Conservative government, and brought with it an optimism around dealing with intractable social problems and a sense of fairness and social equity. However, not only have these issues seemed more like short-lived fads in a constantly self re-inventing government, but so have these significant investments in cities also appeared to become inextricably, and problematically, linked to questions of security, safety, and a new social order more generally. In fact, the project of a British urban renaissance bears the signs of a number of tensions and contradictions. These tensions specifically relate to a linking of crime and social control to the life and revitalisation of the city in the shape of a paternalistic communitarianism within the wider context of a neoliberalisation of the city and its social fabric.

These tensions were evident in the differing emphases of the design and planning-led renaissance envisaged by Rogers (DETR, 1999a) and in the agenda of social equity and reduction of neighbourhood disadvantage that emerged from the Social Exclusion Unit's series of Policy Action Team reports. Not only were these differences strongly evident but their respective plans were scaled and targeted in different ways. While the renaissance agenda was generally focused on cities and the design of their interstitial public spaces and centres, the social exclusion agenda looked more towards residential neighbourhoods. Neighbourhoods subsequently became a primary scale of intervention and point of policy delivery for interventions tackling a range of social problems including schooling, employment, enterprise, truancy, area renewal, and health and now, more emphatically, a crime and disorder agenda.

All of this brings us to another key point relating to the conflict that appeared to lie within the renaissance agenda and that can be traced to the stark difference in the evidence base of these two programmes. On the one hand Lord Rogers and his Urban Task Force drew heavily on Southern European cities and the vitality of public spaces and quality of design, a kind of 'Barcelona turn' in urban policy making. Meanwhile the Social Exclusion Unit, on the other hand, looked more widely to North America and Europe and within the UK at existing best practice and policy innovation. This meant that there was no single 'front' in the assault on British city renewal but a more discursive, contested and, at times, not fully coordinated or overlapping approach. This may help to explain the growing consensus that emerged around crime and disorder that helped to focus attention and coordinate efforts during the second wave of the urban renaissance and to which we will now turn in more detail.

Safety, security, and urban regeneration

Surveying current debates of British urban policy points not only towards an increasing entanglement of social policy and urban agendas, but also to what we have already described as a criminalisation of urban policy. In contrast with changes over the past thirty years within crime control, its practices and theories, different authors (Garland, 2001; Hughes & Edwards, 2002) have conceptualised these changes as a paradigmatic shift. This has seen the increasing abandonment of rehabilitative models of crime control and punishment in favour of a new body of techniques and controls by which crime should be prevented. With the emphasis on situationist understandings of crime, the need to understand causes of crime has become less important while the knowledge of how to prevent the incidence of crime (its environment, the motivation of the offender, the vulnerability of the potential victim, etc) has become the key focus of crime prevention tools and policies. A situational approach to crime prevention has proved to be highly sympathetic to the aims and objectives of urban regeneration, since it was a focus on design and security aspects of crime control that first entered the consciousness of urban planners and practitioners. Defensible space and crime prevention through environmental design (Clarke & Mayhew, 1980) had surfaced in the planning debates of the 1970s, notably in relation to concerns of crime control in the recently built large-scale housing schemes in British inner cities and peripheral locations.

Yet there is another, even more forcefully argued strand within concerns for safety – or more accurately, security – that have entered public consciousness and debate. With the attacks on the World Trade Centre in 2001 and the state of permanent emergency and international war declared by the US administration, notions of fear, crime, and panic have become firmly embedded within concerns of urban security more broadly. At the same time, however, it is important not to forget that security – defined as homeland (as in the US) or the 'inner' (as in German) security – has long been connected to concerns over one country's terrorist threats, such as the IRA in the UK, ETA in the Basque Country and Spain, or RAF in West Germany in 1970s. However, international terror has most recently been experienced as a growing set of anxieties about minority ethnic groups and security threats in British cities, particularly following the home-grown terrorism experienced in London in 2005. This again highlighted concerns about the social cohesion and integration of minority ethnic groups that echoed the earlier analyses of disturbances in British cities. In this volume Murakami-Wood and Coaffee's (Chapter Six) contribution on the 'lockdown' of central cities in relation to fears around such threats appears timely. In all of this it seems more clear that the domestic buttressing of security is indistinguishable from military and international agendas on organised crime and terrorism (Haubirch, 2006), which make this sense of an integrated assault on crime from multiple faces of government more apparent.

New Labour has been clear in its pursuit of a political philosophy linking communitarian values of community cohesion, moral decency and respect. Such a vision has informed British policy since the late 1990s. With the 1998 Crime and Disorder Act being one of its first major legislative projects, it introduced, with the Anti-Social Behaviour Order (ASBO), a previously unprecedented legal construction to pursue undesirable behaviour that might induce feelings of alarm, fear, or harassment. In so doing, New Labour has continued, as Gilling (2001) observes, to pursue community safety using strong communitarian themes and founded on a "civic intolerance of incivility" (p 391). He, alongside Hughes and McLaughlin (2002) in their discussion of the origins of partnership working, sees this organisation of criminal justice policies as congruent with Conservative views of Home Office politics, favouring prevention and risk-based exclusion of social integration models.

Community safety has become a key service function of local authorities and a policy field in its own right at local level with the establishment of a range of organisations designed to tackle crime, disorder, anti-social behaviour, and 'liveability'. Through new institutional arrangements a new emphasis on security and community safety has become embedded in the governance practices of many neighbourhoods by co-opting new agents, like neighbourhood wardens, as well as new institutions, such as registered social landlords. In practice this has proliferated the governance of crime and disorder with multiple new groups and actors now involved to some degree in the management of conduct and social disorder. In particular it has also meant setting up new partnerships between government, the local state, quasi-public agencies (such as some housing providers), and official law enforcement agencies, to say nothing of the local citizen for whom an agenda of cooperation and duty to intervene and improve has been scripted and put in place by New Labour. Proposals for greater local accountability for policing arrangements as well as neighbourhood management and caretaking have created a de facto new tier of complex and intersected governance within which the aim for social, physical, economic, and political well-being is seen to intersect closely with the need to reduce crime and disorder.

As a solution to British urban ills, a strengthening of community values, based around what "of course, the overwhelming majority of people understand ... intuitively", as Blair (2006a) put it in his speech at the launch of the *Respect Action Plan*, has been promoted. It is at this new policy 'junction' that the government's 'social inclusion' agenda and the urban renaissance meet. With the Respect agenda, which emerged at the beginning of 2006 and which extended debates about anti-social behaviour and civic pride, the Prime Minister pushed again the importance of people taking seriously their responsibilities. Such a mode of civic renewal explicitly connects an urgent need for action on disorder with a geography of poor neighbourhoods. The roots of this can be found in the early New Labour government and the inception of its Social Exclusion Unit where there has been a regular and forceful connection made between low social capital, trust, and respect and its primary residence in deprived neighbourhoods. Here respect was defined as "a duty and a responsibility on the citizen to respect the rights of others; a duty on the state to protect the vulnerable from significant harm and a duty to uphold the rule of law in a system that is efficient and fair"(Blair, 2006a).

In short, a familiar theme has re-emerged, relating to the need for communities to take better control of the problems within them and highlighting the connection between an agenda that seeks to physically and socially revitalise British neighbourhoods and cities on the one hand, and, on the other, a logic of disorder that has been firmly attached to these same spaces. Nevertheless, it is important to point to the historical lineage in which particular popular and moral dangers have become identified as dangerous to a public's safety and a city's vitality. In the 1970s Cohen's (1972) work on *moral panics* was influential, but we can trace this further back to debates of the dangerous classes in Victorian urban Britain (Stedman Jones, 1971) where the promotion of the first urban sanitation programmes and establishment of the New Metropolitan Police were infused with appeals to morality, decency, and respect as Victorian values. Yet, by defining underclasses as consisting of anti-social individuals who threaten communities, 'class', which remains to this date one of the underpinning dynamics in which poverty is socially produced, does not enter the equation but is, instead, addressed through the criminal justice system as the outcome of an individual's failings, again highlighting the contradictions of a communitarian agenda played out in individualistic terms.

While these understandings of crime and dangers to public safety are not new, the current government has been able to focus policy attention on crime and respect and to join these with social and physical renewal. Linking these policies not only to social policy (as welfare reform) but also to urban renewal (as a spatialisation of social policy) has enabled the government to promote a politics of public safety, which, in its logic, also implies a politics of public dangers and fears that have often been highly publicised. While Margaret Thatcher merely promised to be tough on crime, New Labour always argued it would be tough on its causes. New Labour has replaced the vacuum created by a denial of mutual obligations under Conservatism with a notion of community that continues to pathologise crime as the failings of individuals even while claiming to acknowledge the roots of social exclusion and deviant behaviour (Young, 1999).

When the narrow limitations of New Labour's meanings of 'community' are more closely investigated we find that hardly ever do young people form part of that community (Rogers & Coaffee, 2005), similarly grassroots organisations still struggle to get their concerns heard (as with public housing stock transfers, in housing management and the latest round of urban and market renewal). Many initiatives tackling regeneration and crime control are based in the same geographical locales, often deprived urban neighbourhoods. It is here that we see a clustering of agencies and programmes in peripheral housing schemes and inner-city communities, alongside a range of initiatives that explicitly target central business districts, their retail and leisure-based economies and clientele. Among this proliferation it would appear that decision-making processes are increasingly obscured by the sheer range of institutions, partnerships, and organisations engaged in urban renewal, community safety, and social inclusion. Crawford (1998) has already pointed towards the similarities of such devolved power to public–private partnerships under New Labour now bypassing local communities and the similar loss of democratic accountability via Thatcher's creation of quangos (quasi-autonomous non-government organisations), often created to bypass unruly local councils throughout the 1980s.

Outline of the collection

This volume is structured in three parts, each part framed by a brief introduction outlining the key themes. In Part I the focus is on the theoretical and conceptual underpinnings of the urban renaissance and crime and disorder agendas and their growing intersection. A key theme in the analysis of New Labour and its policies relating to cities has been a growing concern with crime, but this is also a galvanising process, as Kevin **Stenson** argues (Chapter Two). In his chapter Stenson considers the way in which urban public space has assumed a contested terrain over which political debates have produced a sense of sovereignty – that is to say, a sense of who might be included and excluded within wider debates about the quality of life within cities. Mike **Raco's** chapter (Chapter Three) goes on to look at the way that security now permeates the latest and most dominant urban agenda that can be found in the sustainable communities plan. Here Raco is highly critical of what he sees as a strong link between this massive expansion of sanitisied new-build estates in the South East of England and their connection with concerns for providing predictability and security for their new residents. In Chapter Four, Lynn **Hancock** continues this critical look at urban policy by asking whether urban regeneration is, not indeed criminogenic, that is, not only productive of crime and disorder but in the process further criminalising those populations in neighbourhoods where regeneration is taking place. Drawing on empirical work in Merseyside, Hancock argues that regeneration has, rather than leading to social inclusion, via its entanglement with the criminal justice agenda, contributed to the criminalisation and exclusion of neighbourhoods and residents touched by these programmes.

Part II, in turn, examines in detail existing and emerging political agendas and policies. This second part begins with an overview by Craig **Johnstone** and Gordon **MacLeod** (Chapter Five) on the impact of liveability and quality-of-life issues on the policy formulation under New Labour. Taking up arguments made earlier by both Raco and Hancock, Johnstone and MacLeod contend that the active targeting of visible signs of disorder, mainly in deprived neighbourhoods, is in danger of cultivating a selectivity by which urban neighbourhoods are made liveable for some residents while other residents and neighbourhoods are actively excluded. This in turn casts doubts over the ability of an urban renaissance to achieve its proclaimed aims of genuinely sustainable communities.

David **Murakami Wood** and Jon **Coaffee** (Chapter Six) then argue that urban policy is increasingly involved in staging the city in a way that privileges particular groups of users. Drawing on the example of the Labour Party conference in Newcastle in 2005 they demonstrate that this event and the fears underpinning its security arrangement effectively closed down traditionally open streets and public spaces. This not only privileged the party attendees but, they argue, also set a wider precedent in offering a legitimacy to such anti-democratic arrangements. There are also links, Murakami Wood and Coaffee suggest, between ideas of renaissance and neoliberal urbanism that has seen significant attacks on those considered not to be the 'right' people to support the kind of liveability agendas that have emerged in British urbanism. These themes are picked up at various points later, notably by Charlie Johnston and Gerry Mooney in relation to council estates as well as by Phil Hubbard and his colleagues in their chapter on street sex work.

In Chapter Seven Andrew **Millie** examines New Labour's action on anti-social behaviour given the emphasis in current regeneration action on improving liveability by reducing crime. Millie argues that because disorder and, particularly, anti-social behaviour tend to be concentrated in deprived areas and linked to dissatisfaction, it follows that regeneration that tackles this dissatisfaction is likely to be effective, yet that powerlessness and low trust remain resilient problems. Supplementing, and perhaps contrasting, with the views in this chapter are those of Charlie **Johnston** and Gerry **Mooney**. In their chapter (Chapter Eight) they describe the preoccupation of the urban renewal agenda with social housing estates and the reproduction of inequalities and misery of poverty. However, they strongly criticise current approaches for making disorder synonymous with spaces of social renting, the estate or scheme, which are perceived by policy makers to stand in opposition to the programme of moral and civic renewal engineered via the Blairite political project. The result of this, they argue, is a persistent discrimination against and stigmatisation of the residents of areas of social renting.

Part III of this volume explores in depth different aspects of the role of communities within the emergent crime and renewal agenda. It is particularly concerned with the ways in which communities are becoming 'responsibilised' in the current policy agenda. While closed circuit television (CCTV) has become a well-established tool of crime prevention in both commercial and residential areas, another tool has more recently seen widespread uptake and application: that of warden schemes and other agents of semi-formal control. The ensuing three contributions examine the role of three types of such schemes. In Chapter Nine Caroline **Paskell** introduces police community support officers (CSOs), who, through Home Office initiatives, have been rolled out across the English and Welsh police forces. Paskell's extensive research into the establishment of the CSOs highlights the importance in looking closely at the particular powers various policing actors are equipped with. As she examines the establishment of various CSO schemes across a range of deprived neighbourhoods she links these policing initiatives to processes of urban regeneration. John **Flint** and

Hannah **Smithson** (Chapter Ten) then examine the attempts of two local police forces to target anti-social behaviour among young people. While Manchester employs a Dispersal Order, Glasgow sees a particular small housing association buying additional police support on their streets. These initiatives provide insights into the ways in which the police, as statutory agent, has become involved in the management of disorder in residential neighbourhoods and, furthermore, in making use of additional powers at their disposal.

In Gavin **Smith's** chapter (Chapter Eleven) the focus shifts from largely residential spaces to those of the city centre, where Smith examines a third group of policing agents. His ethnographic study into the late night economy details the interactions between pub and club door staff with CCTV operators. While the late night economy has risen to a mainstay of 'post-industrial' urban economies, Smith makes it clear that it is also producing some of the public disorder targeted under new campaigns for urban liveability. Phil **Hubbard**, Rosie **Campbell**, Maggie **O'Neill**, Jane **Pitcher** and Jane **Scoular** turn their attention to one field of economic activity that has been subjected to sustained control: street prostitution (Chapter Twelve). They ask to what extent an urban renaissance is inclusive in terms of the groups it might deliver for. In so doing, they emphasise the earlier tendencies of current urban policy to exclude and marginalise, not only deprived neighbourhoods (as Hancock, and Johnston and Mooney demonstrate earlier) but also these groups, including prostitutes and deprived residents.

In the final contribution for Part III, which deals with questions over whose community and whose safety, Joe **Hermer** and David **MacGregor** take a look at the case of the legal beggar in Scotland (Chapter Thirteen). One of the most visible and often controversial instruments of urban regeneration are efforts to criminalise those who beg and other types of 'disorderly people'. Hermer and MacGregor offer a paradigmatic example of such legislation, the Ontario Safe Streets Act, as a background to their main discussion of the case of how the City of Edinburgh Council sought to convince the Scottish Office of a need to re-criminalise begging. The authors approvingly note that the refusal of the Scottish Office to make begging illegal is again a small but highly symbolic example of how the 'criminalising' of urban policy can be resisted by appeals to principles of social justice.

An urban renaissance secured?

Part of the urban renaissance blueprint is an attempt to lure back affluent middle classes to the core cities, often achieved through the modernisation of city cores and the creation of affluent enclave styles of development, including 'loft living' (Atkinson, 2004, 2006). That such policies amount to gentrification, including its concomitant consequences of political marginalisation and community displacement, should not be surprising. While policies of regeneration have focused on the recycling and modernisation of adjacent and deprived areas and on mixed tenure and use, the reality has often been the sacrifice of affordable and social housing components in order to retain private developer interest as well as prospective buyers. Even with an apparent emphasis on 'mixed ownership' these issues beg the question of how this kind of renaissance will benefit a broad urban constituency.

While many new urban projects are promoted and justified by the objective of developing post-industrial economies (Coleman et al, 2005), particularly around retail and leisure activities, the abiding sense has been of new investment that produces attractive and safe public spaces to draw down capital and human investment. People and business will not be attracted to re-modelled cities that do not provide spaces of safe sociability. Yet the charge of gentrification is important precisely because it reveals a tendency to displace social problems that have created friction and disorder in cities. Instead local authorities have sought to displace problem people through the use of ASBOs as well as planning regimes wherein a place for affordable housing is not effectively sought. To this end the securing of an urban renaissance has been achieved only insofar as it has offered a shiny new space for more affluent groups. As the chapters in this volume highlight, much of the new ground that has been won and revitalised via the social exclusion and urban renaissance agendas has been carried out without consultation, via the dislocation of unwanted communities and with increasingly punitive strategies. While much of this speaks of a need for inclusion and vitality, the links between safety, investment, and urban fortunes have continued to produce an entrepreneurial form of city governance, albeit one that now combines the tenets of neoliberalism with those of zero tolerance and community policing.

A large number of the many urban policy initiatives and programmes take up arguments to do with criminal justice, liveability, and respect – a combination that points towards an increasing interlinking and meshing of British urban policy with crime and disorder policies, in a way that we earlier called the criminalisation of urban policy. Geographically, many of these are, in addition to the city centre and core business areas, targeted at deprived and working-class neighbourhoods and communities. Many of these have, often since their development via post-war slum clearance schemes, been subjected to various area-based initiatives. As these areas became more socially residualised they also became sites of increasing stigmatisation, as Johnston and Mooney (Chapter Eight, this volume) and others (Hastings & Dean, 2003) have argued. Through the criminalisation of urban policy and its justification through a simplified version of communitarianism (Hughes & Mooney, 1998; Hancock, Chapter Four, this volume), these stigmatising and punitive approaches have moved to the central political stage, expressing the paternalistic tensions of the project. To many progressive policy analysts these now appear as the central problematic to be unpicked in a critical political project.

This punitive turn in policy (Wacquant, 1999) has revealed a targeting of key spaces and social groups who are seen to have neglected their social duties, while abusing the responsibilities of the state in its duty of care for the marginal. Within this discourse it has become apparent that the discussion of rights and responsibilities has been articulated in asymmetrical terms with a stress on the primary obligations of citizens, rather than on their rights. To take Blair's domestic agenda alone it is important to recognise that criticism has been strong and that this has come both from within and outside central government. Richard Rogers himself was critical, for example, of how the government did not go far enough in translating the urban renaissance report into effective action via the 2000 urban White Paper.

As policy has moved on we hear that Whitehall officials are no longer interested in an urban renaissance and that the idea of sustainable communities has become the central focus of current action. Nevertheless both the Urban Task Force (2005) and the Conservative Party have recently attempted to take on renewed visions that might compete and bring a return of attention back to the cities. Indeed, while crude indicators of population re-filling in the hearts of Dundee, Liverpool and Manchester have been taken as signs of a renaissance (IPPR, 2006) it is equally easy to draw on the failure of these changes to promote more inclusive and socially diverse communities (Hubbard et al, Chapter Twelve, this volume), also seen in the rise of gated communities (Atkinson, Blandy, Flint & Lister, 2005) and the continuing out-migration of families from British cities (Champion & Fisher, 2004).

In joining urban policy to the criminal justice agenda, New Labour has been able to 'do something' about those dangers, fears, and insecurities that seem to threaten an idealised notion of community and respectable society. This criminalising of urban policy has been reliant on the punitive treatment of low-level disorder (Young, 1999), particularly as incivilities have gained importance through high media visibility. While the emphasis on crime and disorder has often been critiqued there is little doubt that, for many local communities, British cities remain places of daily fear and anxiety. The resilience of many spaces to continued waves of policy intervention, often dealing with symptomatic malaise, rather than the structural conditions under which poverty is reproduced (Dabinett, Lawless, Rhodes, & Tyler, 2001) has been significant. Nor is this interpretation of disorder and decline a new one, which was observed during the first fully functional Community Development Project set up in 1969. When the 12 projects across the UK first reported back in 1973 they were keen to emphasise that what they faced were not local, isolated problems but symptoms of much wider underlying processes (CDP, 1973). Yet, in the context of this volume we want to argue that these wider underlying processes are still being sidelined, albeit in a different manner, by, this time, emphasising individual responsibilities towards imagined communities. By identifying the urban problem as one of anti-social behaviour, a lack of respect, and too much low-level disorder, urban policy serves to criminalise large parts of the urban population.

Similar discourses and strategies have emerged in other western countries, in the riots and discontent of French banlieues in 2005 and 2006, the almost total systemic breakdown of coastal cities like New Orleans in the US, and the layering of fears about immigration, economic performance, identity, and regeneration in European metropolitan regions like those within Denmark, France, the Netherlands, and Germany. In short, the magic bullet that might engineer a revitalised social and physical fabric of liveability, to use the British government's own terminology, has not only to deliver a methodology capable of treating these as interconnected matters. With policy now operating in a climate of permanent emergency and in a culture of broader social anxiety (Glassner, 1999; Furedi, 2005), it needs to be able to ameliorate the fears of citizens. Being tough on crime and its causes is only one part of this equation; delivering a more inclusive society is undoubtedly a further key part of the strategy that has faltered in recent diagnoses of the urban policy/crime nexus. Attempts to secure the rejuvenation of urban centres have become a more significant crossroads, or leitmotiv, for a noteworthy resetting of the political system in which fear of crime has permeated the agendas of economic development, central city renewal, and neighbourhood revitalisation.

Is the current ratcheting-up of the crime and disorder agenda only the beginning of a much larger shift towards fearfulness and aggressive programmes in British cities? Certainly this would appear to be illustrated in urban fortification, surveillance, interdictory public (and privatised) space, and gated communities, all of which suggest that increased socio-spatial segregation and target hardening for the affluent will be a key route by which high-income households are able to venture into cities for the wealth they provide. There is little doubt that the diet of media panics around dangerous classes and spaces have contributed to this current climate. The prospects for a renaissance-style Southern European street life, vital public spaces, and high-quality design may ultimately be tempered by democratised access to bland executive homes, mono-tenure affluent neighbourhoods, and an increasing segregation along the lines of income (Meen, Gibb, Goody, McGrath, & Mackinnon, 2006). In this context the need for visions and vitality very much remains with us.

Part I
Theories and concepts

Renewed interest in urban policy and British cities has been a defining feature of New Labour's government since coming to power. As detailed in the book's introduction, this focus on the urban became strongly linked to several major policy strategies, notably the presentation of Lord Rogers' Urban Task Force report and the subsequent urban White Paper, *Our towns and cities* (ODPM, 2000). Getting to grips with the intellectual framework for this set of policies, in particular in relation to previous regeneration programmes, presents us with the key theme for the first section in this volume, and forms the backdrop for the first three chapters.

Various commentators have pointed to the visionary nature of the British urban renaissance while drawing similarities with North American new urbanist planning and development (Lees, 2003b; Talen, 2005). These visions of 'reborn' British cities are imbued with wider assumptions not only about the way these cities work and are constituted physically; they also contain implicit beliefs about city economies and its social relations. Many policy commentators have sought to uncover and prise apart these assumptions during the course of New Labour's administration. This, in turn, has meant a significant focus on the tenor and content of key policy debates as a key feature of academic engagements with New Labour's urban policy framework.

In the course of this engagement, the seeming pragmatism of 'what works' has become identified as one of the core techniques of pursuing a particular vision of state–social relationships. In particular there has been an emphasis on favouring quantifiable outcomes (such as the 'floor targets' of the New Deal for Communities Programme) and a need to ensure tangible indicators of 'best value'. This 'new public management' has been central in shifting the nature of social and economic modes of regulation from one characterised by centralised government to one of multiple and far-reaching governance – no less coordinated centrally perhaps, even for all the talk of community engagement and devolved governance arrangements. Crawford's (1998) earlier work on the establishment of community safety partnerships serves as a useful pointer that highlights the way in which such arrangements have pushed towards the embedding of business practices in public service delivery, and indeed continued earlier Conservative attempts at introducing neoliberalism (Hughes & McLaughlin, 2002).

In setting out the content of this section the conceptual context that appears to surround current public policy becomes crucial. In this first part of this volume more detail is given to the conceptual and theoretical underpinnings of the way in which a turn from a singular preoccupation with urban policy was ultimately, to use New Labour's own terminology, 'joined up' to concerns for security and community safety. This lies at the heart of our broader concern in this book to understand more about how this agenda developed and what its implications have been for the broader project of an urban renaissance. These first three chapters situate British urban policy within a much broader process of political restructuring that has seen state–society relations move much closer to concerns with the economy. This has, in turn, driven a vision that combines an agenda of social justice and social cohesion together with a broader emphasis on economic competitiveness, stemming from a repositioning of British cities as powerhouses of creativity as well as commerce. These opening chapters apply and develop analytical tools for studying the conditions of contemporary British public policy, and the ways in which it now attempts to reorganise British cities. All three contributions in this section provide a critical reading of the underpinning of current policy thinking and the way in which it links, more and more strongly, urban regeneration to crime and disorder.

A kind of 'authoritarian communitarianism' has developed within the urban policy agenda. As the authors in this section remark, much of this project is an attempt to deliver community empowerment as a means of enforcing a stricter regulation of disorder and misconduct. That this is conflictually coupled with the attempts to commodify central city spaces as a means of opening up a path for economic development through retailing, leisure, and entertainment can be seen in increased disorder problems with the night-time economy as heavy drinking has accompanied this kind of development.

A further result within this essentially neoliberal form of urban renewal has been the creation of newer affluent neighbourhoods that are often segregated from those targeted by various social inclusion and other regenerative efforts. A geography of renewal has targeted the residents of those poorer spaces, seeing them as places producing both the victims and perpetrators of disorder. Importantly the residents of such neighbourhoods have been written in as the route to salvation for such spaces as exhortations to intervene, collaborate, and support formal agencies of law enforcement have become apparent. The ways in which such policy discourses have sought to locate such spaces and populations lie at the heart of Kevin Stenson's treatment, which asks searching questions about the governance of urban space and the kind of projects that seek to assert such governance (Chapter Two).

Mike Raco continues and expands this perspective of governmentality by examining the sustainable communities initiatives and the role of planning for the provision of not only new, more sustainable communities, but also new kinds of citizens (Chapter Three). His chapter pinpoints the increasingly short timeframes given to particular initiatives before new ones are rolled out. In this sense, Raco argues, the programme laid out for the development of the new sustainable communities may be regarded as an attempt to overcome some of the limitations of the earlier blueprint provided for urban renaissance by Lord Rogers' Task Force. Yet, lying at the centre of Raco's analysis is the question of whether this new name and flagship programme actually means a substantially different set of policies, practices, and theories.

In the third contribution, Lynn Hancock adopts a more explicitly political approach by critically examining the limitation of New Labour's policy discourse on regeneration and crime (Chapter Four). In so doing, she stretches the perspective opened up by the preceding chapters and goes back to ask important questions about power and legitimacy in local politics. She does so by questioning the basis of several of its assumptions and asks, provocatively, whether much of the crime that is found in urban Britain may not be indeed a product of urban regeneration policies. Sceptical of the ability of such policies, and to some extent their intentions, too, she presents empirical research from Merseyside, pointing to the limitations of regeneration policies to bring about their stated aims of social inclusion. These limitations, she argues, exist precisely because regeneration policies are now so closely interconnected with an exclusionary criminal justice agenda that they have ultimately criminalised, rather than 'included', their subjects.

These three chapters taken together contribute not only to a further illumination of this twin theme of a neoliberalisation and paternalism at the centre of New Labour's urban politics and criminal justice agendas. They also broaden the frame of reference to identify the ways in which, as Stenson suggests, 'problem-solving frames' are being drawn up. For both Stenson and Raco, these frames are strongly situated within a struggle for sovereignty, indeed for *state* sovereignty, reworked by the tools of the new public management and thereby suffused with notions of best value, social markets, and communitarian agendas that have done little to engage and resolve older structural social problems in many towns and cities. Yet, as Hancock argues, these problem-solving frames arise from, and take as their objects, the political economy of deindustrialisation, articulated through residualised working-class neighbourhoods. It is with the conjoint perspective provided by these opening chapters that the links between crime and disorder control and urban regeneration can be much more clearly observed.

TWO

Framing the governance of urban space

Kevin Stenson

Politicians, planners, and academics use terms like 'sustainability', 'security', and 'regeneration' in persuading us that we need to manage the social dislocations and urban decay of late modernity and globalisation. Yet cities have always been a fulcrum of trouble. They grew at points of intersection: crossroads, river fords, and ports where streams of diverse travellers would collide and settle, in pursuit of trade, adventure, excitement, riches, romance, survival, conquest, and intrigue. They were always vulnerable to the ebb and flow of markets, human migration, military competition, and struggles between people divided by clan membership, 'race', ethnicity, wealth, religion, and other markers of difference and tribal solidarity. This complexity and danger could be viewed as the sources of the city's creativity and power (Jacobs, 1997). From this perspective, the productive volatility of city life is in tension with competing visions of urban renaissance and of utopian orderliness.

This chapter will explore some of the current tensions in these competing frames of interpretation and strategies of action. It assembles an uneasy mix of ideas from colliding worlds: journalism, high and low; ideological, political networks; policy makers, civil servants and think tanks; the major corporations and their well-financed lobbies; the universities; police, security, criminal justice, and welfare institutions and professions. It also draws on the perspectives of those maintaining the infrastructure of the city from sewage treatment to the transport and emergency services. These frames of interpretation underpin attempts to govern city life from above in the public interest, and in the name of the institutions of law, state, and the big corporations. These constitute the key actors, or, to use current parlance, the 'stakeholders', involved in trying to govern city life from above.

For those trying to drive political agendas for change, rational argument and appeals to evidence and science are limited. Leaders resort to simpler messages conveyed through rhetorical (persuasive) arts of emotional manipulation and rich figurative language: the use of metaphor, analogy, and allusion. Democratic politicians' use of the rhetorical arts, filtered through and shaped by the mass media, involves a recognition that citizens also attempt to govern their domains from below. This is so whether as individuals or in collectivities. These can range from the family, to religious institutions, sports and leisure associations, to organised crime and terrorist conspiracies. They pursue their own agendas, perhaps with alternative visions, that may be resistant, accommodating, or indifferent to agendas of governance from above (Hayward, 2004; Stenson, 2005).

This analysis emphasises the universal struggle for control of populations and territory. In raw form, in cities from São Paulo to Mogadishu, where the central state authority is weak or non-existent, this involves vying for dominance by male groupings united by ties of kinship, ethnicity, religion, and neighbourhood. In the face of this universal struggle, in the advanced societies, there is also the struggle for sovereign control of populations and territories, in the name of law and state authority. This operates through trying – and often failing – to monopolise the use of coercive force. Increasingly, with growing urban fears in the post-9/11 world, the governmental problems of city life and how to regenerate it are disproportionately coded under the terms of security, crime, disorder, and anti-social behaviour (Stenson, 2005).

The chapter will try to unpack some of these issues, firstly, by describing frames, or imaginaries of interpretation, noting the tensions between the attempts to impose orderly visions and the creative energy of city life. Secondly, it traces the roots of the current interpretive frames that take a systematic, rational, and textually visible form. These are the ideological and academic discourses that impinge on notions of urban problems and renaissance. This account identifies the key ingredients and distinguishes between early Victorian laissez-faire conceptions of city governance, late Victorian social liberalism, the social democratic welfare states of the 20th century, with their faith in the power of the state to provide safety nets and guide the economy. This is followed by New Right critiques of the welfare state's belief in 'Big Government', and then New Labour discourses updating social liberalism and the re-coding of social problems under the heading of security and crime control. Thirdly, having identified the key political rationalities generating and authorising rule, the chapter identifies some of the key technologies (or instrumental means) and themes of government, through which these new rationalities operate. Many of these routine technologies at the front line of city management take on an apparently non-political, technical, problem-solving form. Fourthly, the chapter explores how the language of urban political leadership needs to connect not just with the constituencies that identify with rationalist discourses but also with myriad groupings with their own agendas of governance from below. These are often expressed through oral, more emotive discourses. This presents problems of political translation between different registers, largely through the mass media. These issues represent dilemmas of liberal democratic politics understood in the widest sense. A pervasive theme historically has been the tension between the liberal emphasis on the dignity and universal rights of the individual, and on the other hand the security and identity of collectivities, up to and including the nation.

Frames and imaginaries

Urban renaissance promises to govern ungoverned spaces suffering the effects of economic change: the ugly, windswept detritus of closed factories, mines, docks, shipyards and decaying, violent, social housing estates and shopping centres that had served these engines of production with labour. This image offers to replace ugliness with beauty, chaos with order, and pessimism with optimism. It promises new life to creaking infrastructures and troubled areas increasingly abandoned by opportunities for legitimate, well-paid work and the institutions and personnel of the state and commerce (Stenson & Edwards, 2003). Images of renewal are shored up with moral visions, which may have a utopian character, of a better life that may be made possible by the appropriate mix of state and market initiatives. However, the nature of that mix may be heavily contested (Pinder, 2005). While there is a practical dimension to governance, reflections on it usually bind attempts to make analytic sense of these problems with 'imaginaries': shared normative visions of how life ought to be better lived. These imaginaries constitute frameworks of meaning and interpretation of varying degrees of coherence and organisation, providing cognitive and moral frames. These can influence the mentalities and practices of those engaged in governance, and also the wider populations governed in the name of the city and the public interest. They are rooted in religious and ideological belief systems, which include images of local civic (including sports-based), regional, ethnic, and national identities and citizenship. For the longer-settled, indigenous population these were fostered during the great period of nation building in the 19th and 20th centuries. The focus here is firstly on the rational aspects of these visions of better urban life.

Rational discourses of government: from laissez-faire to the New Right

Human science academics can rarely claim the cloak of objectivity; their analyses usually align with particular value or ideological orientations. Yet, they have a vested interest in describing and analysing the world through the lens of rationality, as if there are clear principles, values, and material interests motivating and shaping thought and action (Stenson, 1991). They focus on the emotionally low-key, rational aspects of the knowledge base of rule. These are embodied in concepts, policy, and ideological texts, maps, software, charts, and tables, mediated through the lens of 'governmental savoir' (discourses of governing), or the perspectives of radical critics wanting to govern in other ways. They include the intellectual instruments and substantive data that drive, shape, and provide rationales for the governing process (Stenson & Edwards, 2004). These are the ideas and instruments, or technologies, in the widest sense, which make problems, populations, and targeted, risky geographical areas thinkable, mappable, and measurable for the purposes of government. Although we may be intoxicated by modernity, our current modes of thinking carry traces of the past. Debates between those who celebrate the virtues of market, and those of the state are still shaped by older 19th- and 20th-century debates between market and social liberals and later social democratic and socialist proponents of various welfare states.

Laissez-faire market styles of governmental savoir were dominant in the early to middle period of the 19th century, characterised by belief in a minimal role for the state, international free trade, and market solutions for domestic problems (Stenson, 2001a). Echoing similar shifts in other advanced societies, with the poverty, disease, and disorder of urbanisation and industrialisation, this was followed by the rise of social liberalism in the late 19th century. This shift was associated with the Liberal administrations of Gladstone and the agendas for boosting local civic pride and welfare by Quaker and other philanthropists and local commercial leaders. They tempered the effects of markets with governmental controls at local and national levels, created the infrastructure that markets could not provide, and built social solidarity among fragmented, unequal, and potentially troublesome populations. At the heart of the urban transformation were attempts to govern the crime and disease-ridden rookeries of the poor. This challenged the power of criminal networks and illegal economies, graphically depicted by Charles Dickens's character Fagin, replacing their authority with that of the police, law, and municipalities. City development could often take the form of the mass clearances of these 'urban jungles' and removal of their populations, anticipating the current clearances of the shantytowns and favelas of third world cities, from Rio to Harare, to Delhi (Stedman-Jones, 1971).

It is tempting to depict this period as a stage in the march of universalistic, Enlightenment liberal values, a common, secular citizenship, individual rights and identity. Liberalism, in the narrowly philosophical sense, is associated with individualism and universalism, as distinct from varieties of communitarianism, which give greater priority to the identity and needs of collectivities. Yet, in real life settings, we should broaden our notion of liberalism, to embrace forms of communitarianism, with which it is usually intertwined (Stenson, 1998). In Britain the universalistic aspects of social liberalism were yoked with community and nation-building projects of solidarity that emphasised particularistic, civic, and regional identities and jingoistic, imperialist, and militaristic nationalism (Dench, 1986; Stenson, 1998). This crystallised an irony and tension that has endured through the generations. The development of urbanisation and nation building created sources of identification that transcended those of the local village. They facilitated and fostered a public sphere and a shared citizenship. The new means of transport and relatively safe public streets, squares, and parks enabled collective assembly by diverse groups for political, leisure, commercial, and other purposes (Reiner, 2000). The codes of civility this engendered, ultimately reinforced by sovereign law, were extended to foreign visitors to a degree. Yet, the cultural framework for this collective, *social*, public life remained particularistic in relation to those defined as outside the club of the nation, or deemed to be troublesome within it. Community and nation building, hence, usually entail the creation of populations defined as 'other' in relation to the collectivities being formed. For example, in late19th-century England, much of the rhetoric about the threat of crime, treason, and insecurity focused on the perceived enemy within the growing cities, notably Irish and Jewish people. The parallels today in relation to other minorities within the city are striking (Pearson, 1983; Young, 1999).

Thus the symbols of the economically and militarily powerful nation, with its burgeoning empire were, and remain, visibly represented in the parks and other common urban spaces and highways. They were filled with the monumental statues and architecture celebrating military, imperial conquest, heroism, and the iconography of the dominant Christian faiths of the nation. This crystallises a particular national narrative (Hastings, 1997). Monuments to the heroes and heroines of the democratic, liberal tradition, from Tom Paine and the Tolpuddle

Martyrs, to the Chartists, Keir Hardie, Ellen Wilkinson, Nye Bevan, and Barbara Castle, are rare in British public spaces.

Some influences on new forms of city governance were Europe-wide, including fear of the mob and disease, liberal Enlightenment values, nascent trade unionism, socialism, and demands for suffrage and female equality and ethnic self-determination. In addition, the political rationalities that drove the urban reform of the British social liberal era included protestant evangelism, Celtic nationalism, bucolic, nostalgia for the mythical golden age of Anglo-Saxon freedoms, the civil war in the 17th century, diggers, and levellers. In addition, the leadership that made possible urban reform was provided largely through local capitalist (often Quaker), industrial dynasties, with Joseph Chamberlain's Birmingham providing the most striking role model (Hunt, 2005). This created an enduring tension between communitarian collectivism and individualistic liberal universalism, between the needs, security, and well-being of the majority, and the liberal emphasis on individual and minority civil liberties and human rights (Hughes, 1998; Stenson, 1998). In the post-9/11 era, this tension is sharpening, reinforcing the creation of secure urban enclaves and a creeping segregation of populations deemed troublesome.

Social liberalism and organised labour launched the social democratic welfare states, sharing the major risks of life in the framework of state government that emerged in the 20th century, reaching their high period between 1945 and 1975 (Esping-Andersen, 1990). While law and order policy was not the touchstone issue it is today, child and adolescent offenders were viewed as often salvageable, with the right input from welfare professionals. In the 1970s and 1980s the growing interdependence and volatility of global markets helped to reorder the international division of labour, presenting challenges to all the advanced countries, particularly in relation to the decline of traditional industries and the impact on urban spaces and communities this entailed. However, political responses to these developments varied. The rise of the New Right had a particular impact in the Anglophone countries, where New Right administrations attempted to reduce the role of the state, reinvent government through partnerships, foster greater entrepreneurship and 'ownership' of problems within civil society, and re-balance the roles of commercial, not-for-profit, and state authorities. This entailed governments encouraging people to take greater responsibility for their own security and to be less reliant on welfare professionals to prevent and reduce crime (Garland, 1996).

In the UK, the destruction of 'smokestack' industries was accelerated by the policies of governments of the New Right in the 1980s, decaying the urban fabric. This reinforced the 'heritage' conception of Englishness. This is expressed in idealised rural images and flight from the decaying cities of English white families, followed by the upwardly mobile from minority communities, in pursuit of houses with gardens in suburbs, new towns, and commuter villages (Stenson & Watt, 1999). Urban regeneration initiatives attempted to counter the equation of cities with decay, conflict, crime, and pollution. The initial models of urban renaissance, associated with London and Liverpool schemes for waterside development, attracted professionals back to spearhead a city renaissance (Atkinson, 2006). Tough law and order policies to regulate the marginalised and disaffected, which might threaten middle-class urban colonists and their children, accompanied this. Already by the early 1990s public rather than private sector actors drove urban renaissance. This was despite largely unsuccessful attempts by Conservative governments to encourage private sector firms, in North American fashion, to take the lead in regeneration. In contrast to many US cities, in Britain since the 1970s, at least, it has usually fallen to national and local state agencies to lead these initiatives (Stenson & Edwards, 2003). New Labour embraced these themes, sought a path between over-reliance on either state or market, and refurbished Victorian social liberalism. Emphasis shifted to targeting state assistance to the most troubled areas and populations (Stenson & Edwards, 2001).

New Labour, urban renaissance, and security

New Labour's urban imaginary from 1994 can be traced back to Anthony Crosland's seminal *The future of socialism* (1956), in trying to build a new constituency among the consumer-oriented skilled working and middle classes. The message was that social democracy could be fun, pleasurable, sophisticated, and *urbane*. Labour should 'level up' the culture of the poor and middling classes, enabling them to enjoy urban public association, as in continental European cities. This imaginary was shared by Anglo-Italian architect Richard Rogers, chair of New Labour's Urban Task Force, with its visions of new, high-density housing in urban sites, and cosmopolitan populations enjoying squares and piazzas, well served by good arts, leisure, public transport, and other public services (Urban Task Force, 1999). Evidence about citizens' reactions to the urban transformation so far is mixed. A recent report on 58 English towns funded by the Office of the Deputy Prime Minister has shown clear evidence of growth and improved public satisfaction with their urban environments. However, they trail leading

European cities on most indicators and security remains a key perceived problem, and prerequisite for further growth (ODPM, 2005b).

Urban diversity in terms of wealth, lifestyle, income, religion, and ethnicity has created huge potential for as yet largely unrealised urban social conflict. Research in Merseyside and Brixton in London has indicated that the benefits of growth and inward migration into the city of the well-heeled often fail to trickle down to the local poor. The artistic and other cultural goods provided for the new professionals do not appeal to the long-settled poor. This creates a criminogenic cocktail resulting in the criminal victimisation of the middle-class incomers, mainly through burglary, theft of and from cars, and street robbery. This is particularly so where class differences, in cities characterised by widening economic inequalities, intersect with ethnic, racial, religious, and age markers of difference (Hallsworth, 2002; Hancock, 2003; Atkinson, 2006). Towns and cities experiencing the decline of traditional industries and the creation of huge student residential enclaves, in Leeds and elsewhere, have become increasingly dependent on a youth-oriented (and old-excluding) night-time economy based on the alcohol retail industry. This has become increasingly associated with what older people perceive as violent, anti-social behaviour. Given that the police are ill resourced to manage the increasingly volatile night-time urban spaces, as Smith argues in this volume (Chapter Eleven), this presents major challenges for order maintenance and has been an impetus for the rapid expansion of a, as yet, poorly regulated, commercial security industry prone to entanglement with organised crime and trade in illegal drugs (Hobbs, Hadfield, Lister, & Winlow, 2003).

In addition, the legislation in the 1980s allowing council tenants to buy their social housing has significantly changed the demography and character of both urban and rural areas of historically social housing and dramatically reduced the national social housing stock. This, plus community care policies dispersing mental patients into the community, has concentrated a range of groups with divergent lifestyles, values, and standards into – in many areas – a volatile mutually distrustful mix. One of the key fault lines is between those still hooked into the rhythms of the labour force and schooling, where night time is for sleep and the day for work and learning, and those dependent on welfare or illegal economies. They have different life rhythms, which may involve a 'partying' lifestyle, creating considerable noise at night (Stenson & Watt, 1999; Flint, 2002). A major plank of New Labour policy, expressed through the 1998 Crime and Disorder Act and the 2003 Anti-Social Behaviour Act, has been to introduce Anti-Social Behaviour Orders (ASBOs), curfews, Dispersal Orders, and other measures to deal with what are perceived to be 'neighbours from hell' and anti-social youth gangs. This is in order to keep faith with New Labour's constituencies among the 'respectable' working poor and, as in the Victorian era, seize back control for sovereign public authority from those involved in illegal economies (Stenson, 2005).

The speeches and surrounding debates over several years by New Labour ministers Gordon Brown, about Britishness, and David Blunkett, about Englishness, indicate a reawakened nation building in current soul searching about how to build a new citizenship of rights and duties (Goodhart, 2006). The hope is that this new citizenship may bind new solidarities in socially fractured cities marked by escalating immigration and the flight of indigenous white people. This was the concern of an influential government report by Ted Cantle on the riots between Asian Muslims and poor whites in northern towns in 2001. It was argued that policy should try to overcome ethnic groups living 'parallel lives' with minimal interaction (Home Office, 2001). There are no grounds for complacency, as riots in 2001 and the tube bombings by British-born extremist Muslims in July 2005 indicate.

This signals a key, and often neglected, feature of public governance. It tries to influence those many networks within the city with their own agendas for governing the lives of their kinship, religious, commercial, and other modes of human association. In pluralistic cities there are myriad groupings – sites of governance – driven by their own imaginaries, ranging from those claiming to represent religious and minority ethnic groups to paramilitary organisations (Stenson, 2005). Many of the young in urban minority populations are absorbed into a secular, hedonistic consumerism. This is less so among older people, and, in more extreme fashion, young religious fundamentalists from evangelical Christians, the more conservative Sikhs, Hindus, and Jews, to adherents of extremist versions of Islam. Many still identify strongly with the patriarchal beliefs, values, customs, clan, and religious identities and traditions of their rural homelands – or evolve new hybrid identities mixing old elements with modernity. This often involves opposing the secular consumerism, hedonistic sexuality, and female emancipation of urban, secular, liberal society, and culture (Armstrong, 2001).

Problem-solving frames

While there may be a struggle between those advocating different ideological or religious visions, it should be recognised that for the legions of workers of the infrastructure, governmental knowledge usually takes a problem-solving form. The common thread running through the polyglot languages of technical expertise is a preferred distancing from the emotive fray of politics, which can be translated into an apparently depoliticised language of technical management (de Lint & Virta, 2004). A good example is the pompously self-proclaimed 'crime science'. Mainly reliant on quantitative, psychological research methods, it focuses on reducing crime through a range of what are claimed to be dispassionate, ethically, and politically neutral problem-solving forms of knowledge (Laycock, 2005). The focus is on the systematic evaluation of what is deemed to 'work' in crime control policy in the light of what crime scientists define as methodologically acceptable research and findings. This remains as yet a highly contested field of knowledge, principally because of disputes over how to conceptualise and measure differences in national, regional, and local contexts and the possibilities of global policy learning (Stenson & Edwards, 2004).

Political issues are re-framed as problems that can be solved by the most efficient, evidentially validated available solutions. The key question is less by which warrant should things be done than how things can be repaired, maintained, or made to work a little better, crises and disasters managed, and the great wheels of the city brought back into motion (Thrift, 2005). Cities always presented challenges for creating the conditions enabling the human hive to function and avert chaos and disaster. How can they: provide water, energy, food, communication, and transportation; educate, train, and tame the wayward spirits of children and adolescents; nurse the sick and bury the dead; manage sewage waste and pollution; and deal with effects of fire, disorder, robbery, disease, war, natural disaster, terrorist violence, and pestilence? Such necessity is the mother of invention in the governance of complex urban spaces and populations, and the third part of this volume looks specifically at the (community) governance of such issues. The crucial roles of the emergency workers and the routine provision of services, the taken-for-granted heartbeat of the city, are dramatically revealed during great urban disasters like 9/11, the flood in New Orleans in 2005, and the Madrid and London train bombings in 2004 and 2005.

Fired by a faltering but sometimes heroic public service ethos, this everyday street level of governance by the foot soldiers of rule, the street-level bureaucrats and technicians, is critical to the maintenance of sovereign rule in the city (Edwards, 2005). This stimulates the gathering of information to facilitate problem-solving governance, moving from material engineering and practical maintenance towards social and moral engineering. Commercial, philanthropic, and state modes of governance have categorised, documented, and measured the conditions of populations and territories and fostered their orderliness, health, wealth, and well-being. This has warranted an increasing intervention into personal, familial, commercial, and community life, requiring new modes of expertise in conceptualising, mapping, measuring, and proposing solutions (Foucault, 1991). The attempts to govern the human soul and behaviour from the 1980s have focused on urban crime and insecurity, and re-coded policies increasingly through the prism of crime prevention and reduction. This involves governing through an emphasis on crime, risk, and insecurity (Simon, 1997).

The institutions of policing and criminal justice perform a range of familiar, enduring functions from the maintenance of order, to deterrence and the warehousing of the troublesome. Yet let us note an emerging range of governmental technologies involved in the governance of crime. The focus in this chapter is on three broad clusters of technologies, operating in varying hybrid combinations. They must be seen against the familiar backcloth of the growing central control of the police, local government, and other public agencies through a focus on performance indicators, local public service agreements, linked with fiscal penalties for non-compliance, and risk management. However, as successive evaluation studies have shown, the rhetoric about the need for integrated, 'joined-up' government is not matched by the reality of pervasive fragmentation of effort and limited information exchange between sectors (Stenson, 2000a). The 2002 Police Reform Act signalled the growing pluralisation of the provision of security across the boundaries of state, commercial, and voluntary self-policing. Having eroded the provision of public guardianship in the form, for example, of park keepers and railway staff, in the name of state reform and efficiency, there are attempts to reinvent guardianship in new forms. By 2006 in the UK there was a record 139,000 sworn public police officers, matched by a similar number of commercial security staff and a projection of 25,000 community support officers (CSOs) ancillary to the police, and aided by exponential growth in closed circuit television (CCTV) and other security technologies. The growth in the tax-funded world of security is matched by analogous commercial growth. By 2005, the commercial security industry employed about half a million people and had an annual turnover of £3-4 billion in the UK (BSIA, 2005).

These technologies can be analytically distinguished in terms of the objects that are targeted for governance. They include, firstly, punitive sovereignty – often labelled with the rhetoric of zero tolerance, or Mayor Rudi Giuliani's New York 'quality of life policing'. They aim to regain control of perceivably ungoverned populations and areas, ultimately by use of coercive measures, including the aforementioned

ASBOs and other measures that blur the boundaries between criminal and civil law. An influential thesis uses Liverpool as an example in highlighting the ordering of the regenerated city into defensible enclaves against encroachment by the poor. It argues that the new urban management reflects principally the interests of the large retail corporations in criminalising the poor and homeless and excluding them from malls, the city centre, and other sanitised and refurbished sites of consumption (Coleman & Sim, 2002). However, the huge international popularity of zero tolerance rhetoric and demands for tough policing of the marginalised comes as much from the poor and working classes as from the privileged (Stenson, 2000b).

Secondly, they include situational crime prevention (SCP), in combination with the measures of actuarial justice, or risk assessment and management techniques. These measures aim to 'harden targets', for example, through the redesign of the urban environment, rather than change offenders through punishment, influence child development, or rehabilitate offenders. With these technologies, the immediate targets of governance are the environments within which people act. The object is not so much the deeper causes of crime in social and economic conditions and psychological states. Rather, the dominant assumption is that most offenders are normal, rational actors who can be diverted from crime by creating greater obstacles to offending, or at least assessing and minimising the risks associated with it. In the commercial world, this is reflected in pressure to build crime prevention into product design, making cars, mobile phones, and other consumer goods more difficult to steal or use. It is also represented in the extraordinary growth, particularly in the UK as a world leader, of the use of CCTV, number plate recognition systems, and other digitally based modes of surveillance, given further impetus by post-9/11 fears about security (Ball & Webster, 2003).

Thirdly, there are community security technologies. These involve a turn to the local, fostering greater community responsibility, to defend affluent and regenerate troubled and decaying neighbourhoods. The objects of governance are more directly the relationships between people and institutions, and environmental and other conditions that may foster a sense of cohesion within populations. At one extreme is the concept of the gated community, with 24/7 security, which is increasingly attractive to the super rich. A variant of this principle includes apparently open neighbourhoods, which are guarded by round-the-clock security and tend to promote sociability among the guarded residents. There are at least fifty such schemes in London and South East England, including Primrose Hill, Battersea, Chelsea, and

Hampstead (*London Evening Standard*, 3 June 2005). However, some elements of this kind of neighbourhood security are also incorporated into local community safety and crime reduction policies, the province of the emerging 'community safety' professions based in local authorities and Crime and Disorder Reduction Partnerships (CDRPs) set up under the 1998 Crime and Disorder Act (Hughes, 2006). They range from Sure Start 'early intervention' parent support initiatives in deprived areas, to restorative justice, mediation schemes, youth crime diversion initiatives, strategies to manage illegal drugs use, a host of neighbourhood improvement initiatives, and those to promote the benefits of local networking and community initiatives, such as the example of neighbourhood policing explored by Flint and Smithson in this volume (Chapter Ten) . These are coded as social capital, 'community capacity' building, and social entrepreneurship, and they revive older ambitions to tackle the deeper social and economic causes of crime and disorder (Stenson, 2005; Hughes, 2006).

While the mix varies locally, these elements are involved in the competing and often hybridised technologies of governance embodied in local community safety measures. A key feature of 'community safety' is the ambition to manage crime, disorder, and its deeper roots holistically, through multiagency partnership arrangements and the building of social capital and cohesion (Stenson & Edwards, 2003). The chapter now turns, finally, to explore how in the messy political world rationality and professional expertise must compete, often unsuccessfully, with more emotively based communications and ways to frame problems of crime and anti-social behaviour.

Translating the rhetoric of crime control

It is unwise to exaggerate the role of rational ideas in policy formation (Crawford, 1997). This is particularly so given that, increasingly over the past two decades, in the advanced democracies as well as in poorer countries, problems of the city and proposed solutions to them have been coded in the highly emotive language of crime, risk, fear, and insecurity (Stenson, 2001b). In wrapping up rational and emotional themes, politicians deploy figurative language. Metaphors have a powerful emotional force as calls to action and operate in clusters to structure our thoughts and understanding of social relationships (Lakoff & Johnson, 1980). Politicians picture the world in terms of moral polarities. This fuels the desire for tough punishment and demonises deviants as alien, even 'monsters', threatening the lives of the law-abiding, respectable, and hard working (Wilkins, 1991). It also enables politicians to create collective solidarity in the face of these perceived common threats. The sources of these mediatised images have deep oral cultural roots, and also literature (Reiner, Livingstone, & Allen, 2001). There is a rich 19th-century tradition, updated in modern media, of literary description and analysis of the ambitions, battles, triumphs, and hubris of city life. In this, issues of crime, policing, and justice were writ large – in Balzac's tales of Paris, Dickens's of London and, in our day, Tom Wolfe's of New York and Atlanta.

Through these mediatised representations, the social and spatial differentiation, moral ambiguities, and intertwined commonalities in the experiences of city folk, high and low, are explored. This offers people frameworks of interpretations to make sense of their experience and perceptions. Furthermore, political rhetoric provides metaphors of leadership, for example, the shepherd to a flock, captain of the ship of state sailing through treacherous seas to his crew, or valiant general in the vanguard of his troops. In the US, the political Right has invested hugely in media campaigns depicting the desirable leader as a strong father of unruly children, while Liberal and Left leaders are presented as unmanly, ineffectual, over-indulgent mothers. Powerful lobbies frame issues in such a way as to foreclose debate and downplay political and ethical alternatives through the medium of simple metaphors for the wider public. This leaves governing to the wise patriarch, served by capable experts (Lakoff, 2004). Mayor Rudi Giuliani successfully deployed a strong father frame in legitimating his New York policing strategies. Operating with similar rhetoric and strategies so did Ray Mallon in Hartlepool and Middlesbrough, as both police chief and, later, popular mayor since the mid-1990s. Like Giuliani, he explains social ills as the product of denigrated, ineffective, or non-existent fathering. Strong leadership and policing then serve as surrogates for a refurbished fatherhood, battered by the breakdown of the family, the rise of feminism, and political correctness (Stenson, 2000b).

Figurative and often earthy language becomes a way of trying to resolve or defuse the tensions between maintaining a recognition of, on the one hand, individualist, universalistic, liberal rights, liberties, and due legal process and, on the other hand, a recognition of the collective rights to security for the fearful majority. This is a political representation of the now live philosophical debates that can be traced back to the era of social liberalism. This involves the aforementioned struggle between individualistic forms of liberalism and versions of communitarianism. In the latter, there is greater attention given to the rights, needs, and security of majorities or particular minorities, conceived of as collectivities, rather than as the individual, and universal human rights. It stresses the need to tilt the balance away from an exaggerated emphasis on rights towards an emphasis on responsibility, duty, and the well-being of social collectivities, from the family to the nation and higher levels of human association (Hughes, 1998). This focuses on threats by predatory, 'anti-social' groups and individuals in the city to weak and vulnerable citizens. These can range from noisy 'neighbours from hell' (Johnston and Mooney, Chapter Eight, this volume), paedophiles, aggressive beggars (Hermer and MacGregor, Chapter Thirteen, this volume), street drug dealers (Hubbard et al, Chapter Twelve, this volume) and robbers, to terrorists (Murakami Wood and Coaffee, Chapter Six, this volume).

Successive New Labour Home Secretaries have deliberately baited the educated middle-class liberal elites with their concerns for civil liberties and due process and minority rights. In addition, a striking example of populist, earthy punitive sovereign rhetoric can be found in the speeches of and interviews conducted with Louise Casey, Director of the Home Office Anti-Social Behaviour Unit. She proclaimed her streetwise, working-class background, claiming to represent ordinary people. She noted the strong support for ASBOs by citizens, recorded in surveys and on the doorsteps to politicians during election campaigns, saying, "Sometimes I wish people like ASBO Concern and some of the people who write letters to *The Guardian* could just see it from the point of view of the people in the communities.... [Those who attack Asbos] ... are not necessarily living in the real world, [Asbo] is a byword for the country wanting something done about a guy who is 50 and looks 70 who gets gobbed on and has stuff thrown at him by a group of teenagers when he leaves the house for a night shift" (*The Guardian*, 10 June 2005). This conjures an image of the state trying to protect harassed, victimised, decent working people against feral offenders and also lawyers and other progressive, liberal professionals whose concerns about human rights render them indifferent to those too poor to escape the nightmare of the urban jungle. Ironically, in practice, the urban regeneration policy of Casey's government, in an effort to encourage professionals to colonise the city, facilitates the formation of more secure middle-class enclaves, enabling privileged liberals to keep the poor at a distance (Atkinson, 2006).

Conclusion

Politicians cannot base urban policy simply on what 'experts' define as scientifically evaluated best practice about what policies do and do not work. They also have to consider anger, resentment, jealousy, insecurity, and a fear of all those who are seen as invaders of the familiar spaces of what is considered to be the homeland or home turf. Visions of controlled, sanitised, safe spaces for consumption and other pleasures enjoy wide appeal across the social spectrum and increasingly among the longer-settled minorities as well as white English and Celtic majorities. Recent images of urban renaissance in this sense join a long lineage attempting to tame the chaotic, vivacity of city life. These have been crystallised, for example, in Haussmann's 19th-century architectural vision of Paris, and the social democratic planning visions underpinning the English new-town settlements like Basildon and Milton Keynes created after the Second World War. In more extreme form, they have been expressed in the totalitarian vision and architectural iconography of power manifest in Albert Speer's Nazi Berlin and Saddam Hussein's Baathist Baghdad.

Now the most powerful visions of order come from the corporate world, from the supermarkets and other massive retail chains. These have replaced bazaars, the randomness and spontaneity of street markets, diverse small shops, and the rich urban texture of identities and relationships they spawn, with corporate, branded clones. One of the key products on sale is the safety of these controlled, carefully monitored spaces. They serve, preferably, the well-heeled shopper, at the expense of the market trader looking for humbler customers. The chair of the up-market British John Lewis retail chain in 2006 called for the pedestrianisation and clean-up of London's Oxford Street, transforming it into the regulated ambience of the shopping mall. Its narrow, crowded pavements, where people spill into the paths of buses, attracts a human kaleidoscope, from high spenders, tourists, suburban families, and flirting teenagers, to hucksters, evangelists, con men, street robbers, and pickpockets. The architecture critic of London's *Evening Standard* newspaper reacted sharply, and celebrated the urban jostle and congestion:

> A city needs an Oxford Street the same way that the body needs an oesophagus or a lower intestine: it's not exactly pretty, but it does a job. Shopping malls, by contrast, are about the removal of sensory choice from the physical environment. They create a uniform orderliness the better to concentrate consumers' minds on the merchandise. They offer choice in abundance, but only on things you have to pay for. In a mall you shape your identity only for a price; in a city you can do it for free. (Moore, 2006)

THREE

The planning, design, and governance of sustainable communities in the UK

Mike Raco

This chapter examines the Labour government's recent shift towards the building of sustainable communities in England and assesses the ways in which these new development blueprints define, identify, and tackle questions of security and safety. During the 2000s the discourse of the 'urban renaissance' has gradually given way to that of urban sustainability with its emphasis on the construction of sustainable communities or places "where people want to live and work now and in the future … [and which] are safe and inclusive, well planned, built and run, and offer equality of opportunity and good services for all" (ODPM, 2005c, p 1). The new frameworks represent an evolution in renaissance thinking by arguing that through imaginative planning, responsive forms of governance, and the physical construction of 'inclusive' urban environments, new places can be created in which citizens can feel secure and new forms of attractive community and neighbourhood can flourish. In the absence of security, it is argued, communities and citizens live in an atmosphere of fear and distrust. Any sense of 'neighbourliness' breaks down and individuals and their families become isolated units living disconnected lives despite living in spatial proximity to each other (Buonfino & Mulgan, 2006). Those who can escape such environments do, further exacerbating socioeconomic inequalities. There is a belated (although understated) recognition in the new agendas that the urban renaissance, for all its visible achievements in transforming the physical environments of Britain's cities, has failed to tackle growing social polarisation and urban insecurity.

In order to deliver on these objectives programmes have been introduced that reflect and reproduce broader trends and ways of thinking about security and spatial regeneration and renewal. There are two primary components to the new strategies. On the one hand, they draw on situational approaches in which the effective design of public places is seen as a vehicle for the reduction of crime and anti-social behaviour. They follow a long tradition in urban planning that elides criminal behaviour with the availability of criminal 'opportunities' and the extent to which these are opened up or reduced by the thoughtful design of urban spaces (see Atkinson and Helms's introduction to this volume, Chapter One). On the other hand, there is a new emphasis on community building and the mobilisation of new types of citizenship and active communities. It is argued that through modernised, enhanced processes of governance, new forms of formal and informal policing and mechanisms of social control will help to deliver safe and sustainable neighbourhoods. In effect, the new approaches claim that crime can be 'governed out' of existence by the effective development and implementation of neighbourhood-based strategies and projects.

The chapter argues that a study of sustainable communities discourses and ways of thinking brings into relief broader conceptions concerning the role that urban and regional planning could and should play in shaping people's lives, the relationships between governance and policy, and the ways in which discourses of community, sustainability, and security are being translated and deployed in the pursuit of wider policy aims. The discussion is divided into two main sections. The first examines the relationships between security policy and urban development in the UK and the recent emergence of programmes for building sustainable communities. The second explores the links between these new programmes and broader concerns with the security of urban spaces. It examines governance-focused and situational approaches to policy and highlights the rationalities and possibilities inherent within the new agendas.

Security, safety, and the discourses of sustainable community building

Safety, security, and the re-creation of place

Coleman et al (2005) point out that research in urban studies has increasingly demonstrated that "a core component of city-building processes [is] the policing of the public (visible) sphere and the regulation and control of degenerate and poorer communities" (p 2511). This enhanced interest in policy and security has been a consequence of five interrelated policy processes, outlined below.

1. The concept of place competitiveness has become embedded in entrepreneurial urban and regional (re)development strategies in the UK, Western Europe, and North America. Most urban development projects now demand that the visible security and safety of places for visitors and investors is top priority. A failure to be seen to be 'safe' can undermine these broader agendas. A number of studies have documented the social, economic, and political implications of these new agendas for urban policy in towns and cities such as Liverpool (Coleman, 2004b), Reading (Raco, 2003), and Glasgow (Fyfe & Bannister, 1996).

2. Many regeneration programmes now target mobile, high income, professional groups, or what Richard Florida (2004) has recently termed a 'creative class'. Such 'creative' groups, it is argued, require high quality, secure environments free from the threat of intrusive and violent forms of crime (see Peck, 2005, for a powerful critique of these ideas). The consequence is that, in Coleman et al's (2005) terms, "regeneration strategies … constitute a form of 'governing through crime' whereby images and discourses on the 'crime problem' sit at the centre of, and provide rationale for, key aspects of the urban renaissance agenda" (p 2512). Particular types of criminality become defined as a problem to be tackled, while other less visible offences, particularly so-called 'white-collar crimes' are given less priority as they do not visibly undermine development objectives and, of course, they are committed by those in relatively powerful positions.

3. In many places governing and policing agencies face greater challenges as a consequence of visibly growing inequalities and the spatial juxtaposition of more and less affluent communities. One of the legacies of property-led regeneration in the 1980s and 1990s was the emergence of gentrified neighbourhoods alongside pockets of severe socioeconomic exclusion (see Imrie & Thomas, 1995). As Robson and Butler (2004) demonstrate in their work on gentrified spaces in London, one manifestation of these inequalities has been the greater incidence of crimes, such as robbery and burglary. Other authors have pointed to the wider, polarising effects of neoliberalism in western societies and see the growth of crime reduction strategies as a mechanism for mollifying and controlling marginalised populations. Peck (2003), for example, equates the rise of increasingly punitive criminal justice strategies in the US with a broader fear of excluded 'others' (see also Parenti, 1999).

4. The issue of crime and anti-social behaviour is politically sensitive. The fear of crime has consistently grown at a faster rate than (officially recorded) levels of crime. A National Audit Report in 2006, for example, concluded that over 60 per cent of people believed that crime was rising despite a consistent 11-year fall in recorded crime (BBC Online, 2006). It has become a priority for many politicians to be seen to be tackling visible crime and broadly defined anti-social behaviour.

5. The new emphasis on security also reflects and reproduces the wider availability of new technologies such as closed circuit televison (CCTV) and electronic tagging (Coleman & Sim, 2000; Gold, 2004; Norris & McCahill, 2006). Development agencies are increasingly keen to deploy such technologies as they are significantly cheaper than other, more labour-intensive security measures and provide visible evidence of the 'seriousness' with which governing agencies are addressing visible crime and anti-social behaviour. Security strategies also create opportunities for local state agencies to capture the involvement of others, particularly business communities, in the creation of crime and disorder partnerships.

The next section looks at the emergence of recent sustainable communities agendas in the UK and examines the ways in which ideas and concepts concerning security have become embedded into the new discourses. It begins by exploring the emergence of sustainable communities in planning policy before turning to a discussion of two interrelated elements of security policies within the new frameworks – the designing out and governing out of crime.

The emergence of the sustainable community

During the 2000s the discourse of sustainability, and in particular that of creating sustainable communities, has become the dominant theme in English spatial planning. Discourses of sustainability were a core part of the earlier urban renaissance policy blueprints of the late 1990s and the urban White Paper of 2000 (see Urban Task Force, 1999; DETR, 2000; Lees, 2003b). The new focus on sustainability has close parallels with these earlier rounds of policy, but with less of a design focus and a greater emphasis on developing sustainable communities through the construction of more socially inclusive environments and the active mobilisation of public, private, voluntary, and community sector actors. In many ways there has been an evolution in urban renaissance thinking and a broadening in the scope and scale of urban (and non-urban) planning ambitions.

In 2003 the Labour government launched its most significant spatial policy statement to date, the *Sustainable communities: Building for the future* plan. The plan set out a new vision for the ways in which spatial planning could be used to facilitate the (re-)creation of communities that will 'stand on their own feet' and 'stand the test of time' (see ODPM, 2003; Raco, 2005). At the heart of the new agendas was a commitment to establish planning frameworks to promote more holistic and integrated solutions to urban problems in the context of a strengthened regional development framework.[1] Subsequent efforts have been made to define and redefine the concept of the sustainable community. The government's (ODPM, 2005c) latest definition presents such communities as: "places where people want to live and work now and in the future. They meet the diverse needs of existing and future residents, are sensitive to their environment, and contribute to a high quality of life" (p 1).

Table 3.1 lists the key dimensions of a sustainable community. It shows that a sustainable place is one in which employment, mixed housing, and social facilities are co-present and available to a range of socioeconomic groups. Sustainable communities are populated by self-reliant, active citizens who, in the longer term, provide for themselves and rely less on an active welfare state. Within such agendas, the character of the built environment is presented as a vehicle for the construction of balanced communities with modernist urban developments and suburbs criticised for their lack of character, sameness, and lack of community diversity (see Hall, 1998). The sustainable communities plan claims to

Table 3.1: Key characteristics of a sustainable community

Characteristics:
Active, inclusive and safe
Well governed
Environmentally sensitive
Well designed and built
Well connected
Economically thriving and diverse
Well served
Fair for everyone

Source: ODPM (2005c)

offer new solutions to this urban bleakness through the promotion of mixed housing, employment opportunities, and a new sense of community belonging. In bringing together the broader discourses of sustainability and community, the new approaches draw directly from the new urbanist ideas now entering British spatial planning from the US and beyond (Talen, 1999, 2005).

And yet the introduction of these new 'inclusive' agendas raises broader questions about how processes of sustainable community building are to be managed and the implications for different groups. If one of the core priorities is to create 'safe' environments then how is this to be achieved? Whose definitions of 'balance' and 'safety' are to be prioritised? What should be done with those groups whose absence might be seen, in policy terms, as an important element in the building of a sustainable community? Moreover, what do the new proposals tell us about imaginations of criminality and anti-social behaviour and what the respective roles and responsibilities of the state, citizens, and communities should be? In addressing these questions the next section examines the ways in which security discourses feature in the recent reforms to the planning system. It argues that there are two principal elements to this securitisation – the creation of new forms of citizenship and community bonds, and the designing out of crime through the direct channelling and control of individuals' mobility and access to public and private spaces. The discussion highlights some of the tensions inherent in these ways of thinking and argues that selective understandings of community, place, and criminality are evident in the proposals. It is important to note that one of the weaknesses in the sustainable communities agenda is that, as yet, there is precious little evidence that such communities are being constructed in the ways that the government has envisaged (Raco, in press). The analysis presented here focuses on the discourses and policy programmes that have been established and the ways in which "truths are mobilised rhetorically to constitute the political realities of community, crime and control" (Ericson & Haggerty, 1997, p 68).

Securing sustainable communities: the rationalities and priorities of the new spatial planning

Governing out crime: partnerships, citizen participation, and neighbourhood policing

The government has made it clear that 'community safety' and security are core elements in the construction of sustainable communities.

In order to deliver on these objectives new forms of 'responsive' and 'participative' governance are required that can facilitate the introduction of more effective formal and informal policing practices. In essence, there is an emphasis on governing out crime, or using new forms of citizenship and decision-making processes to enhance the security of sustainable places. The process began with the publication in May 1999 of the document *A better quality of life: A strategy for sustainable development for the UK* (DETR, 1999b), in which each government department was asked to develop its own priorities for building sustainable communities. Following this consultation exercise the Home Office developed a set of Sustainable Development Indicators based on six interrelated themes: reducing levels of crime; reducing the fear of crime; improving the delivery of justice; reducing drug use; increasing voluntary and community engagement; and reducing 'race' inequalities and building community cohesion (see Home Office, 2005a). These indicators promote a mixture of objectives based on the implementation of top-down policing strategies alongside bottom-up community-based programmes through which "citizens, communities and the voluntary sector [become] more fully engaged in tackling social problems and there is more equality of opportunity and respect for people of all races and religions" (Home Office, 2005a, Objective 5).

For the government, building sustainable communities provides a new opportunity to restructure the governance of policing and establish new "creative partnership[s] and an integrated approach to delivering communities that people want to live and work in" (ODPM, 2005d, p 1). Under the new arrangements, when faced with competing priorities, "planning decisions must therefore be made in full consultation with all partners and be based on policies for planning and crime prevention which reflect the local situation and the views of those who will manage and live with the outcome of those decisions" (ODPM, 2005d, p 1). This new emphasis on partnership governance is to be propagated by reformed decision-making frameworks in which operational and strategic decision-making powers are to be moved away from formal policing bodies to local communities and citizens. For the Labour government this shift is a necessary response to the changing character of policing and security threats, as in the words of former Home Secretary Charles Clarke (2005a): "the nature of crime is changing ... at the local level, communities are increasingly menaced by anti-social behaviour. As the threats to our security change, so must our police to create a service that responds better to individual needs and local circumstances" (p 1).

In order to respond more effectively to "individual needs and local circumstances" the Labour government has, therefore, placed significant faith in the power of local governance structures and practices to deliver on its wider objectives. There is a particular emphasis on the twin subjects and objects of neighbourhoods and active citizens. The former not only represent the contexts within which criminality and social disorder are present or absent but also provide the spatial frames of reference through which active citizens can be mobilised to enhance their own security and support those who have suffered from the ill effects of crime.

A series of interrelated initiatives are to be established in sustainable communities in which policing will be conducted through: 'improvements' in the experiences of those who have contact with the police; a rolling out of neighbourhood-based policing; effective community engagement; enhanced public understanding and local accountability of policing; and organisational and cultural change on the part of policing agencies (Home Office, 2005a). A new type of citizen-focused policing is called for that the government defines as "a way of working in which an in-depth understanding of the needs and expectations of individuals and communities that receive and use police services [is developed and this is] responsive to those needs" (Home Office, 2005a, p 1). The purpose of the new agendas is to institutionalise "the primary responsibility of government ... to ensure that law-abiding citizens and families are safe and secure ... neighbourhood policing is central to achieving this" (Clarke, 2005a, p 1). Effective, neighbourhood-level policing is seen as an opportunity to "better tackle crime and anti-social behaviour, help instil respect and decency in local areas and build more cohesive communities" (Clarke, 2005a, p 1).

The neighbourhood, therefore, becomes a definable unit, an object of government whose members will take on greater responsibility for ensuring that policing policies are effectively implemented. While appearing to represent groundbreaking initiatives that will facilitate community inclusion and empowerment, the new agendas will, in practice, represent a wider state strategy of responsibilisation. The focus is on those defined as 'law-abiding', with the addition that it tends to be 'families' whose rights and needs take precedence. Their inclusion in the governance of policing "provide[s] the kind of information that will lead the police to catch the serial car vandal, the persistent burglar, the drug dealer or terrorist ... catching more criminals, in turn, brings greater reassurance to local communities" (Home Office, 2005a, p 4). In this vision community becomes a self-regulating and self-policing unit that identifies its undesirable elements and draws on the formal resources of the police to remove them and make their neighbourhoods 'safer' and 'more secure' environments. It represents an extension of community policing that seeks to "organise and channel thought and action at every level, from official statements of policy to everyday practices on the street" (Ericson & Haggerty, 1997, p 68).

The recent emergence of community support officers (CSOs) and neighbourhood wardens exemplifies the character of this wider move. The Home Office (2005a), for example, estimates that by 2008 there will be 24,000 CSOs in England. New neighbourhood police teams are also to be established to oversee this process and they are designed to "respond quickly to local concerns about anti-social behaviour. Their local knowledge will enable them to focus rapidly on trouble-spots and trouble-makers" (Clarke, 2005a, p 1). By 2008 every community – defined as an area of one or two wards – will have its own dedicated team of named police and CSOs based permanently in their area. They are to be "driven by local priorities and answer the community's concerns" (Clarke, 2005b, p 1). The police, therefore, take on a new role as strategic overseers who coordinate local initiatives and help to establish local strategic frameworks for security policy. In theory they represent new types of flexible, pluralist, and directly accountable state institutions that are able to tap into existing bonds of allegiance and in so doing become more efficient and effective.

However, these new arrangements raise a number of, as yet, unresolved issues. Lines of accountability are unclear and while the government is keen to emphasise the 'bottom-up' nature of decision making, it is likely that the same dynamics that skew community empowerment programmes elsewhere, such as selective forms of representation and the uneven process of community identification and selection, will also feature in community-based policing (Taylor, 2000; Raco, 2003). As Crawford (2006) argues, the new emphasis on neighbourhoods is underpinned by a core tension between building trust and social capital within neighbourhoods on the one hand, and developing new insecurities about the 'dangers' posed by particular individuals and groups within those communities on the other. In this context the rise of sustainable community building agendas "may not be best served by an over-dominant focus on insecurities ... [so that] security may be a precondition for, but also an obstacle to, the construction of open and tolerant neighbourhoods" (Crawford, 2006, p 974).

In addition, the urban renaissance agendas of the 2000s have fuelled significant changes in the socioeconomic make-up of many urban communities. In some cases wealthier in-migrants have taken advantage of the growing availability of exclusive and expensive properties and, as Savage, Bagnall, and Longhurst (2005) argue, their presence has often had a quantitative and qualitative impact on the character of local service provision with the priorities of public and private sector service providers increasingly reflecting *their* needs over and above those of existing residents and businesses. The empowerment of neighbourhood-focused policing partnerships, as a part of the broader sustainable communities agenda, carries the obvious danger that the local domination of such groups, who tend to be well organised and resourced, will be reinforced and that policy agendas will be restructured to secure the interests of an already relatively privileged majority. One of the renaissance's most important legacies could be that in gentrifying urban neighbourhoods it has made the prospects for making urban areas more secure and more sustainable (in the government's terms) less likely.

The process of responsibilisation has also become bound up with the wider objective of enhancing the efficiency of public service delivery. This generates tensions in the government's approach to neighbourhood-focused policing with the empowerment of citizens conditional on the ability of local actors to fulfil their responsibilities in relation to wider, public management agendas and priorities. For example, the new emphasis on (sustainable) community safety requires local actors to engage with a broad range of public sector agencies, not just the police (see Crowther, 2004). It therefore empowers professionals and those with the 'appropriate' skills to manage, coordinate, and implement the new agendas at the local level. As the Office of the Deputy Prime Minister and Home Office (2005) make clear:"planning's contribution to crime prevention must be based upon analysis of the local situation (carried out by someone equipped with the relevant interpretation skills)" (p 8). It is up to experts to diagnose and define the security problems faced by communities and to outline strategies to deal with them. Professionals, such as the police and local planners, therefore, still have a key role to play in the new arrangements and it remains to be seen how and in what ways power over policing policy is delegated to communities and other non-formal policy actors.

This emphasis on improving efficiency is being institutionalised through the government's wider reforms of the planning system in which the concept of mainstreaming has become a key mechanism for funding the construction of sustainable communities. Local Area Agreements (LAAs) are to be created in which local actors develop strategies and programmes that maximise the efficiency of government spending. For all the rhetoric of community ownership, partnership, and a new citizen focus to the reforms, the new governance arrangements are to be underpinned by a greater desire for state efficiency so that agencies can "co-ordinate and maximise the impact of the approximately £8 billion spent each year by public bodies and the private sector on the quality of the local environment" (ODPM, 2005c, p 1). The hand of central government will be ever present through rigorous auditing and regulation. In this sense the governance of policing represents only one part of a wider set of reforms that seek to maintain central government's grip over local policy-making processes (see Counsell, Haughton, Allmendinger, & Vigar, 2003).

Overall, then, there are some contradictory trends within the wider shift towards building sustainable communities and the governing-out of crime and anti-social behaviour. The new agendas have the potential to break open the often inaccessible and remote accountability structures of policing in England. Their vision of community-driven governance in which citizens take on greater responsibility for the security of their neighbourhoods is likely to change the ways in which policing priorities are established and programmes implemented. For the government, the relationships between sustainable communities, governance, and security are clear. Sustainable communities can provide a focus around which new forms of community identity and state institution-citizen relationships can be forged. As such the 'new' agendas represent an extension of existing ways of thinking about how criminality and anti-social behaviour are defined and how they can best be tackled. And yet, there are also tensions inherent in these ways of thinking about the governance of security and sustainable communities. The politics of responsibilisation represents a complex process in which local actors are required to address broader objectives, priorities, and targets in the setting of their 'own' agendas. At the same time, the needs of particular groups are prioritised over and above others and as with community-based programmes in other policy fields, the power relations *within* (sustainable) communities will inevitably have an impact on the setting of any priorities and objectives.

Designing out crime: situational approaches to the security of sustainable communities

At the same time as the new approach to building sustainable communities draws on particular conceptions of citizenship and neighbourliness, it also reinforces and adapts established ways of thinking about the use of environmental planning and engineering to design secure spaces. Table 3.2 summarises the government's definitions of the relationships between sustainable communities and crime

Table 3.2: Seven attributes of sustainable communities relevant to crime prevention

Attribute	Link to crime prevention
Access and movement	Places with well-defined routes, spaces, and entrances that provide for convenient movement without compromising security
Structure	Places that are structured so that different uses do not cause conflict
Surveillance	Places where all publicly accessible spaces are overlooked
Ownership	Places that promote a sense of ownership, respect, territorial responsibility, and community
Physical protection	Places that include necessary, well-designed security features
Activity	Places where the level of human activity is appropriate to the location and creates a reduced risk of crime and a sense of safety at all times
Management and maintenance	Places that are designed with management and maintenance in mind, to discourage crime in the present and the future

Source: Adapted from ODPM and Home Office (2004)

prevention. The attributes it identifies put the onus on sustainable community planners and developers to design urban spaces that channel and control selected forms of mobility. There is, of course, nothing new in the principles underpinning such approaches. There is a long history of planners, architects, and states using urban planning to try to control the behaviour and movement of populations (see Zedner, 2006). This emphasis on controlling mobility has been a recurring element of modernist planning discourses, with locational stability elided with order and efficiency and instability perceived as subversive and threatening (Urry, 2000; Cresswell, 2001; Sheller & Urry, 2006). Indeed, it could be argued that the structures of modern policing are particularly well suited to tackling the problems that emerge within established, settled populations but are less able to address the challenges raised by transitory and mobile groups such as travellers (see James, 2006, for a broader discussion).

The principle that urban design can be used to control and order mobility is embedded in the design guidelines for sustainable communities planning. The emphasis is on ensuring that there is an 'appropriate level' of human activity and mobility through public spaces in order to optimise their sense of security and sustainability. Designers are called on to use environmental tactics and practices to shape the form and character of public spaces and development areas so that they become less attractive to potential criminals and undesirables. The strategies work, for example, by changing

> ... offenders' immediate decision-making through deterrence and discouragement, including through conventional law enforcement and situational prevention. By excluding or deflecting them from crime situations, whether keeping children from crowding sweetshops or attracting rowdy youths to clubs and shelters. By increasing the crime resistance of targets (eg, through redesign of cars, mobile phones), lowering their value and removing them altogether. (ODPM and Home Office, 2004, p 7)

There is an attempt to use design to shape how and when defined groups use public spaces. Deviant behaviour will, as a consequence, be reduced and this will create a positive spiral in which a new sense of security will foster new attachments to places and communities, thereby reducing the motivations for crime.

There is also an emphasis on the role that urban design can play in increasing levels of surveillance. Long-established principles concerning the relationships between built environments and human behaviour are drawn on to justify the expansion of security technologies and the power and scope of those who design and build them. Surveillance is portrayed as a 'natural' mechanism for controlling human behaviour, with architecture and design playing an important role in facilitating it. The feeling of 'being watched' encourages individuals to act appropriately and change their interactions with others.

Other relationships are also evident in these security attributes. It is argued, for example, that there is a strong link between building 'attractive' environments and encouraging community ownership within places. A broken windows syndrome logic (cf Kelling & Coles, 1998) pervades such discourses with simplistic understandings put forward of the motivations that underpin criminality and anti-social behaviour. If an area is visually unappealing, it is argued, this will be reflected in the behaviour of its citizens and will attract other, less desirable individuals. Such conceptualisations are evident in, for example, the strategies of the Home Office's Crime Targets Task

Force that draw on binary conceptions of 'healthy' and 'unhealthy' communities to establish what they claim to be specific links between physical disorder and anti-social behaviour. Healthy environments are those in which "criminal behaviour does not thrive", whereas unhealthy environments encourage and attract more problems (ODPM and Home Office, 2004, p 2). Conversely if a place is perceived to be attractive it "promotes a sense of ownership, respect, territorial responsibility and community" (p 2), qualities that are at the heart of the government's sustainable communities agenda. A failure to establish a healthy and secure local environment will result in the absence of the types of creative and entrepreneurial citizens who are seen as 'vital' to the prosperity and social cohesion of a sustainable community.

At the same time much of the emphasis is also on how to restrict the mobility of more "purposeful criminals", and hence the drive to encourage planners and communities to "think criminal" or to

> ... think about how criminals or disorderly people might react to, or exploit, the use, layout and development of land. How might the environment, and what it contains, affect the criminals' assessment of risk, effort and reward, and hence their decision to offend? How might it actually provoke them to offend? How might offenders' wider life circumstances (eg lack of leisure facilities) motivate them to offend? (ODPM and Home Office, 2004, p 2)

This form of empathic policy making is put forward as a mechanism for the mobilisaton of collective imaginations within communities, with citizens asked to imagine what sorts of public spaces and public space users would be most desirable in their areas. It also has the potential to foster divisive and relational imaginations of citizenship where citizens are asked to consider who might constitute uncontrollable and 'dangerous others'.

The security attributes in Table 3.2 have also been incorporated into the government's recent root-and-branch reforms of the principles that guide planning policy in England. *Planning policy statement 1: Delivering sustainable development* (ODPM, 2004a) makes explicit connections between the planning process and insecure and unsustainable neighbourhoods. For example, its opening paragraph argues that "poor planning can result in a legacy for current and future generations of run-down town centres, unsafe and dilapidated housing, crime and disorder" (p 4). The built environment becomes a key determinant of citizenship interaction and community building and sustainable planning should, therefore, "promote high quality inclusive design in the layout of new development and individual buildings in terms of function and impact ... such policies should consider people's diverse needs and aim to break down unnecessary barriers and exclusions in a manner that benefits the entire community" (p 4). A failure to ensure that environments are well designed and that socioeconomic opportunities are available to a wide range of citizens will condemn unsustainable places to a negative spiral of decline. Crime is a critical component of this because:

> Community safety is an aspect of the quality of life, in which people, individually and collectively, are sufficiently free from or reassured about a range of real and perceived risks centring on crime and related misbehaviour; are able to cope with the consequences of those incidents that they experience; and if unable to cope alone, are helped to do so. All this establishes the conditions for them to pursue the necessities of their cultural, social and economic life. (ODPM and Home Office, 2004, p 9)

The significance of the *Planning policy statement 1* is that planners are now forced to consider such issues when permitting any local development to take place. However, what is not clear from the statement is the extent to which developments should balance short and long-term needs and objectives. Sustainability is premised on actions and plans that will benefit future generations as well as existing communities (see Whitehead, 2004). Within the *Planning policy statement 1* the security implications of these new agendas are not spelt out in detail. Instead, it is assumed that if a community is established (or redeveloped) – that is, well designed – its longer-term future will be assured. In this sense the agendas are less explicit about other causes of crime and anti-social behaviour, such as economic change, labour market exclusion, and changing housing markets, a theme addressed in the conclusion below.

Overall, then, the principle that crime can be designed out through spatial planning is therefore becoming embedded and reinforced within the new sustainable community frameworks. In this sense there is much continuity with earlier rounds of policy thinking and practice, such as the 1998 Crime and Disorder Act in which local planning authorities were compelled to approve only developments that could be shown to be 'secure' (see Raco, 2003). Some aspects of sustainable community design are not discussed openly in the new agendas. They have little to say, for example, about the desirability or otherwise of increasingly segregated, voluntary 'gated communities' or the extent to which planning for sustainability should support or challenge the principle that certain groups of citizens should build barriers between themselves and the rest of society. The concern with making places attractive for certain types of citizens and potential in-migrants has taken precedence over other priorities and objectives for building sustainable communities.

Conclusion

This chapter has examined the relationships between the emergence of the sustainable communities agenda and broader questions of safety and security. It has shown that the new concern with security reflects and reproduces, in large part, the broader emphasis now given to the (imagined and real) relationships between place attractiveness and desirable forms of community mobility and change. In the UK these processes are taking on a particular form as security is being elided (unproblematically) with the malleable discourses of sustainability and community. The new frameworks have extended those evident in the urban renaissance discourses of the early 2000s. Community 'safety' has become a core objective of planning policy and new mechanisms of neighbourhood governance and 'secure' urban design are presented as the primary vehicles through which the new policy agendas will be developed and delivered. In essence, it is argued that there exists a dialectical relationship between security and sustainable community building and that each is a necessary element in the construction and continuity of the other. Involving people in the design and implementation of security strategies, it is argued, not only makes those strategies more effective but also engenders inclusive forms of governance that have the power not only to transform places but also to foster new types of active citizenship within neighbourhoods. In this sense, the relationships between questions of security and the building of sustainable communities reflect and reproduce broader trends of governance in which the state is only part of a wider "matrix of power-knowledge ... and that within civil society there are numerous semi-autonomous realms and relations – such as communities, occupations, organisations, families – where certain kinds of policing and order are present but where the state administration and police force are technically absent" (Hopkins-Burke, 2004, p 14).

However, at the same time there has been little or no discussion within these agendas of the broader questions surrounding why particular types of crime actually happen or what the root causes of any type of criminal behaviour are. The frameworks have little to say about socioeconomic changes, such as the relentless flexibilisation and polarisation of labour markets or the growing difficulties faced by many communities in relation to the cost and availability of housing and the increasingly restrictive character of the welfare state. Security is treated as an identifiable problem that can be resolved through specific, targeted action, rather than being presented as a symptom of these wider changes, many of which are excluding and alienating whole sections of the population from the benefits of economic growth. Despite the 'holisitic' tone of much of the sustainability and community rhetoric, the introduction of these new ways of thinking also reflects the broader relationships between power and dominant perceptions over what constitutes acceptable and unacceptable behaviour. It is certain types of visible criminality and anti-social behaviour that are identified as problems to be tackled through the planning system. Other types of crime such as financial fraud or the corruption that results from the close, informal activities of elite networks are not labelled as 'problems' in the same way. Indeed, they are barely represented at all in the new frameworks, as such actions are not seen as standing in the way of successful sustainable community building.

It seems likely that existing trends will continue into the foreseeable future. There seems little prospect that in the current policy climate the significance of place 'attractiveness' will dwindle within development programmes or that the perceived and actual security of public and private spaces will become any less significant. Much of the publicity given to London's successful Olympic bid and the attacks that took place in the city in July 2005, for example, was focused on the impacts on the city's image and subsequent economic development (see, for example, Smith, 2006) and this is symptomatic of a wider concern with place competitiveness and attractiveness. For the Blair government, anti-social behaviour, the so-called 'Respect' Agenda, and the wider criminal justice system have become core policy concerns and even with the election of a new leader or a new government, it seems certain that existing policy trends will be continued. And yet without a wider engagement with some of the causes of crime and an acceptance that different types of criminal behaviour also exist outside of those that are 'visible', it seems likely that efforts to secure sustainable communities and public spaces more broadly will continue to treat the symptoms rather than the causes of identified problems.

Note

[1] The sustainable communities initiative has a particular focus on the South East, where it lays out plans for the construction of 260,000 houses in Milton Keynes, Cambridge, and Ashford and a further 120,000 in the Thames Gateway areas to the east of London. Beyond this it also involves the establishment of market renewal areas in nine northern English cities that aim to promote new rounds of investment in their most deprived neighbourhoods.

FOUR

Is urban regeneration criminogenic?

Lynn Hancock

This chapter examines some of the taken-for-granted assumptions in the relationship between urban regeneration and crime and disorder reduction and opens them up to critical scrutiny. Against a backdrop where public–private partnerships are vigorously marketing their localities in efforts to secure inward investment, the place of crime and disorder in these imaginaries are outlined. The chapter comments on the assumptions underpinning neighbourhood regeneration and in particular their relationships with crime and disorder reduction strategies in the contemporary setting. It shows how initiatives, which have the ostensible aim of addressing the problems of social exclusion and urban crime and disorder in a 'holistic' way, are nevertheless exacerbating, rather than ameliorating, 'social injustice' in a range of ways in the contemporary setting with the consequences bearing down disproportionately on the most marginal groups. Indeed, urban regeneration strategies and policies are beset with irresolvable tensions that arise from attempting to marry neoliberal economic policies with a moral communitarian social project. The chapter draws on and applies recent criminological insights, informed by empirical observations from Merseyside, UK, and studies conducted in city-regions elsewhere, to support the view that urban regeneration has both criminogenic and criminalising consequences under current frameworks.

Social inclusion and 'radical urban policy'

A number of writers have advocated the development of radical urban policies to prevent crime by addressing social injustice, economic exclusion, and political marginality, which lead to crime and victimisation (Donnison, 1995; Hope, 1995). They observed that reliance on the private market for the distribution of goods and services, particularly housing, has meant that those suffering the greatest economic and social hardships increasingly live in close proximity to each other, in the poorest quality housing stock, the concentration of crime closely reflecting poverty and disadvantage (Hope, 1998). The gap between the most disadvantaged and most affluent areas within cities widened between the 1981 and 2001 Censuses. Over these decades, wider social, economic, and political shifts brought in their wake chronic shortages of decent employment opportunities for economically disadvantaged groups and reductions in the value of welfare benefits that further impacted the living conditions of those living in already distressed localities.

It is in this context that the New Deal for Communities (NDC) programmes and *A new commitment to neighbourhood renewal: A national strategy action plan* (SEU, 2001a) was welcomed by commentators. As a long-term strategy, its stated aim was to close the gap between the poorest neighbourhoods and the rest of the country over 10 to 20 years. The wide-ranging objectives to improve health, reduce crime and unemployment, and improve education, housing, and the physical environment in a joined-up way were commended, although not without some disquiet based on the failure of earlier multiagency initiatives (Hancock, 2003). In view of the evidence on the 'dynamic' relationship between urban social policies (especially housing) and crime (Hope, 1998; Wiles & Pease, 2000; Hancock, 2001) the promise of 'joined-up' government and strategies to address the range of problems faced by disadvantaged communities crystallised in the government's *National strategy for neighbourhood renewal* (SEU, 2000a), promoted renewed optimism. The government's commitment to address 'social exclusion' signalled an opportunity to address a range of urban social problems, including crime, 'holistically', and represented a step towards 'social justice' (Hope, 2001a).

Opportunity knocks

Section 17 of the 1998 Crime and Disorder Act offered the *possibility* that a range of criminogenic conditions could be ameliorated; local authorities (with the police) were charged with the duty to consider crime and disorder reduction through various duties. Moreover a chance to address a range of harms that could not be encompassed within narrow legal definitions of 'crime' was opened up (Wiles & Pease, 2000). Some commentators, however, had already expressed concerns about the 'criminalisation of social policy', which followed from the way in which welfare agencies had become increasingly involved in crime prevention under earlier urban policy frameworks and, in these circumstances, social exclusion and disadvantage diminished as important issues in their own right; they were the object of intervention simply because of their implications for social disorder and crime (Crawford, 1997; Gilling & Barton, 1997).

However, following the Act's implementation, it was not the wider interpretations of 'community safety' that aimed to transgress narrow, conventional definitions of 'crime' and encompass a wider conceptualisation of social harm that were mobilised by policy makers and practitioners at local and national levels. Instead "community safety" was equated with "crime reduction" and "crime and disorder reduction", as anti-social behaviour ascended the political agenda (Hughes, 2002, p 128). In as much as this may be read as a 'narrow' view of 'community safety', the definitions employed in the increasingly draconian anti-social behaviour (ASB) policies that followed have also been widened and stretched ("behaviour that has cause, or is likely to cause, alarm, distress or intimidation": Home Office, 2003, p 15) and the summary justice processes have been increasingly truncated for those subjected to sanctions. It is now clear that clampdowns on ASB have placed the safety of the most marginal sections of urban populations in jeopardy (Coleman & Sim, 2005). Moreover, the regeneration of distressed neighbourhoods and, in turn, the strategies adopted to 'socially include' disadvantaged groups rely on the eradication of behaviour and lifestyles deemed to be socially problematic as much as 'anti-social'.

Opportunities missed

The *National strategy for neighbourhood renewal* and supporting documents recognise that factors external to neighbourhoods and related to the restructuring of local and national economies (as well as local and national government policies) explain to a greater or lesser degree the spiral of neighbourhood decline in urban neighbourhoods (Hastings, 2003). Nevertheless, regenerative efforts in NDC areas and elsewhere remain firmly focused on the deficiencies of working-class families and 'communities'. ASB strategies rely on a wholly uncritical acceptance of Wilson and Kelling's (1982) 'broken windows' thesis, and the rather flawed direction of causality – disorder leads to neighbourhood decline – implied in the thesis (see Matthews, 1992, 2003; Hancock, 2001). The *range* of conditions (for example, local labour market prospects) that cause distress in neighbourhoods and promote outward migration are ignored or downplayed. In contrast, addressing 'anti-social behaviour' is regarded as being of paramount importance if social inclusion is to be achieved:

> At the heart of this Government's determination to tackle
> social exclusion is the National Strategy for Neighbourhood
> Renewal. That strategy must tackle and reduce the
> incidence and perception of anti-social behaviour if the
> Government is to achieve its aims of revitalising the most
> deprived communities. Communities drive this agenda. It
> is Government's role to empower them to succeed. (Home
> Office, 2003, para 4.53)

The ambiguity and confusion surrounding working-class communities is clearly reflected in this quotation: "communities drive" these efforts although, at the same time, they need "empowering". They are an "object of policy" and "policy instrument" (Imrie & Raco, 2003, p 6). In this manner the government both assumes, and seeks to create, a community of interest around the objectives of current disorder reduction policies and the means of bringing them to fruition; the government in short "operate[s] with a simplistic communitarian vision" (Matthews, 2003, p 7). Lying outside the communitarian vision are those groups with the least political power and the most limited of economic resources who are frequently reconstructed as *the* problem.

The 'problem' of 'young people hanging around' receives copious commentary in the official documents of national and local governments. Nevertheless, the 'evidence base' most frequently used to justify these policies, the British Crime Survey (BCS), in fact excludes young people. Interestingly, however, the 2003/04 survey showed that 'teenagers hanging around' as a category of 'anti-social behaviour' was behind vandalism and graffiti, misuse of fireworks, problems associated with rubbish and litter, and illegal or inconveniently parked vehicles when 'very' or 'fairly' big problems were reported by respondents (Wood, 2004). The greatest cause for concern was 'speeding traffic'. Moreover, a significant proportion of 'incidents' in the 'teenagers hanging around' category involved young people 'just being a general nuisance' (43%) or 'not doing anything in particular' (6%), especially in more affluent areas. Moreover, "In over a third of incidents (36%), those perceiving problems acknowledged that young people were not being deliberately anti-social" (Wood, 2004, p 25). The survey showed also that in these instances and for the most part those involved did not know the young people involved in the 'incidents' they commented on in the survey.

Regeneration and punitive crime control policies

The relationship between those who observe or report ASB and those who are regarded as its perpetrators is important, but such relationships are challenged under current urban regeneration frameworks. Where young people causing 'annoyance' are regarded as 'part of the community', there is evidence to suggest that residents are more likely to be sympathetic to the plight of young people (Hancock, 2001). This is not to say they wish to 'tolerate'[1] 'anti-social behaviour'.[2] Yet local people may exercise toleration precisely because the impact of a criminal justice response is seen to be more damaging for the alleged 'perpetrator' than the 'annoying' behaviour that is witnessed or experienced. This may be especially the case where the relationship between the 'community' and key agencies such as the police has, historically, been one of antagonism (see Hancock, 2001). In localities where regeneration or gentrification is promoted a more 'punitive' response may emerge because the nature of 'social solidarity', definitions of 'out-groups', and "local theories about the causes of crime", which flow from and, in turn, are influenced by the local "social-cultural context" (Podolefsky & Dubow, 1981, p 15), are re-configured. At least as far as collective actions around crime and disorder are concerned, it is these contextual factors and conditions that are far more important than the nature and extent of 'crime' for understanding community action around crime and disorder (see Skogan, 1988; Hancock, 2001). The kind of 'social mix' promoted in the consumption-led, regenerating city and the fragmentation of community life that has accompanied neoliberalism (Currie, 2002) point towards particular kinds of draconian anti-crime (and disorder) activities.

Urban regeneration versus 'community'?

Urban regeneration in the contemporary period is market-driven and entrepreneurial, 'facilitated' by local authorities and their 'strategic' partners whose efforts centre on competing with other cities, regionally, nationally, and globally, to attract inward investors. In this context, places are 're-branded' and space 'reconstructed' in efforts to attract wealthy visitors, tourists and shoppers (Raco, 2003); consumption-based and 'culture-led' projects lie at the heart of regeneration partners' efforts in the current period (Jones & Wilks-Heeg, 2004; Mooney, 2004). City partnerships proclaim the arrival of a new 'urban renaissance' as a means to achieve inward investment, through image management, as much as regeneration is an objective to be achieved. That said, as Lees

(2003b) argued, much of what is advocated under the heading of 'urban renaissance' is often a thinly veiled attempt to gentrify urban areas. If this position is accepted, there are a number of disturbing implications, not only for the possibility of achieving 'social inclusion', but because the conditions under which crime and criminalisation become more likely are intensified.

The government's communitarian vision, which underpins its 'social inclusion' and community safety/crime and disorder reduction policies, comes under question in this context. For, as Skogan (1988, cited in Hancock, 2001) argued, "in gentrifying areas there may be divisions that preclude community-wide support as new residents and property developers' interests (exchange values) may not coincide with those of long-term residents. Their influence may result in actions against undesirable people and land uses" (p 153). This can, on the one hand, result in campaigns on behalf of property developers and residents to exclude less affluent groups in the 'preservationist' manner Skogan (1988) outlined. Preservationist groups may well avoid direct reference to the threat to their property values; instead, the challenges that people suffering social and economic hardships represent for the 'lifestyle' of people in the 'community' are invoked along with the widespread belief that their presence will be inextricably linked with ASB and crime. An example of this was observed recently in Liverpool when the City Council approved a site near the city centre for use as a homeless hostel, a development that was, reportedly, met with widespread anger: "Problem people attract problem people. They should not be placed so near families with young children in an *up-and-coming* residential area" (Coligan, 2006, emphasis added). On a day-to-day basis, however, it may be more likely that affluent groups will seek protection via the private market in security (Hope, 1999, 2001a), especially where affluent groups are less well established. Either way, the result is a reconfiguring and strengthening of the 'boundaries' of securitised enclaves (Hope, 1999).

Furthermore, the government has stressed the importance of communicating the fact that action has been taken against crime and ASB – via the media, leaflets, public meetings, and so on – to improve 'community confidence' and to facilitate the reporting of sanction breaches. But the aim is not just to tackle 'incidents' of ASB; rather, as paragraph 4.53 in the urban White Paper (Home Office, 2003) cited above shows, *perceptions* must also be addressed; they influence inward investment. Perceptions are, arguably, more important; the 2003/04 BCS shows that "for those measures where trends are available, there have been significant recent falls in the level of [specific] problems perceived"

(Wood, 2004, p 6), although at a general level respondents regarded ASB to be a growing problem. Moreover, if addressing 'perceptions' is the key concern, and the value of 'regeneration' or the 'community' is stressed, above individual interests (including freedoms), as it is in the most radical communitarian thought (see Hancock & Matthews, 2001) – the limitations of this stance need to be recognised. As Buchanan (cited in Hancock & Matthews, 2001) has argued, in more moderate versions of communitarian thought the rights of individuals are recognised for the part they play in *protecting communities*.

In the 'new urban renaissance', the vision of 'normality' is emphatically middle class where norms and lifestyles are concerned (Lees, 2003b; Jones & Wilks-Heeg, 2004; Mooney, 2004). The target residents for re-populating city centres and other inner-urban enclaves are young professionals whose disposable incomes will boost the consumer city. The apartments are "expensive and for the most part, because of limited space, high cost and lack of facilities for children, are only attractive to better-off professional singles and couples without children" (Lees, 2003b, p 71), with predictable consequences for their long-term commitment to and the stability of localities (Lees, 2003b). Typical developments do not attract, nor do developers wish to accommodate, lower-income groups. At the same time, inflated property prices in areas attractive to middle-class re-population mean that established local residents and their children find it difficult to buy into the local property market, even if they earn good local incomes comparatively. Furthermore, despite widely welcomed mixed tenure developments, there is evidence to suggest that "mixed tenure schemes secured through planning conditions and developed by private sector house builders often fail to integrate the affordable housing units sufficiently. Physical barriers (dividing walls and roads) frequently divide tenures" (Cowans & Sparks, 2003). And, of course, developers' design remits include 'security' as an integral feature of the new city centre and emergent inner-urban middle-class enclaves and warehouse conversions alongside the reshaping of crime control practices in city centre public spaces (Coleman & Sim, 2005).

In contrast to the mediated image of the working-class community (see Johnston and Mooney, Chapter Eight, this volume), and perhaps too the middle-class suburb, the gentrification process and the professional city dweller is presented as 'forward looking' in a way that satisfies appeals to 'diversity', 'difference', and the desire for modern 'cosmopolitan' living (Haylett, 2001a). Social interaction, nevertheless, in areas experiencing gentrification is more likely to occur *within* rather than *between* social groups (Butler & Robson, cited in Lees, 2003). This is important because

> ... in locales which are characterised by a high degree of urbanism ... people are less socially integrated, less likely to think of the neighbourhood as 'our community' and less likely to view the youth as 'our kids'. People who are concerned with the upkeep of the community may frequently be concerned with their financial investments as much as the social effects of a criminogenic environment on neighbourhood youth. (Podolefsky & Dubow, 1981, pp 140-1)

In these settings, community groups are more likely to emphasise 'victimisation prevention', rather than social crime prevention (Podolefsky & Dubow, 1981). Furthermore, since ideas about the 'causes' of and 'solutions' to crime and disorder will be conditioned to a greater or lesser degree by dominant discourses around the 'what works' paradigm in crime and disorder reduction in the contemporary setting, these discourses could be expected to influence people's responses (through the 'local social cultural context' in Podolefsky and Dubow's [1981] terms). In this way strategies that appear to be possible, effective, or funded are likely to be promoted, not least because of the potential alliances that can be made with 'primary definers' in the city (Coleman & Sim, 2005), for whom public participation has become increasingly important and in a setting where alternative discourses are quiet or crowded out. Such strategies effectively counter the ideals of 'inclusion'.

'Inclusion' policies and communitarian discourses conceal the way class divisions are reconfiguring and obscure the manner in which power relations are defended in the contemporary city. The problems of crime and disorder are purportedly shared by the 'community' as a whole, and it is the community who, it is assumed, will benefit from crime and disorder reduction policies and the regenerative effects that are expected to follow from their implementation and enforcement. The benefits to be gleaned from claiming moral and cultural superiority over others are downplayed (Haylett, 2001a). And, as Young (2001, pp 30-1) has argued, in the late modern world where ontological insecurity is commonplace 'essentialisms' help to create a 'sense of self', and a major way of achieving this is through the denigration of others. In Young's (1999, p 118) analysis these observations apply as much to 'included' groups as those deemed to be 'socially excluded', but structural exclusion erodes one's sense of identity and facilitates the embracing of essentialised statuses which, in turn, can become self-fulfilling. These increasingly intensive strategies of control have counterproductive effects in this context (Hayward, 2002).

Discourses around social exclusion itself "reproduce, rather than successfully address, cultural aspects of injustice" (Morrison, 2003, p 139; see also Young, 1999; Haylett, 2001a, 2003), which make crime and criminalisation more likely (Young, 2001). Drawing on the work of Nancy Fraser, Morrison (2003) shows how urban regeneration policy discourses portray the 'socially excluded' as 'the problem to be fixed' or corrected. The nature of economically disadvantaged communities, families and their abilities are devalued; they are contrasted with the 'included' – the 'we' in the policy documents. 'They' are 'misrecognised', that is, they are "denied the status of a full partner in social interaction, as a consequence of institutionalised patterns of cultural value that constitute one as comparatively unworthy of respect and esteem" (Frazer, cited in Morrison, 2003, p 140). 'Communities', in this context, are both 'victimised' *and* 'problematic' on a range of indicators. People are described by their deficiencies, young people portrayed as "threatening and potentially dangerous" (Morrison, 2003, p 152). Importantly, as Young (2001) has argued, these kinds of essentialising processes effectively locate deviance within the individual or group – and *not* in the included majority. Simultaneously, they "reaffirm the normality" of the included and "allow, in a Durkheimian fashion … the boundaries of normality to be drawn more definitely and distinctly" (Young, 1999, p 113). What is important, as Young's analysis indicates, is that the 'socially excluded' are often deeply included culturally. Indeed, Young (1999) drawing on Merton (1938), centres the significance of 'inclusion' in the dominant culture, which centres individualism, consumerism, competition, and success, coupled with structural exclusion for understanding discontent and crime in the late modern period.

It is against the dominant economic and cultural forces of contemporary neoliberalism that Hall and Winlow (2004, 2005) locate their analysis of the way social relations between young people are being reshaped. Put briefly, the shift from the industrial city to the neoliberal consumption-led city has fractured working-class communities and social relations that used to be characterised by mutualism, interdependence, and knowledge about the life events of others in the industrial city. Now, in the contemporary context, young people's friendship practices are characterised by individual self-interest and instrumentalism often centred on consumption in the night-time economy. These 'atomising' forces have profound consequences for social cohesion and criminality (Hall & Winlow, 2004, 2005).

Consumption versus citizenship

In as much as economic benefits are supposed to 'trickle down' from the more affluent to those on the margins, the benefits of city centre consumption-led regeneration are also assumed to 'trickle out' to less well-off communities beyond the city centre. However, the kind of 'inclusion' that becomes most manifest in the regenerating city is associated with 'consumption' rather than 'citizenship'. The dominant inclusionary mechanisms therefore sustain and reflect the cultural values associated with consumption, especially in its conspicuous forms. Their importance is magnified because inward capital investment in the city centre is frequently less forthcoming than city planners would desire (Hobbs, Lister, Hadfield, Winlow, & Hall, 2000) and in this context, "the type of 'culture' promoted is often *popular*, rather than so-called 'high' culture" (O'Connor, cited in Hobbs et al, 2000, p 703). In this context, the development of licensed premises is encouraged by city authorities, but not without disquiet, despite the high prevalence of bars in some city centre spaces.

Businesses respond to such congestion by offering cheap drink and other promotions to greatly facilitate consumption (particularly mid-week). The concern to more closely regulate disorder strengthens. These tensions are neatly reflected in Liverpool City Council's (2005) response to the 2003 Licensing Act, for example, which alerts us to the "potential benefits to Liverpool's economy (in terms of business viability and success, increased customer choice and access, increased job opportunities, and greater visitor/tourist potential) [which] must however be balanced against any potential disadvantages, such as an increase in anti-social behaviour, noise nuisance and crime" (para 1.3.1).

Since disorders of this nature pose risks for commercial, retail, and city centre property interests, we see the further intensification of control mechanisms and responsibilisation strategies under contemporary crime control frameworks, and the risk of criminalisation is enhanced. Meanwhile, the 'rehabilitation of public space' places increasing emphasis on the public rather than private sphere, and in so doing obscures the victimisation of a range of social groups who occupy 'the street' (Coleman & Sim, 2005). Those seen to cause 'nuisance' are regarded as 'in' but not 'of' the desired or imagined 'community', their misrecognition reinforced.

Economic and social divisions and victimisation

The need to boost the local economy is the overriding concern for city authorities and regeneration partnerships. Participation in the labour market is, of course, envisaged as the primary route to 'social inclusion' (SEU, 2001a; Young, 2001) and old Thatcherite notions that economically disadvantaged groups will benefit (or are benefiting) from the 'trickle down effect' and the 'trickle out effect' of city centre regeneration (and also of new business parks on urban fringes) remain pervasive. For New Labour, the reform of welfare benefits, tax policies (for example, Tax Credits), and greater access to childcare (for example, Sure Start and the New Deal for Lone Parents) will 'facilitate' access to paid employment. Of course, the government's Etzioni-style communitarianism (Etzioni, 1993, 1997; Hancock & Matthews, 2001) emphasises the idea that developing 'social capital', 'community involvement', and 'participation' will also help to secure benefits (including employment) for disadvantaged groups in distressed localities, with little evidence to support these claims.

What is important to acknowledge here is the tension between efforts to 'narrow the gap' between the most disadvantaged areas and 'the rest of the country' and local regeneration partnerships utilising the 'comparative advantage' of low pay in specific sectors in their efforts to attract increasingly mobile capital:

> Within specific sectors, Merseyside has a clear advantage
> – for example, starting salaries in call centres are generally
> lower on Merseyside than in the North East, South West,
> Wales and Scotland. (Mersey Partnership, 2005, p 48)

Contemporary strategies aimed at 'getting people to work', especially tax and welfare reforms, sustain rather than challenge the inequalities that accompany urban economic restructuring: the National Minimum Wage and Tax Credits may relieve absolute deprivation for many[3] but relative deprivation and its criminogenic consequences (Lea & Young, 1993) are exacerbated in this setting. Since relative deprivation generates "sources of discontent which are liable to generate high crime rates" (Young, 2001, p 46), and new forms of 'misrecognition' produce disaffection, the consequence of the combination, informed by Young's (1999, 2001) analysis, would suggest higher crime rates, particularly violent crimes, under current urban regeneration frameworks.

Furthermore, while the link between poverty and criminal victimisation has been well documented (Hope, 2001a, 2001b), their relationships in space are becoming less visible, it appears, when employing traditional measures and indicators in the contemporary urban context. Although there is no simple geographic distribution pattern as far as income inequalities are concerned, the large concentrations of poverty in the post-industrial towns of Glasgow, Liverpool, Middlesbrough, and the like are thoroughly documented, and need not be rehearsed here. Improvement on some indicators has been observed. Following regenerative efforts since the 1990s in Merseyside, for example, private sector investment in retail, hotels, offices, call centres, and tourism has increased the number of employment opportunities in these sectors; but more recently questions over the stability of these jobs have been foregrounded as the 'new economy' has suffered job losses in the region (Hornby, 2006; Johnson, 2006). Jobs in manufacturing have continued to be shed. While there has been a marked increase in affluence in some postcode areas, entrenched poverty remains (Jones & Wilks-Heeg, 2004). Not surprisingly, analysis of Index of Deprivation data (despite some methodological problems associated with comparison over time) shows that "by and large Merseyside's position was unchanged" between 2000 and 2004; some areas experienced improvement and others deterioration (Mersey Partnership, 2005, p 13).

One consequence of middle-class re-colonisation of inner-city localities and the development of new urban enclaves targeted at the better-off is that the data traditionally drawn on in analyses of spatial and social divisions – ward, postcode, and other area-based indicators – are less able to distinguish divisions with the same degree of accuracy without sophisticated use of GIS (Geographical Information Systems). Recent BCS data on patterns of victimisation appear to be somewhat less certain than previous sweeps. Accepting the usual limitations of the BCS, analysis of findings for 2003/04 shows those who lack security measures on their homes are the most at risk from burglaries and, while it can be reasonably deduced that the more affluent are more likely to afford protection through the private market, the survey also reveals that young people aged 16-24, single parents, people living in affluent urban areas, the economically inactive, and private renters and also people in inner-city localities, on low incomes, and occupying flats or maisonettes, are among the most at risk from burglaries (Dodd, Nicholas, Povey, & Walker, 2004). For 'criminal damage', people in 'urban areas and low income areas' in particular localities, although the survey reveals 'no distinct patterns', younger respondents (16-24 years) and those occupying terraced houses or maisonettes face the greater risks (Dodd et al, 2004, p 56). For violent crimes measured in the survey, young men, unemployed people, single people (especially parents), private renters, and young women followed by those living in flats or maisonettes as well as more prosperous urban professionals were among those most at risk (in order of magnitude).

What remains clear is that the more economically marginal groups can occupy several of these categories at once, which increases their risk (Hope, 1998). The overriding picture from the BCS is one where the least well-off and some more affluent groups in urban areas face greater crime risks than the population as a whole. That said, the ability to 'insulate' properties against crime risk lies with the more affluent, who are also able to benefit from the activities of 'market intelligence companies' (such as Experian) which are increasingly able to identify with ever greater precision the way patterns of advantage and disadvantage (and the risk of victimisation) are reconfiguring in the late modern city. Therefore, in as much as the primary role of the market must be emphasised in an analysis of urban regeneration, the potential for urban social policies, and crime prevention policies too for that matter, cannot be appreciated without the wider context of market responses to reconfiguring inequalities.

Conclusion

The desire to address a range of urban social problems in a 'holistic' manner as it manifested under the auspices of NDC and the *National strategy*, for example, was commendable and strongly supported by criminological research evidence that had revealed the compounded nature of disadvantage in urban communities. Section 17 of the 1998 Crime and Disorder Act, at the same time, opened up the possibility that 'community safety' (broadly conceived) may become a priority for local partnerships. However, the widespread assumption that securing the regeneration of post-industrial cities is dependent on reducing (the perception) of crime and ASB has been used to justify targeting the most marginal groups whose behaviour, lifestyle, or hardships are deemed obstacles to regenerative efforts. For some of the most disadvantaged and politically powerless – such as the homeless and young people – the 'right' to occupy public space has been effectively suspended (Hancock, 2006). Property-led gentrification is reshaping the social 'mix' of inner-city communities in ways that not only undermine rhetorical communitarian ideals, but promote intolerance. National and local policy statements stress the benefits to be gleaned for all sections of the community, neatly encapsulated in Liverpool's City of Culture slogan, 'the world in one city'. However, the discourses surrounding 'inclusion' policies have remained firmly focused on the perceived deficiencies of working-class families and communities, relative deprivation and its criminogenic consequences continues unabated, and the 'cultural injustices' perpetrated against the urban poor continue to be compounded by higher risks of criminal victimisation among these groups.

Notes

[1] Toleration generally refers to "the deliberate choice not to interfere with conduct or beliefs, with which one disapproves" (Hancock & Matthews, 2001, p 99).

[2] However, the reporting of particular behaviours to the police, or in surveys, does not automatically mean that a punitive response is desired; most will simply want annoying behaviour to cease.

[3] Although not all; many asylum seekers, for example, are expected to subsist below minimum income levels.

Part II
Policies and agendas

In this section the focus is on key examples of the kind of policies and practices that mark out the newly criminalised urban policies, operating through a combination of policing, anti-social behaviour strategies, and partnership working by a broad range of agencies and actors. These agencies and actors have the task to work in accordance with new targets, co-working protocols, or broader urban visions in fields that are at least to some extent concerned with urban problems and disorder.

In the first part of this volume we saw how residential spaces and housing has continued to be central to urban policy. In this section Johnstone and MacLeod (Chapter Five) expand on this theme by arguing that urban policy addressing the criticism levelled at design in the renaissance blueprint, as well as its middle-class orientation, raises questions about the extent to which recent urban policies address the social organisation of the city. Johnstone and MacLeod focus on the inner suburbs, rather than council estates, and see the sustainable communities plan as a possible means of alleviating the inequalities suggested by the urban renaissance documentation. Critically they argue that if we accept that anti-social behaviour might be stemmed by reducing residential turnover, thereby building local social bonds, the sustainable communities plan may be effective by its efforts to create places people want to live and remain in.

Perhaps the most visible impact of the New Labour criminal justice legislative programme has been the 1998 Criminal Justice Act. This Act was used to create the Anti-Social Behaviour Order (ASBO), among a range of other orders designed to regulate and control behaviour. ASBOs are now well-discussed and researched (Burney, 2005; Flint, 2006) but were set up particularly to tackle problems in residential neighbourhoods and as a tool for local governments and social housing providers to deal with perceived problem tenants. Of course a key result of this initiative has been to provide a discretionary tool to regulate behaviour that has been unevenly distributed in its implementation. Local authorities, like Manchester City, have become hotbeds for their use and the range of conduct considered 'anti-social' has highlighted the interplay of a discretionary tool with local community assessments of acceptability and civility.

This specific geography of anti-social behaviour in relation to residential neighbourhoods is a salient theme as it marks one of the strong links between urban renewal and criminal justice. This broad agenda, such as it is linked to social housing and areas of exclusion and deprivation, marks strong connections to wider concerns at urban and moral regeneration. ASBOs have been used against prostitutes and traveller communities in an effort to clean up the streets of unwanted groups or 'others' who are displaced to adjacent locations. While ASBOs have undoubtedly served useful corrective functions, the apparent eagerness with which politicians have used such tools has provoked soul searching among those who have been keen to reiterate the importance of reforming, rather than excluding and criminalising, sections of young people.

Two of the following contributions examine the wider issues of anti-social behaviour in relation to urban spaces and their renewal. For Johnston and Mooney (Chapter Eight) the New Labour battle to control anti-social behaviour has been based on a sensationalised representation of spaces in decline, particularly areas of social renting. Their central argument is that a focus on anti-social behaviour has become synonymous with neighbourhoods comprising almost exclusively social housing. Like Hancock, they argue that this has had the effect of criminalising communities who are effectively tarred with a broad and indiscriminate brush wielded by policy makers. The effect is the further reinforced exclusion of precisely those groups who need assistance in dealing with very real local problems and who are often called on by politicians to 'take a stand'. All of this has created a politics of problem spaces and people, largely seen through a punitive legislative regime that was spearheaded by the Crime and Disorder Act and the populist ASBO culture beneath it.

These geographies of decline have a long history, as Johnston and Mooney argue, and it is mandatory to see the reconfiguration of 'dangerous classes and dangerous spaces' as a continual theme of urban policy. Here New Labour's communitarian project marks only the most recent attempt in a much longer lineage of policy interventions. For Millie (Chapter Seven) the key concern is with how effective policies might be produced to tackle anti-social behaviour. In a detailed study of anti-social behaviour and policies designed to address such problems he sees policies often parachuted in without prior consultation or ensuring effective champions on the ground. The effect is to produce uneven outcomes. While acknowledging that if anti-social behaviour is concentrated in areas of relative deprivation and is associated with neighbourhood dissatisfaction, then tackling anti-social behaviour alongside regeneration work will have mutual benefits. Ultimately the benefits of coordinating these efforts is not achieved, particularly since generating the engagement of people on the ground may be thwarted by situations where communities have been let down in the past.

As we argued in the introduction (Chapter One), policy responses to disorder are not only connected to urban regeneration and residential neighbourhoods. Instead, recent events highlight the fears over terrorist attacks on central city infrastructure, notably of recent landmark projects and vital nodal points such as airports or government buildings. Here, Murakami-Wood and Coaffee (Chapter Six) show how the urban provides a theatre within which fears of otherness and terrorism are projected in the current state of acute anxiety. Under these circumstances rights of citizens to access public space may be suspended under conditions where such rights are considered by authorities to be threatening. As conference tourism provided revenue streams for local economies, now conferences where political parties gather en masse are seen as targets that require defending and securing. Clearly these issues pose important questions for our current understanding of urban citizenship and rights to the spaces of the city that, perhaps, are only likely to be debated further.

A key critique of the current government's agendas and initiatives has been the need to provide new initiatives and modes of working. This has been particularly evident in relation to policies and practice in the fields of urban policy and criminal justice. As cities and crime have provided a key focal point for policy making in the past decade so have the crime sciences, performance indicators, newly invented partnerships, and other programmes provided commentators and practitioners with great difficulty in keeping up. The implications for practice, in particular, have been profound with community groups and other partnerships attempting to attract strategic funding that has mutated or shifted in its objectives, sometimes almost overnight. This unstable framework has undoubtedly adversely affected the effectiveness of what have often been innovative and enthusiastically received ideas from policy makers. The result has been fatigue in the competitive funding arena and reduced force on the ground in many cases.

FIVE

New Labour's 'broken' neighbourhoods: liveability, disorder, and discipline?

Craig Johnstone and Gordon MacLeod

This chapter investigates the approach to urban renewal adopted by Britain's New Labour government in the early years of the 21st century. We contend that the Labour administration's initial concern to foster an 'urban renaissance', articulated most vividly in its 2000 urban White Paper (DETR, 2000), appears to have at least partly been displaced by an explicit endeavour to create 'sustainable communities' (ODPM, 2003). At the heart of the sustainable communities agenda is the acknowledgement that places and neighbourhoods need to be economically viable, effectively governed, and, literally, 'liveable'. In doing so it recognises that any revitalisation of distressed neighbourhoods – whether inner city, suburban or peripheral housing estate – requires them to be clean, safe, and attractive, places where people would actually choose to live rather than places to which people are simply shunted at the whim of some bureaucratically administered diktat (ODPM, 2005a).

In the endeavour to create such 'sustainable communities', the government, we contend, is actively targeting visible signs of 'disorder' within England's 'broken' neighbourhoods,[1] ranging from void housing and a degraded urban environment to forms of anti-social behaviour (ASB) that are likely to unsettle the sensibilities of 'respectable' citizens. One notable consequence of this is that such neighbourhoods have become the projected state spaces where strategies for urban renewal intersect with those for criminal justice and labour market regulation (see Peck, 2003), the motivation being to purge these spaces of any perceived signs and symbols of disorder while simultaneously disciplining the purportedly inappropriate habitus of marginalised groups.

This chapter is concerned to critically evaluate three themes. The first relates to a notable modification of the geographical horizons of

New Labour's urban renewal agenda. For while the earlier trumpeting of an urban renaissance clearly implied further revitalisation of the commercial and industrial heartlands of Britain's towns and cities, the sustainable communities agenda seems to signal a notable stretching beyond the city centre and a more concerted endeavour to revive distressed inner and outer suburban neighbourhoods. In turn, these spaces have become the testing grounds for new public policy tools and their inhabitants objectivised – and indeed in Foucauldian terms 'subjectivised' – as the targets of communitarian discourses of civic responsibility and inclusion (cf Etzioni, 1998; Johnston and Mooney, Chapter Eight, this volume).

The second theme examines the substantive significance of 'liveability' to the 'sustainable communities' agenda. Pre-election commitments to social justice and equality of opportunity have meant that, since coming to power, the New Labour government has been concerned to address the entrenched disadvantage bedevilling the most deprived urban neighbourhoods and, consequently, has invested heavily in its *National strategy for neighbourhood renewal* (Kearns & Turok, 2003). What appears to differentiate these interventions from those of previous administrations, however, is an attempt to confront in a more holistic approach, the manifold problems facing deprived neighbourhoods. This includes getting to grips with concepts such as 'liveability' and 'quality of life', both of which are subject to considerable contestation and hard to measure in practice. Indeed, as a consequence, it seems that contemporary endeavours to enhance liveability have become inherently politicised, not least in the way that one of their fundamental concerns – 'anti-social behaviour' – has been propelled into the mainstream of political, public policy, media, and lay discourses (Squires, 2006).

In the final section, we aim to interpret the broader implications of the sustainable communities liveability agenda through the lens of a range of distinct, although we would argue potentially interlinked, conceptual approaches. In briefly discussing communitarianism, the penal state, the 'dispersal of discipline' thesis, and the revanchist city perspective, we conclude that certain policies designed to purge the *signs* of neighbourhood 'disorder' and to discipline the purported *agents* of such disorder are, in effect, serving to penalise the very existence of socioeconomic marginalisation. In so objectivising the deprived neighbourhood as a space of discipline and control, and thereby reinforcing the very exclusion being experienced by certain segments of society, it may be that the New Labour government is creating sustainable communities for a selective rather than a universal 'public'.

Urban renaissance to sustainable communities: extending policy horizons

Shortly after coming to power in 1997, Britain's New Labour government dramatically enlivened the political discourse about cities and moved swiftly to identify as one of its key objectives the stimulation of what became termed an 'urban renaissance' (Holden & Iveson, 2003; Johnstone & Whitehead, 2004). An Urban Task Force was quickly mobilised. Chaired by the illustrious architect Lord Richard Rogers, the Urban Task Force (1999) produced a report that boldly proclaimed, "We must bring about a change in urban attitudes so that towns and cities once again become attractive places in which to live, work and socialise" (p 7). Its overriding concern was to revitalise the distressed commercial and industrial heartlands of Britain's towns and cities. Considerable emphasis was placed on good urban design, effective land-use reclamation and, in particular, the restoration of 'brownfield' sites. Interpreted by some as a 'gentrifiers' charter' (Smith, 2002) or as an aspiration to create an 'urban idyll' focused around city centre living (Hoskins & Tallon, 2004), the Task Force report and the subsequent urban White Paper (DETR, 2000) were certainly nudging towards a movement 'back to the city'. Nonetheless, and while the urban White Paper itself takes on board many of the ideas encapsulated in the Task Force report, the latter's ostensibly middle-class, cafe culture-oriented excesses are tempered somewhat, largely as a consequence of the involvement of the government's Social Exclusion Unit (Lees, 2003b). However, as Lees (2003b) contends, the fundamental shortcoming of the White Paper is that, despite all the sanguine rhetoric of social inclusion and sustainability, it offered little in the way of substantial plans to do anything about them.

In its post-2000 policy proclamations, however, New Labour seems to be offering a more meaningful approach towards tackling social exclusion which, it is worth recalling, has long been one of its purported commitments (Commission on Social Justice, 1994). The rhetoric has been modified: the luminously upbeat discourse of 'urban renaissance' at least in part superseded by the more ostensibly earnest concept of 'sustainable communities' (ODPM, 2003, 2005a). As a signatory mantra underpinning all elements of urban policy in England,[2] the sustainable communities agenda has seen the launch of a number of initiatives designed to reduce inequalities and to improve the quality of life in inner urban and suburban neighbourhoods. All of which, in turn, implies that the geographical horizons of urban policy have been extended beyond the erstwhile preoccupation with city centre revitalisation (cf Coleman et al, 2005; Bannister, Fyfe, & Kearns, 2006).

To be sure, the sustainable communities approach promises to foster sustainable economic growth in designated high-profile zones like the Thames Gateway (ODPM, 2003; Raco, 2005). However, a notable primary concern is to confront the seemingly intractable problems that are deemed to compromise everyday life in deprived urban neighbourhoods. Of course, British urban policy has long been associated with the problems of deindustrialised inner cities or the 'sink' estates of the urban periphery (Hill, 1994). But while the sustainable communities agenda retains an interest in these, especially the social housing estates where some of the most acute concentrations of deprivation continue to be found, its prime target appears to be those neighbourhoods in the ageing inner suburbs. Often forged out of the Industrial Revolution and heavily concentrated in the towns and cities of northern and central England, such neighbourhoods have endured prolonged deterioration since the 1960s, as the redundancy of the factories, docks, and sites of heavy industry on which the majority of residents relied directly or indirectly for employment has been paralleled by substantial out-migration. In some locations demand for tightly packed byelaw terraced housing, built to house working–class families tied to local industry had, like the factory work, almost completely collapsed by the end of the 1990s and countless properties stood vacant (see SEU, 1999; Lee & Nevin, 2003; Cole & Nevin, 2004). Put another way, some towns and cities now possess a substantial surplus of dwellings relative to their population: for example, Liverpool has seen its population halve from 852,000 in 1931 to 439,000 in 2001 (ODPM, 2005f).

The decline of the inner suburbs has profound implications for individual trajectories, family life, and community cohesion. In what is held to be a classic investigation into what happens to neighbourhoods when work disappears, Wilson (1987) argues that the departure of the more skilled and formally educated residents – those best placed to seek out new employment opportunities elsewhere – tends to strip communities of their leaders and positive role models, the glue that helps bind communities together. Whether or not one subscribes fully to Wilson's perspective – which, it is worth emphasising, is based on research undertaken in Chicago – it seems that this population drain can often impact quite profoundly on the viability of community institutions and neighbourhood services, be this in the form of local shops, decent pubs, or health provision. There is also a terrible irony here in that it is those who are most in need of good local services – the sick, older people, single parents on low incomes, and long-term unemployed people – who predominate in deindustrialised neighbourhoods. The availability of cheap accommodation also leads to a further influx of those in the lowest income brackets, further concentrating disadvantage in them. In reviewing the situation in Britain in the 1990s, the Social Exclusion Unit (SEU, 1998) claimed that "the poorest neighbourhoods have tended to become more rundown, more prone to crime, and more cut off from the labour market.... They have become no go areas for some and no exit zones for others" (p 1).

In almost every post-industrial town and city, this concentration of inner suburban decline appears to be forming a necklace of neglect that encircles dramatically revived, sometimes glittering, urban centres. In more general terms, of course, this is the fractured geography we associate with the so-called post-modern city, comprised of enclaves of wealth and poverty often sitting cheek-by-jowl (Dear, 2000; Soja, 2000). Aside from being an urban nightmare for the growing army of city image makers (Hoskins & Tallon, 2004), as David Garland (2000) observes, a decaying inner suburban belt fuels wider public unease about crime and disorder, particularly among the middle classes. For unlike the problems of peripheral 'sink' estates, which to a great extent are 'out of sight out of mind', the inner suburbs are routinely witnessed by thousands of residents and commuters. Each day passers-by are exposed to visible signs of dereliction and disorder, not least crumbling and sometimes burnt-out buildings, vandalised public spaces, and congregated groups of putatively feral children. Thus, and importantly from the vantage point of New Labour, any endeavour to remake the visual appearance of a community has significant implications that stretch beyond its own individual boundaries.

New Labour's most recent response is the sustainable communities plan, which set in train a substantial physical remodelling of the worst-affected areas through the introduction of nine housing market renewal (HMR) pathfinders (ODPM, 2005f). Their task is to reinvigorate demand for local housing and to narrow the gap in housing market performance that exists between pathfinder areas and the regions in which they are located. To achieve this, pathfinders are involved in three interrelated tasks: first, a programme of selective – and in some cases extensive – demolition backed by compulsory purchase powers; second, the renovation of the most viable properties; and third, facilitation of the construction, by private developers and housing associations, of properties that would meet the consumer preferences of 21st-century owners and tenants. In essence, such neighbourhoods are viewed to be sustainable only if they are fundamentally transformed and made appealing to new types of residents. Yet while HMR is a significant (and costly) intervention, it impacts directly on a very small number of communities. Of much greater national significance are those aspects of the sustainable communities agenda concerned with enhancing liveability more generally.

The term 'liveability' is widely used but hard to define. The most recent *State of the cities* report (Parkinson, Champion, Evans, et al, 2006) contends that:

> Liveability is concerned with the quality of place and the built environment. It is about how easy a place is to use and how safe it feels. It is about creating a sense of place by creating an environment that is both inviting and enjoyable.... The liveability agenda is essentially about creating places where people want to live. (p 156)

The report is careful to point out that liveability should not be conflated with 'quality of life', which it views as much broader in scope, dependent also on factors such as health, education, and poverty. Within government, however, definitions of liveability still vary. Public Service Agreement (PSA) 8 sets targets for improving liveability for local authorities. All seven targets are concerned with environmental considerations such as litter, abandoned vehicles, quality of parkland, and so on. In contrast, when asked in Parliament to explain what liveability meant, Tony Blair stated: "Liveability is the ability of local communities to be free from crime and fear" (Prime Minister's Questions, 2006). Even though a certain amount of inconsistency prevails, there seems to be general agreement – evident in policy and more recent legislation from the Office of the Deputy Prime Minister/Department for Communities and Local Government and summed up by the *State of the cities* report (Parkinson et al, 2006) – that liveability is influenced by a mixture of urban fabric, environmental, and community safety considerations.

In disadvantaged neighbourhoods nationwide, poor quality public spaces, unrepaired vandalism, graffiti, abandoned vehicles, litter, and fly tipping are all likely to erode the quality of life for existing inhabitants while equally rendering such neighbourhoods less attractive places for prospective residents (Shaw, 2004). These dimensions of liveability were the focus of New Labour's 2005 Clean Neighbourhoods and

Environment Act. This legislation and other interventions[3] seeking to ensure that neighbourhoods are clean, pleasant, well maintained, and well managed are premised on the assumption that physically presentable neighbourhoods are those in which residents will take pride and, because they have the general impression of being cared for, may be less prone to crime, whether low level or otherwise (see Wilson & Kelling, 1982). Not only are these ills viewed to be detrimental to community well-being in their own right, they are also purported to compromise any potential gains of regeneration. Indeed, the *Respect Action Plan* (Home Office, 2006a) observes that in order to ensure quality of life is actually improved in deprived areas, "we must make sure that anti-social behaviour does not undermine it" (p 28). It is the apparent convergence of urban policy objectives with criminal justice agendas under the rubric of 'liveability' in deprived neighbourhoods to which we turn in the next section.

Fixing 'broken' neighbourhoods: the intersection of urban regeneration and criminal justice policy

> • Tackling anti-social behaviour is a fundamental part of the drive to improve the quality of life for people in our towns and cities and is key to creating sustainable communities. (Yvette Cooper, Regeneration Minister, speaking at the Home Office Anti-Social Behaviour Conference, October 2003)

English urban regeneration programmes, from Urban Development Corporations (UDCs) to the urban renaissance, have long been concerned with enhancing the physical appearance of run-down areas. However, not since the responsibility for urban policy was removed from the Home Office in 1977 have area-based regeneration initiatives devoted so much attention to questions of social order. For in early 21st-century England, it has become paramount to purge neighbourhoods of any visible *signs* of disorder and to discipline the *agents* of this disorder. The sustainable communities of New Labour rhetoric are to be pleasant, attractive, clean, tolerant, respectful, friendly, and inclusive places rich in social capital and a 'collective efficacy' and where the bonds between residents are strong (Atkinson & Flint, 2004). Disorder, or at least 'disorder' as perceived by governmental technologies – whether signalled by void and derelict housing, benefit scroungers, or anti-social teenagers – has thus become a primary target of urban regeneration and criminal justice policy (Shaw, 2004).

Matters pertaining to crime and 'anti-social behaviour' have each featured prominently in national schemes like the New Deal for Communities, neighbourhood management and neighbourhood renewal, and the publication of the *Respect Action Plan* has only intensified such concerns (CRESR, 2005; SQW & Partners, 2005; Home Office, 2006a). In neighbourhoods where residents have had the opportunity to shape the priorities of regeneration schemes, community safety issues have invariably been identified as most in need of attention. Concern typically focuses on low-level disorder and behaviour that is not strictly criminal, such as young people hanging around on the streets, although in some areas prostitution and drug dealing are known to be prevalent. Regeneration schemes have responded by contributing funding to improve street lighting, the extension of closed circuit television (CCTV) coverage, the gating of alleyways and blocking off of other crime-prone locations, additional policing, patrols by neighbourhood wardens, and Youth Inclusion Programmes (Bannister et al, 2006). Whether any of these measures prevent offending and offensive behaviour or simply displace them to surrounding neighbourhoods is unclear but they are, nevertheless, illustrative of a governmental concern to identify and remove or risk manage individuals who threaten the liveability of these places. Most significant in realising this end, however, are the new criminal justice powers introduced to curb ASB.[4] Crucially, it seems that ASB has swiftly become a virtual metaphor for the condition of contemporary Britain, and indeed British youth now stands as a byword for rudeness, loutishness, intolerance, selfishness, disrespect, drunkenness, and violence (Squires, 2006).

To combat ASB, New Labour has produced an extensive menu of legal sanctions and new powers for state agencies. The most high profile is the Anti-Social Behaviour Order (ASBO). Imposed by the civil courts,[5] recipients of ASBOs are required to desist from certain types of behaviour and often also to refrain from entering specific geographic spaces and from associating with named individuals. An order is valid for a minimum of two years and there is no upper time limit. Significantly, breach of the stipulations of an ASBO can result in a maximum of five years' imprisonment. Its status as a civil order means that it is not the police but local authorities and housing associations that are central to their successful implementation: from the collation of dossiers of evidence on the anti-social, through giving evidence in court, to ensuring that any breaches do not pass unnoticed.[6] Another important pre-criminal intervention over which these agencies exercise control is the Acceptable Behaviour Contract (ABC). Such contracts are drawn up by social housing landlords and usually signed by the 'anti-social' children of tenants (or if the children are under 10 years old the tenants themselves). Breach of the contract can speed the forfeiture of tenancy and/or be used in court as evidence in support of an ASBO application (Home Office, 2003; Flint, 2006).

There are a number of further measures to note here. The Dispersal Order is particularly significant because it focuses not on individuals who are deemed anti-social but on the actual geographic spaces in which ASB is considered to be especially prevalent. Any public area identified by a senior police officer and city authority chief executive as being prone to persistent ASB and which has been the site of related public harassment or distress can be subject to a Dispersal Order. There is no centrally imposed restriction on the size of the area that can be designated but an order automatically expires after six months. It provides the police with powers to disperse groups of two or more people and remove minors to their homes between 9pm and 6am if their presence "has resulted, or is likely to result, in any members of the public being intimidated, harassed, alarmed or distressed" (Home Office, 2003, section 30.3). For adults, failure to comply can result in imprisonment for up to three months. Local child curfews, if imposed, similarly allow under-10s to be returned to their homes if found in pre-designated public spaces after 9pm.

While these measures aim to manage the geography and sociology of ASB, Parenting Contracts and Orders approach the problem from a different angle. Parenting Contracts are voluntary agreements between the government's Youth Offending Teams and the parents of children convicted of ASB whereby parents agree to exercise certain responsibilities and typically to attend training to improve their parenting skills. A breach of contract or failure to agree to a contract can result in the imposition by the courts of a Parenting Order and failure to meet its conditions usually leads to a return to court for further sentencing. The *Respect Action Plan* (Home Office, 2006a) has also called for a renewed endeavour to enforce parental responsibility, and the possibility of 'neighbours from hell' being temporarily removed in order to secure training facilities for intensive intervention has been floated by government. As Fyfe, Bannister, and Kearns (2006) argue, ABCs, Parenting Orders, and Tenancy Agreements all seem to be pointing further in the direction of a contract-based citizenship in which rights and entitlements are conditional on particular duties and obligations.

How are we to account for this proliferation of legislation and initiatives designed as a crackdown on 'anti-social behaviour'? Tony Blair himself maintained throughout his premiership (cf Blair, 2006b), and in the face of some trenchant criticism of ASB legislation (Napo, 2005; O'Malley & Waiton, 2005; YJB, 2005), that his government was quite simply responding to the demands of decent 'hard-working families' living in deprived communities whose lives are made unbearable by the ASB of others (see Field, 2003). These people are Labour's natural constituency, as much as one still exists and, in political respects, improving their quality of life might be seen as the early 21st-century equivalent of the slum clearance programme pursued with gusto by the Wilson Labour administration during the 1960s. Yet as Cummins (2005) points out, through the rhetoric of ASB, politicians have actively coaxed citizens to comprehend modes of human behaviour in new ways. Feeding on perceptions of a rising tidal wave of crime and armed with a novel and powerfully evocative discourse with which to demonise others, and backed by a raft of no-nonsense stoutly authoritarian legislation, some residents in distressed neighbourhoods have successfully waged the power of the state against other families and groups within their own 'communities'. In this context it is hardly surprising that the European Commissioner for Human Rights (2005, para 110) was moved to observe that civil orders like ASBOs "look rather like personalised penal codes, where non-criminal behaviour becomes criminal for individuals who have incurred the wrath of the community". It is interesting to note here the significant concentration on youth: for, aside from the fact that curfews and Dispersal Orders are specifically designed to shape young people's use of public space, a disproportionate number of ASBOs have been imposed on teenagers (Napo, 2005; Squires & Stephen, 2005; Shilling, 2006).

Conclusion

So far in this chapter we have examined how the discourse of urban renaissance has been superseded by that of sustainable communities, and explored some of the socio-spatial implications of this. We have also outlined some of the policy interventions that are emerging from this sustainable communities agenda and, in doing so, reveal a growing convergence of urban and criminal justice policies around issues of liveability and quality of life. In signalling these intentions, it would appear that the Labour government is no longer content to render deprived neighbourhoods as mere holding pens for the poor: spaces essentially beyond the reach of public policy. This contrasts with earlier eras, when entrepreneurial downtown renaissance was – as in the US (Smith, 1996; Mitchell, 1997) – interested primarily in clearing signs and symbols of disorder from high-value urban spaces and not unduly concerned with the eventual consequences, whether this be the geographical displacement from such premium spaces of prostitution, street brawling, or working-class street culture (Short & Ditton, 1998; MacLeod, 2002; Coleman et al, 2005). Indeed, the sustainable communities approach is notable for attempting to neutralise the threat to community cohesion posed by so-called 'problem' residents without displacing them en masse[7] and is doing so, New Labour maintains, with the support of large segments of the communities concerned.

In these regards, then, the sustainable communities schema might offer some scope for a socially inclusive approach to urban regeneration. While it is easy to sneer at some of the methods adopted by government to achieve its objectives, progressives of whatever politico-ideological persuasion would be hard pushed to contest the criteria through which the sustainable communities model is being defined (ODPM, 2005c; Raco, 2005). There can be little doubt that a neighbourhood will only reach a sustainable condition if it becomes a place where current and prospective residents actually want to live. Only then will 'churning' of population slow and the cohesive bonds of community, on which New Labour places so much emphasis, have a chance to emerge. Nonetheless, we have reservations about the implications of the agenda being pursued and so, in the remainder of this chapter, we interpret the sustainable communities agenda, and Labour's attempt to transform deprived communities into liveable spaces, through a number of theoretical lenses.

First, on some levels New Labour's disciplinary route towards establishing sustainable communities sees it drawing resonances with the language of the communitarian philosophy, which was so central to Blair's premiership. Communitarianism laments the erosion of civil society and its institutions, particularly the family and the community, blaming in particular the perceived dominance of liberal values since the 1960s (Etzioni, 1998). It posits that individual rights, which it contends have increased sharply in the latter decades of the 20th century, have become disconnected from any sense of social responsibility and that citizens should only be earning such rights by accepting that they have responsibilities to wider society (Home Office, 2003). Thus, while the focus on quality of life acknowledges that all citizens have the right to live in clean, well-managed, and safe neighbourhoods, it also underlines that residents have a responsibility to respect the rights of others, a responsibility that the state will enforce if it is not exercised through choice.

Related to this, and indeed central to the more right-wing brands of communitarianism (Etzioni, 1998; see also Levitas, 1998; Hale, 2004), is the re-moralisation of society as a crucial first stage in the rebuilding of families and communities. Labour's *Respect Action Plan* (Home Office, 2006a) is a good example of this re-moralising agenda in that it seeks to re-instil seemingly lost social values (cf Whitehead, 2004). Essentially, the power of the state is being mobilised here to discipline the so-called 'hard to reach' or 'hard of hearing' (McLaughlin, 2002), those who cannot, due to their marginalisation within society, or will not, due to their disaffection, participate in the enterprising and civilising neoliberal project being pursued by New Labour. While the workfare regime introduced by the Treasury perhaps illustrates this disciplinary tendency most effectively (see Peck, 2003), the targeting of threats to liveability in deprived communities is also symbolic. Critics, however, contend that the nostalgic, conservative, and utopian vision of community that New Labour shares with communitarians fails to acknowledge that strong communities can become 'pockets of intolerance and prejudice', 'intrinsically exclusive' in that they are inward-looking entities that define themselves in opposition to other groups or geographic areas (Johnstone, 2004; Herbert, 2005).

Second, by relying increasingly on the instruments of criminal justice rather than those available to social and urban policy per se, the sustainable communities liveability agenda resonates powerfully with recent pronouncements about the onset of a penal state in advanced countries. While the burgeoning of highly visible punitive solutions to urban problems can be located partly in a political desire for public and tabloid popularity (Garland, 2000), Wacquant (2001, 2006) sees such attempts to govern through criminal justice as part of a more general attack on the dispossessed. In his recent book, *Punishing the poor: The new government of social insecurity*, Wacquant (2006) contends that contemporary policies

> ... purport to attack head-on the problem of crime as well as urban disorders and the public nuisances that border the confines of penal law, baptised 'incivilities,' while deliberately disregarding their causes ... to do so, they claim to rely on the recovered or renewed capacity of the state to durably submit so-called problem populations and territories to the common norm. (p 2)

The drive to create sustainable communities has arguably extended the pervasiveness of the penal state. In recoding certain types of behaviour as anti-social and such behaviour as deviant in the eyes of the law, Labour has brought "a whole range of persons, predominantly the young, within the scope of the criminal justice system and, often enough, behind bars without necessarily having committed a recognisable criminal offence" (European Commissioner for Human Rights, 2005, para 83). While the legal instruments designed to enforce pro-social behaviour do not automatically funnel recipients into prison, critics, including the government's own Youth Justice Board (2005), argue that those in receipt of ASBOs are in many respects set up to fail as it is often difficult for them to abide by the stringent conditions imposed on their daily life. Furthermore, in defining ASB so vaguely and only requiring those bringing a charge to prove that the behaviour in question was 'likely' to cause harassment, alarm or distress, the government has made it very easy for those on the margins to be caught up in the fine mesh of the criminal justice dragnet (Squires & Stephen, 2006).

Third, certain measures to enhance liveability resonate strongly with Cohen's (1979, 1985) 'dispersal of discipline' thesis. Cohen argued that non-custodial and ostensibly less punitive criminal justice interventions work by spreading discipline, in a truly Foucauldian sense, throughout the social body. They enable the locus of social control to migrate from within the walls of the prison to the communities in which deviance is claimed to occur. Sanctions relating to ASB encourage those who are targeted to take responsibility for their own fate: breech and be punished, conform and escape further sanction. Dispersal Orders approach the problem in a slightly different way by laying a blanket of enhanced social control over a demarcated geographic space. What is perhaps more significant to this discussion, however, is the enrolment of families and communities as agents of social control. Parents who fail in their child-rearing duties can risk tenancy forfeiture or legal sanction. For their part, 'responsibilised' members of communities play a crucial role in bringing ASB to the attention of the authorities, giving evidence against those they construe as anti-social, and providing informal surveillance of the deviant once restrictions on their behaviour have been secured. The European Commissioner for Human Rights (2005) has noted that those found guilty of ASB are those whose behaviour has incurred the collective wrath of their community. It is possible, therefore, that government attempts to make communities more sustainable may only serve to entrench pre-existing divisions within neighbourhoods, as those who are deemed responsible and thus 'worthy' are empowered to shape how the allegedly irresponsible minority should be controlled.

Finally, and while not wishing to overstate the case, there is a risk that New Labour's latest solution to urban problems may give rise to a further 'revanchist' retaking of urban space from the poor and dispossessed by the affluent middle classes, and the intensified intolerance and growing fear of 'the other' that this often evokes (see Smith, 1996, 1998). The work of Garland (2000) in particular highlights how the punitive and exclusionary political responses to crime and disorder common in contemporary Britain are not simply occurring at the whim of government but reflect "the deep sense of vulnerability, of insecurity, of precariousness" (p 361) felt by the middle classes as a consequence of the profound socio-cultural and economic changes that swept Britain in the latter decades of the 20th century, and the growing intolerance of deviance and difference among these influential professional classes, the liberal elite. Further, as Walsh (cited in Squires, 2006) has noted, curfew and Dispersal Orders go much further than simply seeking to control the criminal behaviour or ASB of young people; rather they aim "to control their behaviour completely … [and] seek to ban groups of young people congregating in public at night, regardless of whether or not their intent is criminal, or indeed, antisocial" (p 160). All things considered, then, it may be that discretionary street-level enforcement action seems more likely to widen rather than close 'justice gaps'. But as Tony Blair articulated during his premiership – and echoing the warning shots of the revanchist thesis (Smith, 1998) – we are no longer interested in understanding the social causes of criminality, "people have had enough of this part of the 1960s consensus … they want rules, order and proper behaviour" (Blair, 2004).

Notes

[1] This chapter focuses on policy developed in England. Although a similar ethos is identifiable in policies deployed in other parts of the UK, Scottish urban and criminal justice problems have long been governed from Edinburgh (see Turok, 2004) and since devolution in 1999 responsibility for most Welsh urban issues (although not criminal justice) has been transferred from Westminster to Cardiff.

[2] Until it was transferred to the new Department for Communities and Local Government in May 2006, urban policy in England came under the remit of the Office of the Deputy Prime Minister, which itself superseded the Department for Environment, Transport and the Regions in 2002.

[3] Examples include neighbourhood management, neighbourhood wardens, the Liveability Fund, the 'Cleaner, Safer, Greener' Agenda and establishing the Commission for Architecture and the Built Environment (CABE).

[4] For definitions of ASB and an exploration of the concept see Millie, Chapter Seven, this volume.

[5] Increasingly ASBOs are also being imposed 'on conviction' in the criminal courts. They typically accompany another punishment or may come into force once an offender has been released from custody in an attempt to discourage recidivism. Of most concern to critics are interim ASBOs imposed by the civil courts on limited evidence often without the accused being present (see YJB, 2005).

[6] In January 2007 the government announced that powers to apply for ASBOs would be extended to selected council estate residents groups.

[7] That is not to say the threat of displacement through, for example, ABCs, is not used as a mechanism for maintaining pro-social behaviour.

SIX

Lockdown! Resilience, resurgence, and the stage-set city

David Murakami Wood and Jon Coaffee
with Katy Blareau,[1] Anna Leech, James McAllister Jones, and
Jonathan Parsons

For almost a week in February 2005, a large section of the newly regenerated south bank of the River Tyne, in Gateshead, was entirely sectioned off from the rest of the Newcastle-Gateshead conurbation by metal fencing, armed police, closed circuit television (CCTV) cameras and road closures. The headline in the *Newcastle Chronicle* was 'Lockdown!' (Smith, 2005), and so it seemed to be. This is an increasingly familiar experience in many British cities: Brighton and Manchester had experienced much the same the year before, Edinburgh would later in the same year. In the former, as in Gateshead, it was the annual conference of the ruling Labour Party, in Edinburgh, the G8 summit.

This chapter examines the Gateshead 'lockdown' and traces this particular event back through three linked and increasingly intertwined contextual threads: disaster preparedness; urban management through territorial defence; and surveillance. It argues that these threads are being woven together in an emerging conception of urban resilience, a combination of security and recovery from disaster that is becoming increasingly central to urban policy, and furthermore that this urban resilience is itself being woven into concepts of urban competitiveness linked to regeneration, one aspect of which being the need for security of the elite-driven urban redevelopment agenda that relies heavily on attracting such 'meetings tourism' as both evidence and product of regional, national, or even global urban economic status. It argues that the intertwining of these trajectories in the resurgent city concept heralds an era of a renewed pragmatic and open control of the city by hyper-mobile transnational 'kinetic elites' who, while participating little in the slow, difficult, and more dangerous spaces of ordinary people, are able to move rapidly in and through urban spaces with little risk to themselves (Slotterdijk, 1998; Murakami Wood & Graham, 2006).

However, it also argues that such controls, like the perambulatory mediaeval court, and like the regeneration strategies they seek to protect, are in many ways superficial and image-centred, or what Williams (2004) calls, the city "not so much materialised, as staged" (p 229), and that this undermines many of the claims to resilience.

Policy responses to urban threats

Cities continue to be sites for both strategic and opportunistic violence. As Warren (2002) notes, "urban areas in many nations have experienced decades of formal and guerrilla warfare in varying degrees of intensity" (p 614). However, the contemporary city requires openness and complex interlinkages in a variety of regional, national, and global flowspaces. It can no longer respond with external fortification or abandonment and retreat (Farish, 2003). It is the continuing centrality of cities in 21st-century life, the concentration of wealth and key societal functions, that also makes cities vulnerable to natural hazards (Henstra, Kovacs, McBean, and Sweeting, 2004) and human threats.

Three main policy responses to urban threats can be identified: first, emergency or contingency planning; second, territorial control and the making of boundaries; and third, increasing and more sophisticated surveillance. However, since the attacks on New York, London, Madrid, and elsewhere, cities have become increasingly scrutinised through a new hybrid lens of vulnerability and resilience, across a range of public and private institutions involved in the governance of urban space. These responses are by no means uniform nor necessarily even cooperative or compatible; however, we argue that global competition between cities for capital is increasingly harnessing resilience to place marketing in the notion of the resurgent city. This response is highly ambivalent, particularly when based on superficial alternations to urban form and policy, and the marketing of resilience may actually undermine genuine attempts to create resilient cities. We will deal with each of these five responses in turn.

The prepared city

Contingency or emergency planning is undertaken by organisations and institutions of government to decrease their vulnerability to attack and increase preparedness in the event of attack. In Britain, until the late 1980s, the predominant policy discourse in this specialist area of government was of emergency planning, "the general term for the work that the government, the emergency services, the health services and the Council all do in preparing plans and procedures for dealing with any emergency that might affect large numbers of people" (Hounslow Council, 2004). This remains key to the way in which local authorities think in this area, however far removed it is from the mainstream of their activities.

From the 1950s, Britain had an organised civil defence structure with regionally based commissioners governing the country should a nuclear attack occur (Campbell, 1982; Fox, 1996). In 1968 this stance was abolished and civil defence put on a 'care and maintenance' basis. From 1974, each local authority had to appoint council emergency planning officers, and make plans for action after a hostile attack, instructing the public, disposing of human remains, and so on. However, financial resources were restrictive. The 1983 Local Government Civil Defence Regulations added a requirement to keep all plans up to date, and the 1980s also saw more money made available to local authorities. Alongside this, the United Kingdom Warning and Monitoring Organisation (UKWMO) was to be modernised. Fox (1996) also describes how the mid-1980s saw the national government responding to the concept that civil defence planning could also be used for peacetime emergencies – an 'all hazards' approach to what was increasingly being called 'emergency planning' – and this led to the 1986 Civil Protection in Peacetime Act, allowing civil defence resources to be used for peacetime emergencies. By 1988 all councils had submitted plans, albeit of variable quality.

In 1992, regulations were introduced to remove civil defence functions from local authorities, although responsibilities were retained for civil protection under the 1993 regulations. In 1991, funding for emergency planning was £24.5 million. This was reduced year on year to £14 million in 1997 where it remained for three years. In 2000, authorities were allowed to bid on a partial and restricted basis of need. Funding then increased to £19 million, before 9/11, but no extra funding was added to respond to the government's expectations for counter-terrorism.

Moves to improve emergency planning were prompted firstly by the so-called '3 Fs' – fuel price protests, widespread flooding, and the Foot and Mouth Disease (FMD) epidemic in rural areas in 2001 – and then by terrorist attacks. The 2004 Civil Contingencies Act established a new framework for civil defence and new Regional Resilience Forums, which are required to draw up detailed plans for dealing with catastrophe. The state's return to military threat-response tactics and technologies has raised concerns that "democracy could be replaced by totalitarianism" (Bunyan, cited in Tempest & Batty, 2004).

The defensive city

The second response has been through internal physical or symbolic notions of the boundary and territorial closure: an 'architecture of fear', the creation of 'exclusion zones' or 'cordon sanitaires' to particular 'at risk' sites and people (Pawley, 1998; Beck, 2002; Graham, 2002), for example, in closed defensive enclaves around residential gated communities, airports, civic buildings, or even whole districts, especially financial centres (Marcuse, 2002; Coaffee, 2004).

This defensiveness initially re-emerged in North American cities as a response to urban riots as well as the perceived problems associated with the physical design of the modern city (Jacobs, 1984). Research had indicated a relationship between some environmental design and reduced violence (Gold, 1970), and there were concerns that privatised security and urban fortification, following a loss of faith among the middle and upper classes with the state's ability to provide safety, were leading to the decline of city centres and social polarisation. Newman (1972a) called for a "range of mechanisms – real and symbolic barriers ... [and] improved opportunities for surveillance – that combine to bring the environment under the control of its residents" (p 3). 'Defensible space' was seen as the physical expression of a social fabric that could defend itself through the subtle manipulation of architectural and design elements in the whole community, and thus offered an alternative to the gating and closure of residential communities emerging at this time in North America and subsequently in other western countries, most notably the UK (Poyner, 1983).

In the British context, such ideas had wider implications in relation to terrorism. Belfast in the 1970s can be seen as a laboratory for radical spatial-security experiments, with a number of distinct defended territories created along sectarian lines to give inhabitants enhanced security, for example, the 1974 'ring of steel' around Belfast city centre, comprising physical barriers and stop-and-search policing Boal (1975). The same language was used in the early 1990s for the City of London (and also the 'iron collar' around London Docklands), but surveillance rather than actual fortification was the key (as discussed later).

During the 1990s, Los Angeles' militarisation and 'fortress urbanism' assumed a theoretical primacy within urban studies (Davis, 1990), portraying the city, like Belfast earlier, as an urban laboratory for anti-crime measures (Dear & Flusty, 1998). In 1991, 16% of city residents were living in "some form of secured access environment" (Blakely & Snyder, 1999, p 1). Davis showed how the boundaries between the two traditional methods of crime prevention – law enforcement and fortification – became blurred, resulting in the creation of what Flusty (1994) referred to as 'interdictory space'. Thus the desire of both Jacobs and Newman for a more open and civil city as the key to safety had been thoroughly defeated.

The watchful city

By the 1990s, electronic surveillance within public and semi-public urban spaces came to be seen as a remedy for many of the problems of defensive architecture and design. The early 1990s saw increased targeting of global cities and their economic infrastructure by terrorist organisations. The Provisional IRA exploded large bombs in the City of London in 1992 and 1993 and in the London Docklands in 1992 and 1996. The reaction of urban authorities and the police to the protection of these key spaces of global finance included both territorial and technological approaches (Coaffee, 2003a, 2004): after the 1993 bomb in the City, what was referred to in the media as a Belfast-style 'ring of steel' was created, although locally this was dubbed the 'ring of plastic' as restricted access areas were demarcated primarily by plastic traffic cones.

These approaches of limiting territorial access were backed up by retrofitting CCTV. Although shops and casinos had long used CCTV, and the police had conducted experiments (Williams, 2003), the first permanent public CCTV scheme was set up in Bournemouth in 1985, for the ruling Conservative Party's annual conference, after the previous year's IRA bombing (Norris & Armstrong, 1999). Stories of the success of CCTV encouraged local authorities and central government to invest heavily in cameras (Webster, 2004). In central London, police, through an innovative partnership scheme, 'CameraWatch', encouraged private companies to work together to install cameras, and in 1997 automatic number plate recognition (ANPR) cameras, linked to police databases, were installed around the 'ring of steel' and at strategic points within it. This digital system could process images and provide feedback within four seconds. In a decade, the Square Mile became the most surveilled space in the UK, and perhaps in the world, with over 1,500 surveillance cameras, many equipped with ANPR.

Following the 1992 Canary Wharf attack, managers had initiated their own 'mini-ring of steel', shutting down access to this privatised space in London Docklands (Graham & Marvin, 2001) with security barriers, no-parking zones, CCTV, and identity card schemes. After the 1996 bomb, amid fears that high-profile businesses might flee, the business community successfully lobbied the police to set up an anti-terrorist security cordon modelled on the City of London's approach covering the whole of Docklands: the 'iron collar'.

The surveillant architecture of 1990s London was not primarily about protecting ordinary people, but about defending capital. Both the City of London and Docklands are strange semi-autonomous districts with unusual and undemocratic forms of governance, the former with its mediaeval Corporation of London, and the latter a Thatcherite capitalist enclave that was considered key to safeguarding London's future as a global city. The 1996 bomb caused far more damage to a nearby housing estate, yet it was the Docklands enclave that received all the investment in security infrastructure, most of which was designed to keep the likes of housing estate residents out.

Over time, such securitisation against certain 'at-risk' sites from terrorism has led to the inevitable dislocation of London into zones of differential risk and security, and allowed a more expansive security blanket over central London. ANPR has now been rolled out across central London for use in traffic 'congestion charging'. This system became operational in February 2003 and uses 450 cameras in 230 different positions. Central London is encircled by a dedicated digital 'surveillance ring' affording London's police forces vast capabilities for tracking movement of traffic and people (Coaffee, 2004). The UK has become the most surveilled country in the world (Norris, McCahill, & Wood, 2004) and by 2008, the ANPR system will operate nationwide.

The resilient city

Now a new response is emerging, combining city emergency planning, territorial strategies, and surveillance into 'urban resilience' (Harrigan & Martin, 2002; Coaffee, 2004; Vale & Campanella, 2005). Resilience has many overlapping definitions. Timmerman (1981) defined resilience "as the capacity to adapt to stress from hazards and the ability to recover quickly from their impacts" (p 5). Pelling (2003) offers a subtle adjustment: "the capacity to adjust to threats and mitigate or avoid harm" (p 5). Vale and Campanella (2005) (and most of their contributors) continue to conflate recovery and resilience, but Godschalk (2003) emphasises the proactive:

> Resilient cities are constructed to be strong and flexible, rather than brittle and fragile. Their lifeline systems of roads, utilities, and other support facilities are designed to continue

functioning in the face of rising water, high winds, shaking ground, and terrorist attacks. (p 137)

In the UK, the British government's Office of the Deputy Prime Minister argues that "Resilience means ensuring that the country is prepared to detect, prevent and respond with speed and certainty to major emergencies, including terrorist attacks" (ODPM, 2004b).

Pelling (2003) writes that resilience has physical, economic, and social components, which could include: 'landscapes of defence' (Gold & Revill, 2000), the provision of adequate insurance facilities (Harrigan & Martin, 2002; Mills, 2002), the development of civic and institutional frameworks to deal with risk management (Beck, 2002; Pelling, 2003); and even individualised responses (Safir & Whitman, 2003).

Some claim that cities are becoming more resilient: Vale and Campanella (2005) show that fewer lives are lost and smaller, concentrated portions of urban fabric destroyed in disasters in western(ised), modern cities, and even human threats now focus on such targeted destruction rather than their obliteration. However, celebrating the resilience of modern cities would appear premature if the example of the aftermath of Hurricane Katrina and consequent flooding in New Orleans in August 2005 is to be taken into account. Even a city such as this in the richest nation on earth remains, at the time of writing in mid-2006, only partially reinhabited and rebuilt, with arguments and accusations continuing over the politics and economics of reviving New Orleans. Indeed some have argued that the over-concentration on resilience to terrorism has undermined structures of resilience to natural disasters: there are multiple dimensions of urban resilience (Graham, 2006).

That said, it has been argued that after 9/11, "military and geopolitical security now penetrate utterly into practices surrounding governance, design, and planning of cities and region" (Graham, 2002, p 589). The "war on terrorism" has already served as a "prism being used to conflate and further legitimize dynamics that already were militarizing urban space" (Warren, 2002, p 614). In the immediate aftermath of 9/11, some, like Swanstrom (2002), asked whether fear and urbanism were now at war, and there were bleak predictions of the demise of the skyscraper, a new counter-urbanisation trend among business and wealthier citizens (Vidler, 2001), or 'concentrated decentralisation' (Marcuse, 2002). These worst-case scenarios now seem pessimistic; however, anti-terrorist defences and heightened surveillance can restrict urban areas as functioning entities. For example, in London after 9/11, London police forces focused on digitalised tracking technologies as well as the crude and overt fortressing of 'at risk' sites against vehicle-borne bombs, such as the US embassy, which has become a virtual citadel, separated from the rest of London by fencing, waist-high 'concrete blockers', armed guards, and mandatory ID cards. Furthermore, in May 2003, in response to a heightened state of alert, a vast number of waist-high concrete slabs were placed outside the Houses of Parliament to stop car bombers. This so-called 'ring of concrete' was later painted black to make it more 'aesthetically pleasing' (Coaffee, 2004). Subsequently, all protest was banned within a one-kilometre radius of Parliament ostensibly also for 'security' reasons.

Surveillance may be less visible, but can form what Lianos and Douglas (2000) call automated socio-technical environments (ASTEs): normative notions of good behaviour and transgression as well as increasingly stipulations and punishments are encoded into the space-time fabrics of cities by using software. Some have gone as far as to demand a pervasive automated surveillance apparatus of micro-sensors (Huber & Mills, 2002), that would observe, smell, or detect all kinds of unusual movement, activities, people, or objects. Furthermore, exaggeration of urban risk in the global media has seen "trust replaced with mistrust and as such 'the terrorist threat' triggers a self-multiplication of risks by the de-bounding of risk perceptions and fantasies" (Beck, 2002, p 44). This leads to areas becoming physically and technologically disconnected from the rest of the city (Graham & Marvin, 2001) through the development of securitised 'rings of confidence' (Coaffee, 2003b), threatening the very freedom of movement and intermixing that produces 'civilisation'.

The resurgent city

The response of urban authorities to threat has particularly serious consequences when militarised security perspectives are bound up with neoliberal agendas on urban regeneration (Raco, 2003), and as such are embedded in attempts of an urban renaissance. Urban resilience exists within a climate of regional, national, and global competition between cities for footloose capital, company relocation, cultural assets, and visitors. Practices of urban social control are, unlike emergency planning, key to mainstream urban governance and strongly connected to competitive economic strategies. However, the period of resilience can now be seen to be hybridising into a period in which emergency policy becomes mainstream and integrated more strongly with urban social control and economic competitiveness. In this environment of standardised market-based solutions, and particularly in the linking of resilience to competition for capital, one finds the notion of the resurgent city. Many cities are now overtly linking security to regeneration, both in terms of the micro-management of new 'cultural quarters' and gentrification initiatives (CCTV, gated communities, etc) and the macro-management of urban image through 'city marketing' initiatives. Presentations of place and the management of these processes often highlight the safety of cities for business as a now vital selling point. However, too much overt security can also demonstrate high underlying levels of risk, which could repel investment. Belfast demonstrates both sides of this issue: businesses were put off as much by the overtly fortified landscape as by the terrorist threat, and as the ring of steel was replaced by CCTV, urban planners also sought to re-image this 'pariah city' in an attempt to attract businesses back (Neill, Fitzsimons, & Murtagh, 1995). Furthermore, the resurgent city sees the securitisation of other policy discourses, most recently in the UK, while the concept of designing out threat has returned with the publication of *Safer places: The planning system and crime prevention* (ODPM, 2004c). Following the North American 'broken windows' debate, it is quite clear that the this return to 'designing out crime' is already incorporating town centre management, CCTV, and urban security into an appropriated discourse of sustainability (see Raco, Chapter Three, this volume), which has now come to mean much the same thing in UK state planning discourse as resilience. These linkages and discursive shifts can lead to superficial outcomes: Williams (2004) has shown that much of the 1990s regeneration agenda has tended to develop the city in a theatrical way, like a stage set, so that it becomes merely a spectacle for the consumption of the privileged, which reflects and is made more extreme by a state of anxiety about the urban. This is the peculiarly British variation on Sorkin's (1992) US theme-park city. There is no better example of this than the reliance of the resurgent city on meetings tourism.

Lockdown!

The example on which we will draw here is a case study of the Labour Party conference which took place from 11-13 February 2005 in Newcastle/Gateshead. The methodology was a combination of site visits, observation, and photography with examination of the local media, Labour Party, and police statements, as well as informal interviews with serving police officers, workmen on the site, passers-by, and many local businesses. The aim was to get as holistic a picture as possible, an overview of the event from the point of view of resilience.

The conference took place in the £70 million Norman Foster-designed Sage music centre, a huge undulating steel and glass structure, funded by the Arts Council Lottery Fund. Important delegates stayed in the nearby, and also new but architecturally less interesting, Hilton Hotel. Along with the Baltic Arts Centre and the award-winning Gateshead Millennium Bridge these buildings are pieces of the jigsaw of the East Gateshead Regeneration Strategy, in creating an arts-based redevelopment of derelict ex-industrial riverside land, which can be seen either as a new 'cultural quarter' or a rapidly gentrifying ghetto. The project has put Gateshead on the map as a cultural draw and an engine of regional growth, although without the creation of the hybrid entity of NewcastleGateshead, it is doubtful how many people would realise this was Gateshead and not Newcastle. Linked to the more business and residential-oriented Newcastle Quayside, it forms an amphitheatre of urban renaissance, but particularly on the Gateshead side, it is physically and socially detached from its surrounding communities (Cameron & Coaffee, 2005).

The conference saw a massive security operation that started six months in advance. For local businesses, the process started with a detailed data-gathering and surveillance operation that saw the vetting of business employees and their vehicles. The buildings were closed to the public for a week before the conference and subjected to detailed external and internal examination and preparation by the police and private security organisation, Group 4 Securitas. Individual officers were placed on every external entrance, structural support, and vulnerable point. What the press releases referred to as 'an enclosed and secure walkway' was also constructed from the Hilton Hotel to the Sage.

Also in the week before, on major roads around Tyneside, random armed police road checks were carried out, under powers from Section 44 of the 2000 Terrorism Act. The public were asked to be vigilant and report any suspicious vehicles or people. The stated aim of the police was to balance the aims of security with those of local businesses and residents: "We have to achieve the right balance between public reassurance, safety and speed of response" (Dave Warcup, Assistant Chief Constable of Northumbria Constabulary, quoted in Thompson, 2005).

The day before, what was referred to (once again) as a 'ring of steel' security cordon was thrown around the conference venues (Figure 6.1). Surrounding roads were closed or restricted in access; the closure of the low-level Swing Bridge across the Tyne caused massive traffic disruption and tail-backs lasting hours in the mornings and evenings. A flight exclusion zone was put in place over the general area of the conference, and the police presence was stepped up to 1,000 officers on duty at any

Figure 6.1: The lockdown zone

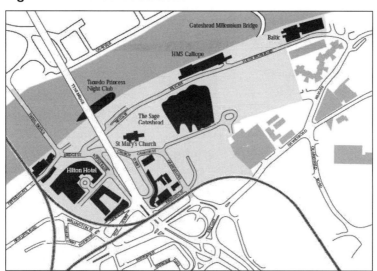

one time, including specialised personnel, but not including members of the armed forces, whose presence was obvious but unacknowledged. River searches and patrols also took place. However, the public were not informed about the impact of the conference until the week before, and up until the day before the conference access to the exterior of the main conference buildings was still possible, yet the Sage itself was entirely closed for a week.

During the conference itself, security became even more overt, with snipers on higher buildings and police on jet skis on the River Tyne, and mobile CCTV units and police vans lining the length of the road from the Sage down to the Millennium Bridge (Figure 6.2). Many expected protests took place from groups including Fathers 4 Justice (F4J), the Countryside Alliance, Stop the War Coalition, and the Association of University Teachers; however, these were contained by both legal and territorial measures on a small stretch of the Newcastle Quayside on the far bank of the Tyne. One F4J protestor, dressed as Spiderman, did manage to get past the supposedly tight security and climbed high onto the Armstrong Bridge, where he remained for several hours, before voluntarily descending.

The impacts of the conference in economic terms are hard to quantify. The costs were estimated to be around £3 million, but conveniently the expected 'economic boom' as a result was also estimated to be the same amount. From questioning traders in the immediate vicinity of the conference, it became apparent that the benefits were far from evenly spread, with claimed loss of trade for some local businesses but

Figure 6.2: CCTV (left) and police vans (right)

with hotels in particular benefiting from advance bookings. The costs of the inconvenience and temporary loss of civil liberties and freedom of movement are also hard to factor in, but for some businesses it was clear that the inconvenience outweighed any benefits.

For Gateshead, one benefit touted by the local authority and Northumbria Police was the retrofitting of permanent security infrastructure (especially CCTV) linked to crime reduction and safety in Gateshead in the longer term. According to the police:

> Many of the things seen over the weekend are not where the money went in the security operation. Around £1.5 million of the total was spent on CCTV, radio communications and technical equipment which will be available for use in future major events and in the fight against crime. (Chief Constable Warcup, cited in Thompson, 2005)

The Labour Party Chairman, Ian McCartney (cited in Ford, 2005), also stressed that "these improvements are not just for the conference but for the long-term benefit of the community as a whole".

One could also see this conference in the wider picture of the attempts by the region and by the NewcastleGateshead Initiative (NGI) in particular to attract further conferences. Such trade has been estimated to be worth £72 million per annum to the region's economy. The NGI claims that the twin city has "a fantastic reputation as a wonderfully creative, cultural city, a great reputation as a visitor city and that is very attractive from a conference point of view" (NGI, 2005), an attractiveness that their 'Creative Conferencing' initiative defines as 'the X factor'. This X-factor conferencing offer includes many measures that temporarily alter the publicness of these largely publicly funded schemes, whether it be simply the projection of corporate logos onto the façade of the Baltic Arts Centre or high security (at the extreme, the ability to close spaces to public use entirely in the case of events involving national security issues). This strategy, claimed an NGI spokesperson, "helps put delegates in a creative frame of mind and ensures they make an active contribution to their conference".

One has to question the links between the rolling out of anti-terror policies like stop-and-search, automated surveillance, and the use of anti-terrorism measures in these provincial and largely unthreatened cities, especially when such measures impact so intensely on the ability of ordinary people to use the spaces paid for from the public purse. Ironically these spaces are simultaneously and contradictorily the sites of economic development and urban renaissance initiatives aimed at improving ordinary people's lives and are predicated on principles of social inclusion. 'Rings of steel' or 'rings of confidence' slowly but surely become more general 'rings of exclusion' (see Coaffee, 2004). It is at this point that the prevention of terrorist threats links up to the wide range of more conventional crime control measures such as in relation to street begging (see Hermer and MacGregor, Chapter Thirteen, this volume) or in relation to the policing of poor urban neighbourhoods (see Hancock, Chapter Four, and Johnston and Mooney, Chapter Eight, this volume).

Equally, the appropriateness of the high cost of the operation was criticised by many, and questions as to who was financially responsible were unanswered until the Home Office clarified that it (or ultimately the general taxpayer) would pay half.

Finally, the depth and real effectiveness of the whole operation must be criticised in its own terms. Much of the rhetoric about the security measures was overplayed and even ludicrous in light of the material reality of the measures in practice. Apart from the F4J protestor, it was relatively easy to get right up to the Sage even during the conference without being approached let alone searched by any security, as we did. The so-called 'ring of steel' was merely ordinary steel-mesh fencing (Figure 6.3), and the much-heralded pedestrian walkway that was supposedly to have linked the Hilton Hotel to the Sage was in fact just a jury-rigged bridge constructed from scaffolding materials that

Figure 6.3: The Sage behind the 'ring of steel'

crossed one single-carriageway road that was in any case already closed to traffic, which in fact made anyone crossing it more exposed to any potential terrorist threat (Figure 6.4). Talking to the workers building this edifice before the conference opened, it was clear that they saw the irony, commenting with a laugh that someone was "paying a million quid for *this*!". Much of the security was theatrical, within an already stage-set regeneration, putting a publicly visible frontage on the still-impoverished core of Gateshead, and thereby prompting further calls into the uneasy relationship with urbanity that Britain has enjoyed in the recent past, highlighted by Williams (2004).

Conclusion

There are key gaps in past and current research on the relationship between security, resilience, and urban regeneration that need to be inspected carefully in order to highlight their operation, and impact. The academic and policy literature tends to separate these things, in terms of security focusing almost without exception on how security professionals, risk management planners, and other key actors can defend the core global cities under perceived risk of attack, especially from forms of terrorism.

Figure 6.4: The 'secure' walkway

But there are many more complex and less easily divisible questions. It is possible that a certain competitive advantage can be gained in the competition to be recognised as a networked global city in being the site of new security initiatives; however, it is equally possible that businesses seeking a secure environment may prefer less visible, and therefore less 'threatened', places. In terms of community development, the UK government is now adopting a discourse of 'sustainable communities' that puts 'security' at the forefront of this sustainability (see Raco, Chapter Three, this volume). And if the exact term 'resilience' is not used here, it could be argued that fundamentally resilience *is* that coming together of sustainability and security, with the former redefined by the latter. Partly at least this is because both security and resilience already have economic and social implications; however, it seems clear that the forms of security and resilience that have emerged from debates about terrorism and crime are the ones colonising the social and economic, to reframe older concerns with urban order: rather than security by design, we have security by sustainable development.

Many commentators have already argued that how authorities respond to the current 'war on terrorism' will have serious consequences for British urbanism. For example, as Swanstrom (2002) noted, "the main threat to cities comes not from terrorism but from the policy responses to terrorism that could undermine the freedom of thought and movement that are the lifeblood of cities" (p 139). And this has to be real human security not the superficial, macho, image-centred security of the stage-set city: the combination of overreaction in a climate of fear and solutions that concentrate as much on image as real human security is a dangerous and wasteful one. Theme-park security is not helpful, nor does it provide what the image presents for ordinary people, who are supposed to be the ultimate beneficiaries of initiatives to improve the urban environment. Instead, many places are increasingly constructed not only as economically separate from their surroundings and their poorer inhabitants, but are also increasingly physically separable in more or less temporary ways, and ironically on pretexts whose justifications are already written in the policy documents as part of the core agenda of community regeneration. Just as one is forced to ask who are the beneficiaries of the resurgent city, one has also to ask who benefits from resilience and the embedding of security in exclusionary urban form. We believe, in contrast, that such security comes from city form following hope, not fear.

Note

[1] Case-study research for this chapter was conducted as part of a Linked Research Project by Diploma in Town Planning students in the School of Architecture Planning and Landscape at Newcastle University, 2004-05.

SEVEN

Tackling anti-social behaviour and regenerating neighbourhoods

Andrew Millie

At the 2005 Labour Party Conference the then Home Secretary Charles Clarke (2005a) stated that the party had to show by the next general election that it had "eliminated the anti-social behaviour and disrespect which still blights the lives of so many". Beyond the simple observation that no party could ever be expected to achieve such a goal, this statement highlights the political importance that anti-social behaviour (ASB) is currently thought to have. With this being the case, what can be achieved by tackling (if not eliminating) ASB? This chapter critically considers some of the definitional issues relating to ASB, where the most serious forms of ASB occur, and some of the potential causes of ASB. Various rationales for tackling ASB are considered; however, the main focus is on a relationship between tackling ASB and regenerating neighbourhoods. In national policy documentation problems of ASB are frequently linked to concerns of neighbourhood decline. For example, in the foreword to the government's Policy Action Team report into ASB (SEU, 2000b) – as part of the *National strategy for neighbourhood renewal* – Charles Clarke[1] states: "Anti-social behaviour destroys lives and shatters communities. It is a widespread problem but its effects are often most damaging in communities that are already fragile. If left unchecked it can lead to neighbourhood decline with people moving away and tenants abandoning housing" (p 6). It is logical from this position that tackling ASB may halt, or even reverse, such decline, thus contributing to a much-heralded 'urban renaissance' (Urban Task Force, 1999). While this may be simplistic, and downplays other factors influencing decline (Hancock, 2006), tackling ASB could have a part to play in neighbourhood regeneration (and conversely, regeneration could lead to reductions in ASB).

This chapter draws mainly from two recent research projects: the first a study conducted for the Joseph Rowntree Foundation (JRF) (Millie, Jacobson, McDonald, & Hough, 2005) involving a national survey of public opinion[2] and interviews and focus groups in three neighbourhoods with problems of ASB; the second a critical review of ASB for the Nuffield Foundation (Jacobson, Millie, & Hough, forthcoming) involving interviews in five areas. Between the two studies, examples are drawn from 'Westerncity' (a relatively deprived estate in a provincial city), 'Midcity', (an edge-of-town estate in a midlands city), and 'Newtown' (a conurbation of several towns and some more rural areas). Further evidence is drawn from a study conducted to inform the *London ASB strategy 2005-2008* (GLA, 2005; Millie, Jacobson, Hough, & Paraskevopoulou, 2005). While the chapter focuses principally on residential neighbourhoods, many issues will be transferable to town and city centre districts.

Defining anti-social behaviour

On the face of it, determining something as 'criminal' should be fairly straightforward as most people simply relate crime to activity prohibited by criminal law. However, if for example the law itself is unjust, or breaches certain basic human rights, determining the 'crime' becomes problematic. It is a problem that criminologists have been struggling with for decades (see Garland, 2002), and to which both Stenson and Hancock refer in Part I of this volume (see Chapters Two and Four, respectively). Determining something as 'anti-social' may be even less straightforward as ASB is almost entirely reliant on subjective assessments. A wide range of behaviours can be potentially anti-social, from the inconsiderate to that which most people would regard as seriously criminal. In a focus group for the London study one participant narrowed ASB down to "other people's stuff". While it is tempting to leave it at that, sociology may help in determining what this 'stuff' is with its talk of 'conduct norms' (for example, Sellin, 1938). In this respect, ASB is something that contravenes certain 'conduct norms'. If the seriously criminal are excluded, the notion of ASB becomes interchangeable with incivility and, to a certain extent, disorder. For instance, LaGrange, Ferraro and Supancic (1992) describe incivilities as "low level breaches of community standards that signal an erosion of conventionally accepted norms and values" (p 312). This at first appears wholly sensible; however, these norms and values will vary both between and within communities. It is complicated further because those perceived as behaving anti-socially are also very much part of any community (Burney, 2005), and they may have very different ideas of "accepted norms and values". There is of course the perennial problem that 'community' is difficult to define and is not tied necessarily to any particular location. Also, within any location there may be any number of 'plural communities' (Crawford, 1997; Jones & Newburn, 2001).

Such ambiguities mean there is no neat categorisation of what is 'social' or 'anti-social' (or, as described in the social psychology literature, 'pro-social' and 'anti-social'). Legislation only helps to narrow the focus to a limited extent. The 1998 Crime and Disorder Act – which saw the introduction of the Anti-Social Behaviour Order (ASBO) – contains the most widely cited definition of ASB: behaviour "that caused or was likely to cause harassment, alarm or distress to one or more persons not of the same household as [the perpetrator]"(Section 1[a]). This is exceptionally broad and, while excluding domestic incidents, includes most other unwanted activity. The Home Office has since produced a typology (Harradine, Kodz, Lernetti, & Jones, 2004) that divides ASB into: misuse of public space; disregard for community/personal well-being; acts directed at people; and environmental damage. This may get closer to the types of behaviour regarded as anti-social; however, it still does not exclude serious crime. In an attempt to provide focus for work on the *London ASB strategy 2005-2008* (GLA, 2005) the following definition was used:

ASB is behaviour that causes harassment, alarm or distress to individuals not of the same household as the perpetrator, such that it requires intervention from the relevant authorities; but criminal prosecution and punishment may be inappropriate because the individual components of the behaviour are not prohibited by the criminal law or, in isolation, constitute relatively minor offences. (see Millie, Jacobson, Hough et al, 2005, p 9)

Admittedly not the pithiest of definitions; however, it does limit pragmatically ASB to behaviour that requires intervention, thus excluding perhaps the more minor irritations to daily life. It also restricts ASB to non-criminal or minor criminal behaviour. An important factor that makes this behaviour anti-social is its *cumulative* impact on individuals or neighbourhoods. With this in mind the Home Office typology can be simplified into:

- interpersonal or malicious ASB (for example, intimidation, hoax calls, or vandalism directed at individuals or groups);
- environmental ASB (for example, littering, fly-tipping, or noise nuisance); and

• ASB restricting access to shared spaces (for example, intimidating behaviour by groups of youths, street drinking, and related disorder or public drug use).

The form the ASB takes will dictate who should deal with it as a problem, and what the appropriate response might be. Of course, there is still subjectivity in determining ASB, making such choices all the more difficult.

As far as the public is concerned, most people appear to equate ASB with youth problems – although, of course, ASB is not restricted to young people. For instance, in the national survey (Millie, Jacobson, McDonald et al, 2005) respondents were asked what they thought the worst form of ASB was where they lived (within 15 minutes' walk of home). Although 17 per cent did not think there was any ASB, 27 per cent considered the worst problems stemmed from rowdy teenagers (Table 7.1). Other concerns came a long way behind.

In political and media discourses ASB is often portrayed as a serious problem for all of us. This is not necessarily true. In the national survey respondents were asked to indicate the impact of seven different ASB issues[3] on their quality of life. Only a minority thought the ASB occurred in their local area and seriously impacted on their quality of life. For instance, for 'rowdy teenagers in the street' 19 per cent thought

Table 7.1: The worst forms of ASB in your local area (*n*=1,682)

Issue	%
Rowdy teenagers	27
Vandalism/graffiti	8
Litter/rubbish	8
Drug use/dealing	8
Drunk/drinking in public places	6
Dangerous/bad driving etc	4
Noisy neighbours	3
Abandoned/burnt-out vehicles	1
Begging	1
There isn't any ASB	17
Don't know	5
Other	12
Total	100

the problem occurred and had a fairly/very big effect on their quality of life (while 32 per cent thought it occurred and had a minor effect; and 48 per cent did not think it was a problem, or, if it occurred, it had no effect on their quality of life) (Millie, Jacobson, McDonald et al, 2005, p 11). Similarly, the 2003/04 British Crime Survey (BCS) (Wood, 2004) indicates that ASB is not a major concern for most people across England and Wales, with just 16 per cent perceiving a high level[4] of ASB in their local area. Nonetheless, this is still a sizable minority, and if spatially concentrated, then concerns are accentuated.

Others (for example, Brown, 2004) have suggested that ASB is found in deprived areas because this is where people look for it. However, the national survey identified greater concerns in such areas. For example, key predictors (using a logistic regression model) of 'rowdy teenagers on the streets having a fairy/very big effect on quality of life' were: living in London; living in social housing; being aged 18-30; having no qualifications; and being of Black and minority ethnic/mixed origin (Millie, Jacobson, McDonald et al, 2005) – factors that broadly point towards deprived and/or urban areas. According to the BCS (Wood, 2004) 34 per cent of those living in inner-city areas perceived a high level of ASB in the local area (using the ACORN classification [Association of Community Organisations for Reform Now] of residential neighbourhoods, the figure was 31 per cent for people in 'hard-pressed' areas, compared to 5 per cent for 'wealthy achiever' areas). Evidence from the 2002 London Household Survey[5] (Millie, Jacobson, Hough et al, 2005) suggests that higher levels of perceived ASB – and crime – are associated with neighbourhood dissatisfaction. For example, of those very dissatisfied with their neighbourhood, 41 per cent also regarded troublesome teenagers/children as a problem, compared to 4 per cent of those very satisfied. Similarly, 59 per cent of those very dissatisfied with their neighbourhood thought litter and rubbish on the street was a problem, compared with 17 per cent of those very satisfied. That ASB concerns are spatially concentrated in deprived urban areas, and are linked to neighbourhood dissatisfaction, points towards strategies that tackle ASB alongside wider neighbourhood regeneration.

Explaining anti-social behaviour

Finding the causes of ASB is not a simple task. However, if the most serious forms of ASB tend to be spatially concentrated in deprived urban areas, poverty – or at least relative deprivation – may have a part to play in creating an environment where ASB is more likely.

That said, the public does not seem to blame poverty. Again drawing from the national survey, respondents were asked to list the three main causes of *youth* ASB (Table 7.2). 'Poor parenting' was by far the most popular, mentioned by 68 per cent. Over half thought causes included boredom/not enough to do, alcohol and drugs, or having low respect for others. Perhaps of comfort to agencies tasked with tackling youth ASB, poor discipline at school was mentioned by only a quarter and ineffective policing by 14 per cent.

Interview and focus group respondents (in the JRF case-study areas) tended to provide explanations of ASB that were rooted in broader ideas of social and cultural change. Three main 'narratives' emerged, although these were not exclusive or discrete. The first narrative sees ASB as a result of social and moral decline. In line with the national survey findings, this was often linked specifically to a decline in family values, poor parenting, and a lack of respect; as one youth project coordinator in Westerncity put it:

> "Things like respect and discipline all seem to have gone out the window. I know people say it's all old-fashioned, but I don't think so because I think it's the very essence of being able to live with others and integrate with others."

The second narrative sees ASB tied to the increasing disengagement from the norms of wider society by a significant minority of youth and, in many cases, their families. This disengagement is sometimes

Table 7.2: Which do you think are the three main causes of youth ASB? (n=1,682)

Issue	%
Poor parenting	68
Boredom/not enough to do	58
Alcohol and drugs	52
Low respect for others	51
Poor discipline at school	25
Ineffective policing	14
Poverty and deprivation	14
A lack of local jobs	9
None of these	1
Don't know	1

Note: Percentages do not add to 100 as the question was multi-coded.

linked to low expectations. The third narrative sees ASB as part of the age-old tendency for young people to push boundaries and test the patience of their elders, that 'kids will be kids':

> "Older people tend to be intolerant; they see young people as sort of an intrinsic threat. The fact that they're not engaged in positive and regimented activities they see as a negative factor." (community safety coordinator, Westerncity)

That young people push boundaries and are often misunderstood by the generation before is nothing new (for example, Cohen, 2002) and the 'kids will be kids' narrative does not assume ASB is necessarily getting worse. Implied solutions will focus on diversionary activities. On the other hand, the narratives of social and moral decline and disengagement do assume problems of ASB are worse than before and solutions may not be so straightforward.

The policies put in place to tackle ASB are very much dependant on how ASB is viewed. For instance, the Home Office's TOGETHER campaign to tackle ASB has had an implicit call for higher standards and tougher discipline. This view has pointed towards the social and moral decline narrative and a response centred on enforcement. Perhaps social and moral standards have declined, and disrespect for authority has grown to a point where action is needed. The past fifty years has certainly witnessed a decline in deference and increased individualism (although this is not all bad). An accompanying growth in alcohol and substance misuse would also be implicated. However, the fact that problems of ASB are concentrated most heavily in areas of relative deprivation lends weight to the narrative of social exclusion and disengagement – "where the losers in a 'winner takes all' society create truly troublesome problems for others" (Millie, Jacobson, McDonald et al, 2005, p 35). This is despite, as noted, most people not regarding poverty as a cause of youth ASB. Such areas have a heritage of low employment and housing policies that have led to large concentrations of socially excluded – and often young – families. This disengagement narrative will lead to an emphasis on various forms of preventative work. In the JRF study (Millie, Jacobson, McDonald et al, 2005) we argued for a balanced approach between enforcement and prevention; and with the recent Respect campaign, the government's rhetoric has shifted to a 'broader approach'. For instance, in the foreword to the *Respect Action Plan* (Home Office, 2006a) Tony Blair states, "We need to tackle root causes with the same rigour and determination as we have taken with ASB" (p 1). However, the stance is still a tough one; in the next sentence the Prime Minister declares, "Everyone can change [but] if people who need help will not take it, we will make them" (p 1).

Of course, the government may have simply 'talked up' the problem of ASB so they could respond and be seen to do something about it (see Burney, 2005). However, it would be wrong to assume public perceptions of ASB are mere artefacts of government policy. ASB is a cause of genuine and serious concern, particularly in deprived urban neighbourhoods. That said, historic policy stances of local and central government may be implicated in explaining ASB. For instance, during the 1980s many local authorities had strained relationships with the police, some having 'police monitoring groups' (Millie, Jacobson, McDonald et al, 2005). Although ASB was certainly evident, partnership action to deal with it would not have been considered too often.[6] At the same time, local authorities were witnessing successive budget cuts – or budgets were being reallocated – resulting in, for example, fewer caretakers or park keepers. This meant fewer people were able to exercise the sort of informal social control that is thought to deter crime, perhaps leaving more minor ASB to go unchecked (for example, Sampson, Raudenbush, & Earls, 1997; Scottish Executive, 2003). Changes in budgets meant local authority property was maintained less frequently. It has been estimated (Urban Parks Forum, 2002) that £1.3 billion in revenue expenditure had been lost to public parks over the past two decades. Changes in policing are also implicated; from the mid-1990s performance targets were imposed on the police that skewed their function away from order maintenance towards crime control, leaving less scope for attention on individually less serious incidents of ASB (a situation that may be addressed through renewed focus on neighbourhood policing; see Home Office, 2005a).

It is possible that there has been a concurrent increase in people's appreciation of personal rights in the UK, sometimes referred to as a 'rights culture'.[7] One interpretation may be that 'it is my right to behave how I like' – either socially or anti-socially. Similarly, there may be a greater expectation for others 'to behave how I would want them to'. While certain conduct norms may be desirable, this has implications for people's tolerance of difference, with non-conformers identified as anti-social, and then excluded from certain spaces (for example, Rogers & Coaffee, 2005). This has particular relevance to young people. It has relevance also to the acceptance of people with mental health problems, which may lead to behaviour perceived as anti-social, including various conduct disorders, hyperkinetic disorders (for example, attention-deficit hyperactivity disorder), autistic spectrum disorders, or personality disorders (for example, anti-social personality disorder: see Farrington

& Coid, 2003). As alcohol and substance misuse can sometimes be linked to mental health problems (BMA, 2006) there is increased scope for such people, of any age, to be identified as behaving anti-socially. In terms of young people, one in 10 children under 16 in the UK has a clinically diagnosed mental health disorder (BMA, 2006). Of course, these will not all behave anti-socially, but there is a risk that behaviour that is outside the accepted norm will be swept up in ASB enforcement. According to a recent survey (Green, McGinnity, Meltzer, Ford, & Goodman, 2005) mental disorders are most prevalent among children and young people in (using the ACORN classification of residential neighbourhoods) 'hard-pressed' areas – the kind of areas where concerns about ASB are at their highest. A recent survey of 54[8] Youth Offending Teams (BIBIC, 2005) found that around a third of young people under 17 given ASBOs were also diagnosed with a mental health disorder or an accepted learning difficulty. Beyond the observation that there must be a more suitable intervention (especially as the strict conditions of the ASBO may not be understood), this does illustrate issues around the tolerance of difference. Spatial concentrations within relatively deprived areas, of people with mental disorders in particular, accentuate concerns.

Connecting anti-social behaviour to regeneration

Current debates on ASB do not occur in a theoretical or policy vacuum. To start with the most straightforward, ASB can be tackled simply because it is a bad thing, it degrades local environments and affects quality of life. While 'quality of life' is a vague idea, in policy discourse (for example, DEFRA, 2005; ODPM, 2005g) it is linked sometimes to notions of sustainable development and environmental inequality (as discussed in more detail elsewhere in this volume by Raco, Chapter Three, and by Johnstone and MacLeod, Chapter Five). Environmental inequality is the more specific, and refers to people's differing access to 'quality' environments (Eames & Adebowale, 2002; Lucus, Walker, Eames, Fay, & Poustie, 2004). While including wider objectives – such as access to healthy food and clean air – ASB concerns such as litter, fly-tipping, graffiti, and vandalism are included. Of course, notions of what constitutes a 'quality' environment may be contested; for instance, shoppers and skateboarders may have very different notions of quality urban spaces (see Woolley, 2006). Nonetheless, in terms of potential linkages between ASB and regeneration this may be a useful starting point. It also links to the earlier observation that ASB is related to neighbourhood dissatisfaction.

Of relevance to the creation of 'quality' environments – and potential regeneration – is the North American literature linking minor disorders or incivilities to fear of crime (for example, Wilson, 1975; Garafalo & Laub, 1978; Taylor, 1999). In the UK, Innes (for example, Innes, 2004) explored this further through what he termed a 'signal crimes' perspective: that crime and disorder are functionally equivalent (see also Sampson & Raudenbush, 1999), but certain incidents have a signal value and disproportionate impact on fear of crime and/or perceptions of security. The perspective has played a part in the UK policy of reassurance policing (Millie & Herrington, 2005), since incorporated under the neighbourhood policing banner. Within reassurance/neighbourhood policing residents are 'involved' in determining neighbourhood 'signals' – an idea that fits in with New Labour's wider communitarian agenda. It also fits in with the government's Respect campaign with its talk of 'neighbourhood charters' and 'respect standards' – this later idea calling for registered social landlords and partners to, "involve the community in setting and enforcing [standards]" (Home Office, 2006a, p 27). Thus, from this perspective, tackling ASB not only eases fear of crime, but increases community involvement – often seen as an end in itself. That said, if this involvement is meaningful, then there is potential to improve social capital (Putnam, 2001), or collective efficacy. Here the work of Sampson and colleagues in Chicago is particularly influential and they define collective efficacy as "social cohesion among neighbors combined with their willingness to intervene on behalf of the common good" (Sampson et al, 1997, p 918). There is the added benefit of hopefully increasing legitimacy and public confidence in agency decisions. This links to a further, purely pragmatic, reason for tackling ASB, that doing so may benefit the agencies involved in terms of lower service costs in the longer term.

ASB may also be tackled because it is viewed, not as functionally equivalent, but as causally linked to crime. There are two versions of this perspective; firstly in terms of criminal careers (for example, Farrington, 1992), that engaging with those who commit ASB may reduce the likelihood of then moving onto more serious criminal behaviour. The second perspective is exemplified in the often quoted 'broken windows' thesis of Wilson and Kelling (1982), that incivilities – such as broken windows – can be read as signs of dereliction, which, if left unrepaired, can damage public confidence and lead to fear of crime. This in turn can disempower local communities as fearful people are likely to withdraw from public spaces, thus reducing informal social control and creating environments where crime can flourish. 'Broken windows' has been interpreted in many different ways and used to justify a range of policies (see Taylor, 2005). Versions are popular among politicians:

> In isolation a bit of vandalism here or graffiti there might seem trivial, but their combined effect can seriously undermine local quality of life. Some criminologists talk of the 'broken window' problem. They argue that a failure to tackle small-scale problems can lead to serious crime and environmental blight. Streets that are dirty and threatening deter people from going out. They signal that the community has lost interest. As a result, anti-social behaviour and more serious criminality may take root. (Blair, 2001)

At its simplest, it is an attractive idea; however, the perspective has its critics. For instance, Harcourt (2001) argues that it is the *process* of order maintenance policing, in the form of surveillance and apprehension, that reduces crime, rather than greater orderliness by itself. A high profile interpretation of 'broken windows' has been the various forms of 'zero tolerance' policing, involving strict enforcement of minor disorder and incivility. The most oft-quoted initiative thought of as 'zero tolerance' was that deployed in New York under Commissioner Bratton (Burke, 1998; Kelling, 1998). From this example, ASB and minor crimes are not tackled solely because they can lead to more serious crime, but because the perpetrators are often also serious criminals.

Many of these rationales will feed into wider regeneration objectives (although zero tolerance has the possibility of being counterproductive by alienating certain groups). For instance, strategies to tackle ASB as an issue of environmental inequality, or in order to foster collective efficacy, will benefit neighbourhood regeneration. Similarly, work to tackle ASB because it makes crime less likely will have obvious regenerative effects as investment in the area becomes more likely. Recently there has been huge investment in socially disadvantaged communities in the UK through, for example, the Single Regeneration Budget and Neighbourhood Renewal Fund; however, ASB continues to be an issue. At its most severe, problems have contributed to 'urban flight' and housing market decline and abandonment (Cullen & Levitt, 1999; Urban Task Force, 1999; Cole & Nevin, 2004). Low housing demand in certain neighbourhoods – particularly in some post-industrial northern English cities – is thought to be due to a combination of housing stock obsolescence, surplus stock, and the existence of unpopular neighbourhoods. These neighbourhoods become unpopular because "a range of factors, such as unpopular property design, stigma and high levels of perceived crime and anti-social behaviour, interact to reduce external demand and result in a high proportion of existing residents wanting to leave" (Cole & Nevin, 2004, p 10). This could be extended to include *actual* as well as *perceived* ASB and crime. By tackling ASB and crime it may be possible to stop neighbourhood decline before it reaches such a drastic stage, a view that has some support in the literature (for example, Skogan, 1986, 1990; Taylor, 1999). Skogan (1990), for instance, elaborated 'broken windows' to include neighbourhood decline: "Disorder erodes what control neighbourhood residents can maintain over local events and conditions. It drives out those for whom stable community life is important, and discourages people with similar values, from moving in. It threatens house prices and discourages investment" (p 3).

The link between ASB, crime, and neighbourhood decline has been picked up in British policy documentation (for example, SEU, 2000b). Skogan was concerned also with the part that informal social control and 'social disorganisation' (for example, Shaw & McKay, 1942) play in creating spirals of neighbourhood decline. The potential impact of poor informal social control has been already noted. 'Social disorganisation' is defined generally as a community's inability to achieve shared goals and exercise social control (for example, Bursik, 1988). According to Sampson and Grove (1989) it expresses itself in poor friendship networks, unsupervised teenage peer groups, and low organisational participation. It is in effect the opposite of 'good' social capital or 'collective efficacy'. Areas with collective efficacy are thought to have high informal social control. To risk oversimplifying things, they may also have less ASB.

Respondents did sometimes link ASB to regeneration. For instance, a local authority director of education from Newtown noted:

> "It can stymie any attempts to improve the neighbourhood
> if you've got a continuing anti-social behaviour and crime
> problem, because the perceptions are, 'well this isn't an area
> worth investing in'. More upwardly mobile residents move
> out. It can cause a decline in the area."

There were variations to this view; a local authority director of environmental health from Westerncity did not think ASB necessarily led to decline, but *reflected* neighbourhood decline:

> "I think in some ways, things like graffiti de-valuing the public space, or the public realm that people live in, is often a sign of the decline of a neighbourhood."

In practical terms it may not be too important to determine precisely what causes what, as a local authority head of litigation from Westerncity put it:

> "Something will start off the decline and then it becomes 'chicken and egg' and then you have a downward spiral."

A community safety partnership officer from Newtown had a broader view in that visible signs of ASB could have an impact on investment in the town as a whole:

> "If you've got visitors it is very off-putting if there's large amounts of rubble, litter, whatever it may be, which then has an impact on the wealth of the area. Because we're obviously affecting business visitors and tourism to the area."

The positive effects of regeneration on ASB, even on a small scale, were noted by those interviewed. A community activist from Westerncity told of how residents on one street did not maintain their gardens or take pride in their neighbourhood: "Well of course, if you live in degradation and poverty then it brings you down". ASB and crime were real problems in this area. However, following housing stock refurbishment and the remodelling of front gardens with new walls (in line with Newman's [1972b] 'defensible space' ideas) improvements were noted:

> "But it [the regeneration] has given you a lift, you know what I mean? They've got more people out in their gardens ... I think it's a different outlook when you don't see the windows closed up...."

The community activist may not have used these terms, but she was describing how refurbishment had moved the neighbourhood closer to being a 'quality' environment. A situation had been created where residents' informal social control is more likely (for example, because they are more likely to be out in their gardens), possibly contributing to greater collective efficacy. An environment is made where ASB – and therefore crime – is less likely.

Some problems with this perspective

Things are, of course, not always straightforward. For instance, the case-study areas in the JRF study were all deprived areas chosen because they had problems of ASB; however, within these neighbourhoods good social ties and collective efficacy already existed to a certain degree, although this could vary from street to street, and between different social groupings. For instance in Midcity, a worker in the local authority neighbourhood office commented that residency turnover could be a problem in one area. However, referring to a particular street, she observed:

> "It is quite a nice close-knit community round here, nearly everybody on this stretch is in the residents group."

Walklate and Evans (1999) have observed that social cohesion is not necessarily absent from high crime – and high ASB – areas; and it is also possible that neighbourhoods that are socially heterogeneous can assert common goals (Hancock, 2001). In the Midcity example of a 'close-knit' street residents still suffered ASB from one particular family that had moved onto the street: "they'd come out at night and cause mayhem" (local authority neighbourhood officer). As noted, Sampson and colleagues saw collective efficacy as leading to high levels of informal social control: "the monitoring of spontaneous play groups among children, a willingness to intervene to prevent acts such as truancy and street-corner 'hanging' by teenage peer groups, and the confrontation of persons who are exploiting or disturbing public space" (Sampson et al, 1997, p 918). However, continuing with the 'close-knit' Midcity street, people were not always willing to intervene; rather most people felt *powerless* to intervene. This was expressed in a fear of abuse or intimidation, as the following quotes from the same study illustrate:

> "Today you can't tell them not to do certain things: it's a case of, 'who are you?'. And half the time they just look at you daft and just carry on." (community activist, Westerncity)

> "My son told me that if I shout at them I will only get a brick through the window, and that's true." (retired person, Midcity)

Atkinson and Flint (2002) found that residents in deprived areas were more likely than their comparatively affluent counterparts "to intervene to prevent crime and disorder". If this is the case, then the evidence from the JRF study indicates that this is still not likely to be the majority, although further research would shed light on this. The JRF study revealed also a perception that authorities are powerless to do anything meaningful to intervene. For instance, in a focus group discussion with parents in Midcity one mother commented:

> "It's not good, I phoned up about five month ago, that lad had my daughter on the floor.... I phoned the police and they didn't come out. Then the second time I reported it, it took them about two hours to come out, they went over to see him and they didn't do anything about it, he's twelve and she's only eight."

Perceived powerlessness, along with a lack of trust in authorities, may have repercussions for those who do intervene. That poorer neighbourhoods have a culture of non-cooperation with the police has been noted elsewhere (for example, Walklate & Evans, 1999). This is illustrated in the following exchange from the same focus group where parents discussed how they might react to ASB:

Male 1: "On scruffy estates like these you just deal with it when it comes to it."

Male 2: "A lot of people around here have been brought up to not phone the police and just deal with it yourself."

Female 1: "It's a no-win situation."

Female 2: "It's like protecting your kids, if somebody's going to whack my kid then I'm sorry but I will whack them, because I am there to protect my kids. If my kids are fighting one-on-one I will stand there and say, 'yes, you fight one-on-one' because that's the way I was brought up. I wasn't allowed to go home and say, 'I've just been battered' because I was battered myself and just told to get out there and deal with it."

Interviewer: "Do the rest of you think like that?"

Female 3: "I would say that you should just walk away, but when you get picked on, it takes a bigger man to walk away."

Conclusion

If ASB is concentrated in areas of relative deprivation and is associated with neighbourhood dissatisfaction, then it follows that tackling ASB alongside regeneration work will have mutual benefits. The case-study areas in the JRF study had existing strategies to tackle ASB and were also receiving funding for regenerative work. However, the two programmes of work rarely overlapped. Such projects need better coordination. This chapter has argued that ASB can be tackled in order, for example, to reduce environmental inequality, to reduce crime, or to improve collective efficacy (so long as there is a balance between enforcement and prevention). All these, and other, objectives will have wider regenerative benefits. Similarly, regeneration work aimed at, for example, housing stock and infrastructure refurbishment, or wider 'quality of life' objectives could benefit work to tackle ASB. In the JRF study (Millie, Jacobson, McDonald et al, 2005, p 37) the scope for a shared governance of ASB strategies was noted, shared between residents and local agencies. I would extend this to link in with community-led, or community-partnered, regeneration efforts. However, as expected, the picture on the ground is not straightforward and, if residents have been let down in the past, or have low regard for authorities, then the potential for success is limited (see Purdue, 2001). In these circumstance, projects or strategies that are 'parachuted in', without considering the views and experiences of residents, will not fully succeed (see Hughes, 2004). Outsiders can only go so far in developing and supporting all important systems of informal social control. Greater success was evident where there were active neighbourhood 'champions', and mobilising residents will depend on the personal qualities of those involved. However, there is a danger of working with self-appointed 'champions' who only represent their own interests, or those of certain groups. Also, as Burney (2005) has observed, those "whose behaviour needs controlling are equally part of the syndrome and part of the community" (p 170). If residents are to be actively involved in deciding limits to acceptable behaviour – as suggested in the government's *Respect Action Plan* (Home Office, 2006a) – then the views of all groups have to be considered, recognising that different groups have different, and sometimes contested, uses for their neighbourhood spaces. They may also have contested notions of acceptable behaviour.

In tackling ASB, net widening should be avoided, where behaviour that has been tolerated for generations becomes unacceptable. For instance, Rogers and Coaffee (2005) have observed that work to promote an 'urban renaissance' of Newcastle's city centre resulted in the exclusion, or at least, "the effective displacement and dispersal of youth from public spaces" (p 334). They ask the question, "Whose quality of life is enhanced, and at whose expense?" (p 321). The same could apply to certain actions against homelessness (see Hermer and MacGregor, Chapter Thirteen, this volume), or directed at youth ASB in residential neighbourhoods (as examined by Flint and Smithson, Chapter Ten, this volume). There are related concerns regarding behaviour by people with mental health or learning difficulties being labelled as anti-social. Any joint ASB/neighbourhood regeneration work will need to be sophisticated enough to recognise such issues.

Finally, there may be scope for work to reduce the stigma of living in relatively deprived areas, and in improving self-worth and engagement. However, as one young person who lived on an edge-of-town estate pointed out, wanting to stay did not mean she lacked ambition:

> "If you stay around here, if you have a good head on your shoulders, you can do what you want really. You can't say that, just because somebody wants to stay around here, they have no ambition. I know what I want to do and I still want to stay." (female aged 16-18, Westerncity)

To maximise the impact of work to tackle ASB *and* regeneration it is a case of building on this aspiration, and encouraging aspiration in others who are disengaged or feel excluded. However, issues relating to a sense of powerlessness or a lack of trust in agencies to do anything will have to be resolved. To use the current political language, for regeneration and ASB strategies to work, agencies need first to earn residents' respect.

Notes

[1] Then Minister of State for the Home Office.

[2] The survey was conducted in England, Wales, and Scotland. A set of questions was commissioned in the monthly Office for National Statistics omnibus national survey (April 2004 – sample 1,678). The survey has a true probability sample of those aged 16 plus and typically has a response rate of around 65%.

[3] Rowdy teenagers in the street; drug use/dealing; vandalism/graffiti; abandoned/burnt-out cars; noisy neighbours; begging.

[4] The measure of high perceived ASB was based on a combined measure of ASB strands: namely, teenagers hanging around; drug use/dealing; rubbish and litter; vandalism and graffiti; drunk or rowdy behaviour; abandoned cars; noisy neighbours.

[5] The 2002 London Household Survey was conducted for the Greater London Authority, with a sample of 8,000 households.

[6] The situation has improved, especially following the creation of Crime and Disorder Reduction Partnerships through the 1998 Crime and Disorder Act.

[7] A 'rights culture' would be influenced by legislative changes such as the 1998 Human Rights Act and the 2000 Freedom of Information Act, by media campaigns and increased demands for 'no win no fee' compensation.

[8] This figure was obtained via personal communication with the report author.

EIGHT

'Problem' people, 'problem' places? New Labour and council estates

Charlie Johnston and Gerry Mooney

> Over the last two decades the gap between these worst estates and the rest of the country has grown.... It shames us as a nation, it wastes lives and we all have to pay the costs of dependency and social division. (Blair, 1998, cited in SEU, 1998, p 1)

> For some, those who from generation to generation, are brought up in workless households in poor estates, often poorly educated and frankly sometimes poorly parented, the rising tide has not helped them. (Blair, 2006c)

This chapter is concerned with the construction and representation of council estates as 'problem places'. Council estates have long been represented as posing a 'problem', to the local state, for agencies engaged in the delivery of criminal justice, and for a diverse range of organisations involved in the management of welfare and welfare-'dependent' populations. In this chapter it is argued that these estates play a symbolically and ideologically important role as a 'signifier', a marker of social problems and spatialised 'dysfunctionality'. In New Labour's much-heralded 'urban renaissance' the council estate is often counterposed against the vision of a revitalised urban citizenship, in which 'responsible' and 'orderly' communities are involved in the management of their neighbourhoods.

Before we proceed, however, some 'disclaimers' are perhaps required. The city has long been portrayed as a place of 'social disorder' and 'social disorganisation', perhaps exemplified by the work of the Chicago School of Sociology. Thus, there is no argument here that it is only ever the council estate that has been portrayed as a 'problem' locale. Nor is it claimed that the council estate is the only urban locale that figures in contemporary representations of urban 'disorder' and decay, with the 'inner city' continuing to occupy a similar role in England, if much less so in Scotland. It is also acknowledged that 'the council estate' as a label encompasses a significant range of area 'types' and includes contrasting forms of housing development, with many of those deemed to be most problematic frequently located on the urban periphery (Hetherington, 2005). In those estates considered more attractive, there has been a marked increase in home ownership through Right to Buy since the early 1980s, together with small-scale transfers of stock to other social landlords. Further, across urban Britain, many estates have been the target of 'initiatives' to promote diversification of tenure in the pursuit of 'balanced', or 'sustainable' communities (see Raco, Chapter Three, this volume). The inclusion of such localities with shifting populations does not erode the potency of the label 'council estate'.

In this chapter the term 'council estate' is used against the general fashion since the 1980s to refer to 'social housing', reflecting in considerable part that publicly provided rented housing is increasingly provided and governed by a range of agencies (today encapsulated by the term 'registered social landlords'). However, while acknowledging the diversity of providers, the term 'social housing' is for us a misnomer in that historically much of state-provided housing (and indeed that provided by many of the large housing agencies today) has, if anything, been 'anti-social' in that the council estate represents relatively highly controlled ways of living, the most regulated of all housing tenures, reflecting wider discourses that the residents of these areas require management and direction.

However, that 'the council estate' is something of a catch-all label does not detract from the way in which this label operates as a powerful metaphor. Space and place play a significant role in discourses of poverty and social exclusion, urban disorder, and decline. Our main concern here is not to detail the existence of hardship, disadvantage, and the effects of structural inequality on working-class areas, not least because these have been extensively documented elsewhere and the existence of concentrated deprivation has been repeatedly confirmed by successive reports over many years. Instead, we are primarily interested in the specific ways in which such estates are problematised leading to particular policy prescriptions.

Representing 'problem places'

It is not only in New Labour and official discourses that council estates feature as a prominent element in the construction of a new moral framework. For example in film and television fiction (for example, *The Bill*, *Trainspotting* and *Rita, Sue and Bob Too*), council estates are frequently used to signify assorted forms of social disorganisation, crime, and disorder. First broadcast in 2003, one of Channel 4's most popular dramas has been *Shameless*, a story of a 'dysfunctional' family living in, of course, a council estate in inner Manchester where 'different rules' are played from 'normal' 'mainstream' society. In fairness *Shameless* does at least avoid portraying people as simply passive victims with albeit anarchic forms of 'making do', creative adaptations, and resistance prevalent.

Elsewhere, in popular travelogues (for example, *Danziger's Britain* by Danziger, 1996) and in journalistic exposés of 'hidden' Britain (for example, Davies' *Dark heart*, 1997 and Wilson and Wylie's *The dispossessed*, 1992), the council estate figures prominently. Other journalists simply regurgitate the commonsense view of council estates that depicts them as "areas that have become morally, spiritually and emotionally disconnected from the rest of society" (Phillips, 1998). Toynbee has questioned key aspects of New Labour's social policy project, including the agenda for increasing resident involvement in community activities on 'run-down' estates:

> Everything on the estate must improve to such a degree that three-quarters of the residents can report that they 'feel involved' in their local community and 85 per cent can say they are 'satisfied with the area'. This target for community involvement struck me as an impertinence. 75 per cent of the people must feel involved with the community? How and why? It is strange that it is always the people with fewest resources, struggling the hardest against the odds, who are the ones who are expected to galvanise themselves into heroic acts of citizenship. Most people most of the time just wish the civil servants or the politician would get on with delivering the things they are paid to deliver. Since no one ever demands the residents of Mayfair get involved with their street lighting or pavements why should these people, whose difficult lives and lack of money make it harder? There is a curiously Victorian notion that 'community' activity is a good of its own, or at least that it is good for the poor on council estates. (Toynbee, 2003, p 130)

The contemporary policy and political preoccupation with social exclusion and disorder on council estates is also evident in debates about working-class masculinity and the state of the 'white working class' in modern Britain (see Campbell, 1993; Collins, 2004), while in his now infamous account of the underclass in the 1980s, Murray is clearly preoccupied by the overwhelmingly white council estate (Murray, 1990). In all of these different forms of writing, place and identity are powerfully linked, the common themes being that council estates are locales of moral deficit.

In important respects there are enduring legacies from the past here. A browse through the literature on housing reveals that the 'problem estate' is probably the one with the most enduring appeal for 'housing experts', politicians, and academics alike. Damer (1989) has produced an exhaustive and compelling critique of the evolution of the 'problem' concept and its changing spatial focus as the term was continually redefined over the years. The first official identification of *problem* families or *problem* tenants was in a government report of 1930. This is what Damer refers to as the beginnings of the 'state representation' of problem estates and problem people. While acknowledging that poverty played a part in the development of the 'problem' tenant it was their 'inability to cope', 'poor standard of hygiene', and so on that was the core of the 'problem'. After the Second World War the concept of the 'problem family' and that of the 'problem tenant' began to be reshaped. What were regarded as 'pockets' of 'problem families' in the 1940s began to multiply in the 1950s and 1960s to form a large proportion of problem estates. Damer refers to this as the social democratic representation of the 'problem'. Basically these accounts emerged as post-war sociologists began to take an interest in the 'decline of community'. Not surprisingly, the 'communities in decline' were working-class housing estates that provided sociologists with a rich source of empirical evidence about how 'problem people' led their lives and allowed them to distinguish between the 'roughs' and the 'respectables'. The final representation that Damer refers to is the 'filtering-down' thesis that emerged in the 1960s and 1970s and influences current debates on 'problem places' with 'anti-social tenants' added to the lexicon of the discourses on 'problematic areas'.

Throughout the 1980s and 1990s the council estate comes increasingly to be seen as a residual locale of spatialised social problems. Arguably more so in Scotland, by the early to mid-1980s it had already begun to replace the 'inner city' as the key spatial problem facing government and policy makers. By the time New Labour came to power in 1997, there was a ready-made stock of largely negative terms, imagery, and signifiers that were to find renewed vitality and generally uncritical usage in the early years of the 21st century.

New Labour's 'problem places'

> The worst schemes that I have ever seen are vast sums of
> public money invested in a vain attempt to change the
> infrastructure of a neighbourhood without touching the
> people who live there. And, within 5 to 10 years, it is back
> to where it started from, without having changed the nature,
> the tradition, or the culture, the aspiration and expectation
> of the people who are there....We are also faced with a small
> group of individuals who actually believe that they can play
> the system. I grew up on a deprived council estate and it is
> called being street-wise. (Blunkett, 1999, pp 4, 8)

As has been well documented (cf Imrie & Raco, 2003; Johnstone
& Whitehead, 2004; and Part I of this volume) 'community' and
'neighbourhood' play a significant role in New Labour's world view.
The neighbourhood has become a central organising principle in
urban renewal strategies, sitting alongside the newly 'rediscovered'
community across a wide spectrum of social policy developments.
Whitehead (2004) argues that "neighbourhood is now being utilised
as a moral framework through which urban problems in Britain are
being identified, codified and addressed" (p 59) and that "certain codes
of conduct and social responsibilities are now being constructed around
neighbourhood spaces" (p 63). It is our argument that within this moral
geography the council estate comes to play a major role as a symbolic
marker of social disorganisation and disorder, in many ways similar to
the imagery of the 19th-century slums.

In his first public speech as Prime Minister, in June 1997, Tony Blair
chose the Aylesbury Estate in Southwark in London to outline key
elements of New Labour's social policy. The choice of location was
significant (as it was in his first speech on law and order in another
council estate later the same month), providing a backdrop to a speech
that proclaimed New Labour's goal of combating "fatalism, and not just
poverty", "about re-creating the bonds of civil society and community",
of "rejecting a rootless morality", and of creating a "sense of fairness and
a balance between rights and duties" (Blair, 1997). Importantly, Blair
also mobilised ideas from 'underclass' discourses as he promised that
New Labour would ensure that the poorest groups would no longer
be the 'forgotten people':

> Today there is a possibility of an alliance between the haves
> and the have nots. Comfortable Britain knows not just

its own forms of insecurity and difficulty following the recession and industrial restructuring. It also knows the price it pays for economic and social breakdown in the poorest parts of Britain. There is a case not just in moral terms but in enlightened self interest to act, to tackle what we all know exists – an underclass of people cut off from society's mainstream, without any sense of shared purpose. Just as there are no no-go areas for New Labour so there will be no no hope areas in New Labour's Britain. (Blair, 1997)

All too evident here are the legacies of the past concerning the 'disreputable poor', the underclass. Throughout the past century-and-a-half, there is a continuing thread in the portrayal of the poor and disadvantaged that seeks to divide them into two main groups: those whose poverty is largely due to factors outside their control, and another group whose behaviour, lifestyle, and/or culture contribute largely to their impoverished position. The fatalistic underclass identified by Blair are, in New Labour thinking, largely to be found, although by no means solely, in the 'worst estates' in Britain; in places 'cut off' from 'mainstream' society, or which are otherwise portrayed as a residual legacy of the past. This 'dual city' metaphor was apparent also in Glasgow's council estates in the 1980s and 1990s (Mooney & Danson, 1997; Mooney, 2004). Amid its 'transformation' from a decaying industrial centre into 'post-industrial' city, Glasgow's council estates, in particular the large 'peripheral estates' were, to borrow from Blair quoted above, 'forgotten locales'. Echoing Engels's account of segregation in Manchester in the 1840s, some journalists have commented:

> There is far less a deep North-South or regional wealth gap than the great social divide to be found within each area, everywhere rich and poor living in the same postal sectors. In every big city rich and poor live cheek by jowl, close together yet far apart, managing to be unaware of each other in their parallel space. (Toynbee, 2003, pp 18-19)

Although we might add that at times policy-making elites are only too aware of what they think exists in this 'other world'!

The same sentiments are expressed in a different way in the launch report of the Social Exclusion Unit's national neighbourhood renewal programme – *Bringing Britain together* – in 1998:

> Over the last generation, this has become a more divided country. While most areas have benefited from rising living standards, the poorest neighbourhoods have tended to become more rundown, more prone to crime, and more cut off from the labour market. The national picture conceals pockets of intense deprivation where the problems of employment and crime are acute and hopelessly tangled up with poor health, housing and education. (SEU, 1998, para 1)

While there is some recognition of inequality and of social polarisation here (and in other government reports), we can again see the influence of underclass notions of an identifiable group and a type of place isolated from the 'mainstream'. That there appears to be at least three discourses of social exclusion in the above quotation from the Social Exclusion Unit echoes Levitas's (2005) argument that New Labour employs three contrasting notions of social exclusion: a redistributive notion in which inequality is recognised; a social integrationist perspective in which participation in the labour market, community, and 'civil society' is given priority; and a moral underclass discourse that emphasises the behavioural mores of the poor. However, as Levitas (2005) and Watt and Jacobs (2000) among others have argued, there is no equal weighting for these discourses and arguably in the quotes from Blair and Blunkett provided elsewhere in this chapter, the moral underclass perspective is predominant, although heavily influenced by ideas of social integration/cohesion. This is evidenced by a language that works to contrast poor neighbourhoods and estates with 'the rest of the country', and which juxtaposes the behaviour of those living in such localities with 'mainstream' society. As Morrison has argued, there is a powerful language at work here that contrasts "us" with "them" (Morrison, 2003, p 144). There is all too frequent reference to high crime rates, drug misuse, teenage pregnancies, and worklessness, as if these are the prevailing moral and cultural characteristics of estate inhabitants.

It is perhaps not surprising that in relation to identifying the 'worst' estates or neighbourhoods, definition comes a poor second to the stereotyping language that prevails. In *Bringing Britain together* it is claimed that there are 'several thousand' poor estates in England alone, while at the launch of the Social Exclusion Unit itself in August 1997, Peter Mandelson outlined the task awaiting the Unit in addressing the five million people living in 'workless homes', three million of whom were to be found on 1,500 council estates: "This is about more than poverty and unemployment. It is about being cut off from what the rest of us regard as normal life" (Haylett, 2001b, p 49).

New Labour has claimed that council estate inhabitants were among the forgotten population during the 1980s and 1990s, although this neglects initiatives such as the Estate Action Programme in England and New Life for Urban Scotland. Arguably there has been a sea change under New Labour in that there is now at the highest policy-making levels recognition that addressing the 'problems' of (or with) council estates is a key objective. This is evidenced not only by the work of the Social Exclusion Unit in London, or of the Social Inclusion Partnerships and more recently the Community Planning Partnerships in Scotland (see Johnstone & McWilliams, 2005), but across a diverse range of social and economic policies and in relation to criminal justice.

We can identify a number of closely related but discrete elements in New Labour's policy approach to council estates which, taken together, provide a clear insight as to the dominant ways in which these estates are understood and conceived as 'problem places'. We have already highlighted that council estates figure prominently in representations of social exclusion and act as a symbolic moral marker in the new urban renaissance. While we can detect in New Labour a view that economic growth in the 1980s, 1990s, and early 2000s has largely 'bypassed' these areas, this coexists with other ideas that the inhabitants are, to some extent, also to blame for their situation. Bringing these groups and their locales 'into' the social and economic mainstream has become a key element of the urban renaissance. Such integration is organised around three dimensions by which New Labour approaches council estates: social capital and active communities; housing stock transfer and the responsible tenant; and crime and disorder. It is important to acknowledge that in New Labour's much-vaunted desire to develop joined-up thinking and joined-up policies, the different policy developments are interrelated in complex ways.

Social capital and 'active communities'

Along with social inclusion and social cohesion, social capital forms an important element of New Labour's policies, a 'Holy Trinity' that underscores much of the urban policy discourse. The promotion of community 'engagement' and 'partnership' is an integral element of New Labour's commitment to neighbourhood regeneration. Set up by the Home Office in 1998, the Active Community Unit was given the task of developing new ways of promoting community self-help. Such policies are integral to New Labour's urban visions in which active communities play a more important role in policy making and are themselves increasingly self-regulating (albeit in very prescribed ways). New Labour's urban renaissance, then, is underpinned by a social project in which active citizenship is seen as a vital component (see Holden & Iveson, 2003; Imrie & Raco, 2003).

As Raco has argued in an earlier chapter of this volume (see Chapter Three), New Labour sees the development of 'stable' communities as a key component in building a socially inclusive society. Here, socially acceptable forms of behaviour are the norm, with responsible citizens engaged in activities that ensure order. Locales with 'cohesive' communities are, in this discourse, clearly distinguished from 'disorganised' communities in which social disorder of varied forms flourish. In this we can detect the coming together of notions of community as understood by communitarians such as Etzioni as well as more recently mobilised notions of social capital (Etzioni, 1998). The re-activation of community under New Labour is in part a key component of a wider strategy of 'civilising' 'disorganised' communities (see Ward, 2003).

Reinforcing and underpinning their vision of active communities is New Labour's commitment to Putnam's thesis on social capital (Putnam, 2001). Under New Labour the discourse of social capital is becoming increasingly prevalent across the policy spectrum, but particularly in the development of area-based community 'regeneration' programmes and it is also central to New Labour's arguments about civic 'renewal'. For Blair:

> A key task for our second term is to develop greater coherence around our commitment to community, to grasp the opportunity of "civic renewal". That means a commitment to making the state work better. But most of all, it means strengthening communities themselves.... Indeed the state can become part of the problem, by smothering the enthusiasm of citizens.... The residents' association that started with enthusiasm but disbands at their inability to convince the authorities to act on their problems. The victims who stop reporting crime because they lose faith that it will lead to a conviction.... Responsive public services are part of the solution. But we also need to give power directly to citizens. That's why we are piloting neighbourhood management of estates, where the tenants and residents will commission their local public services.... As Robert Putnam argues elsewhere ... *communities that*

> *are inter-connected are healthier communities. If we play football together, run parent-teacher associations together, sing in choirs or learn to paint together, we are less likely to want to cause harm to each other. Such inter-connected communities have lower crime, better education results, better care of the vulnerable.* (Blair, 2002, pp 11-12, emphasis added)

For New Labour the attractiveness of the notion of social capital is in part that it can address social exclusion. Civic regeneration and the development of social capital are seen as integral to neighbourhood regeneration and to the redevelopment of disadvantaged communities, notably including council estates. Here the argument is that the socially excluded have either 'fallen out' from 'civil society' (or are likely to do so) and fail to participate, especially with paid work, but also volunteering, running clubs, and so on. Once again we can detect enduring legacies of underclass discourses: that the poor and disadvantaged fail to engage with those activities that are assumed to be 'normal'. However, what is neglected in this discourse is that such 'normal' activities are, in fact, not prevalent in high-income and middle-class localities where a high-quality environment is all too evident.

Given the limited space of this chapter, we cannot examine the wide-ranging critiques that have been made of the ideology of social capital (see Fine, 2001; Law & Mooney, 2006a, 2006b), save to note some of the ways in which these can be used for the stigmatisation of particular places. In other words, the mobilisation of normative notions of social capital enables the construction of particular locales as 'problem' places. Communities, groups, and individuals are poor and disadvantaged not simply because they suffer from low income, but because they have not networked enough and have insufficient social capital. This is implicit in the quote from Blair provided above. What we have here is a rather sheltered middle-class outlook, a world of neighbourliness, painting classes, neighbourhood-watch schemes, a world in which the community is responsible and self-policing. Communities that fail to match this ideal model (which for the Social Exclusion Unit and the National Neighbourhood Renewal Programme, includes the bulk of Britain's remaining council estates), require 'bringing into line' – notwithstanding the fact that such a notion of normalcy is in itself a stark idealisation. In the place of a concern with material inequalities and with unequal power relations, we see an emphasis on individual and/or community dysfunction. We have all been here many times before: social capital allows for the re-entry of some of the worst kinds of stigmatising discourses. The significance of this is that it reminds us of the need to critically engage with the notion of social exclusion as much as with social capital (and social cohesion). In much of New Labour social policy, social exclusion is perceived as *self*-exclusion, notably in relation to worklessness, that is, an unwillingness to work.

That the populations of housing estates, particularly the poorest ones, are all too often depicted as lacking in social capital, that is, *officially sanctioned* social capital, leads to a view of such locales as characterised by social disorganisation and social disorder. However, while seeking to avoid a simple relativism that suggests that one person's disorder is another person's order, it is crucial that such language is problematised and the underlying ideologies exposed for critical scrutiny (see Mooney, 1999). That council estates and poor working-class communities may be characterised by particular cultures and identities does not mean that these are dysfunctional or pathological, as is frequently implied by some of the more populist and New Labour interpretations of social capital. As has been argued elsewhere, day-to-day survival strategies, epitomised in *Shameless*, often conflict with publicly sanctioned ways of living (see Smith & Macnicol, 2001; Watt, 2003). Thus, following Haylett, we would argue that there is an urgent need to recognise "that working-class identities and cultures exist in positive ways in spite of economic inequality – ways of well being that may have their problems (like another class position) but that are not always and ever problematic" (Haylett, 2003, pp 56-7).

Housing stock transfer and the responsible tenant

In the field of 'social' housing, New Labour has promised to bring about a 'transformation' in the lives of tenants. The key vehicle for achieving this is housing stock transfer, involving the wholesale restructuring of social housing and the new provision of 'new' forms of housing management. Throughout all of this the key notion is 'choice'. As Flint (2003) has argued, "Social housing is ... rationalised as a point of distinction between autonomous individuals, capable of self-government, and dependent individuals to be targeted for government intervention" (p 615).

For New Labour the restructuring of council housing is not simply a 'bricks and mortar' strategy, but is founded on the promotion of choice and the transformation of the council tenant from state-dependent to active consumer of rented housing (Marsh, 2004). Here the tenant is no longer conceived of as a passive consumer of their housing, but someone who can exercise judgement in the choice of landlord or provider, and who will want a greater say in the management of their housing. Passive dependency will be replaced by an 'empowered' consumer who will seek to engage with others in the management of their community. As Flint (2003) has again pointed out, owner-occupiers are accorded an identity as rational and responsible consumers of housing. Not so the council tenant.

It is important to acknowledge in the policy towards the 'selling off' of what remains of Britain's publicly rented housing stock an implicit attempt to 'get rid' of council tenants also. Through housing stock transfer, the attempt to reconstruct tenants as morally responsible citizens who have responsibility for their own housing (to a very limited degree), the 'welfare' or 'estate culture' that is said to permeate many working-class areas, will be eroded.

The council estate as a locale of crime and disorder

In a recent reworking of classic social disorganisation theory, especially in its Chicago School variant, under New Labour those estates and localities that have high rates of crime are said to suffer from low community involvement and a lack of social cohesion. Again here we can see notions of social capital coming into focus. As Atkinson and Flint (2004) have argued, however, there are other mechanisms of social ordering at play in such localities, through more informal processes. The image of the council estate as a crime-'ridden' place 'from hell' has long featured strongly in media representations of crime and disorder. For Haylett (2003) negative working-class subjects are very much central to the mainstream cultural imagination about a wide range of social 'problems', from teenage pregnancy and youth offending through to nuisance neighbours and drug misuse. Throughout such imagining the council estate is often not far from view. 'Estate cultures' are violent, disordered, criminal, and/or dysfunctional and deviant in other ways. Arguably council tenants and council estates probably represent some of the most regulated forms of housing tenure and this has reached unparalleled heights under New Labour. There is a marked toughness to New Labour that is sometimes obscured by the deployment of 'softer' language of social inclusion, social justice, and social capital (Jones & Novak, 1999). Alongside new benefit systems, backed up by the threat of more punitive sanctions, there are a host of curfews, orders, and social regulations that govern parenting, youth offending, young people in general, and unemployed people. And then there are Anti-Social Behaviour Orders (ASBOs). While there are different objectives here, alongside the increasing responsibilisation, there is a marked shift towards criminalisation.

Such developments lend weight to Jones and Novak's (1999) arguments of a 'retooling' of the state under the Conservatives and New Labour, with a harsher, tougher ethos permeating criminal justice and welfare delivery. Central to the 'rescue packages' for council estates is a harsh law-and-order message, reinforced by tough sanctions. Here we have the *hyper*-regulation of particular groups of people in particular places where criminal justice and other agencies work to 'seize back' estates and neighbourhoods from those considered to be disorderly. The localisation of many criminal justice policies reaches a different level in many working-class estates from 'normal' areas. For example, there are the well-publicised youth curfews in three council estates in Hamilton (see www.scotland.gov.uk). Introduced in 1998, these imposed a 'dawn to dusk' curfew on under-16s with the police given new powers to force young people from the streets. Curfews have since been implemented elsewhere, reinforced by the use of ASBOs. 'Anti-social' families and neighbours will now face local authorities equipped with more draconian powers of eviction. There is little clearer manifestation of New Labour's world view that such estates are beyond 'normal' or 'conventional' society.

Conclusion

Throughout the history of place stigmatisation, similar themes constantly reappear in different periods: 'disorder', 'disorganisation', 'pathological', and so on. There are dominant recurring themes in the story of the representation of council estates. While over time the language used might have become somewhat more sophisticated (although not always), underlying ideologies and hostility to working-class ways of living are all too present. As Haylett (2001b, 2003) among others, has argued, working-class cultures are seen as highly problematic by politicians and policy makers, cultures that are seen to find their strongest expression in council estates. The language used by officialdom betrays the class contempt that often underpins policy making, with 'sink estates', 'dump estates', 'estate cultures', and 'benefit/welfare dependency' figuring prominently in the policy-making frame today. Here echoes of the 'deserving' and 'undeserving' poor of the 19th century and, more recently, of the underclass continue to find a prominent place in policy prescription designed to 'deal with' such areas. While class is rarely named, there is a language of class at work here, underpinning the wide range of moral euphemisms that are frequently deployed in official discourses (see Skeggs, 2005).

As is well documented, New Labour's preoccupation with social exclusion and social disorder has a strong geographical referent. This is not to deny that problems of social exclusion and crime rates are geographically uneven in their intensity. However, the policy response to this geography has a strong moral undercurrent, one that is all too often imbued by stigmatising discourses. However, in other ways council estates have been rediscovered under New Labour, this time as offering a yet to be fully utilised reservoir of labour. In the new wisdom that preaches of links between 'competitiveness and cohesion' there is a new-found role for the council estate in the pursuit of global economic competitiveness (see Boddy & Parkinson, 2004).

While there are echoes again here of 'dual city' thinking, a key shift is that council estates are now to be 'included' in the drive for economic growth, thus their portrayal as a residual locale of anti-competitiveness is being tackled head-on by New Labour. In addition, that there have been widespread processes of urban renewal and 'regeneration' should not go unremarked. Many of the 'problem' areas or 'bad spots' of the 1970s and 1980s are no longer visible, either having been demolished (a marked feature of the recent urban landscape across Britain), or having been subjected to processes of 'gentrification'. In other places once regarded as 'dangerous places', we can now find locales of retail consumption and leisure, often staffed by the descendants of residents of the estates who once lived there but who now provide a significant source of often very cheap labour.

Council estates may no longer be the abandoned or forgotten places that they were under the Conservatives, but they remain 'foreign' places, an internal 'exotic' amid the wider urban renaissance. The early 1920s aside, for much of their history, council housing has been viewed as second-class housing and, in recent decades, increasingly as the tenure of last resort; a tenure requiring significant 'makeover' and 'rebranding' (see IPPR, 2000). Arguably, through housing stock transfer and other policies targeted at council estates, this is what New Labour aims to bring about. However, in the process, despite claims of 'partnership', of greater tenant involvement and of self-management, existing problems of social marginalisation are reproduced and indeed intensified in some respects through the utilisation of a stigmatising language. In part the new managerialism that pervades policies for these estates/schemes together with stock transfer are fuelled partly by suggestions that the council estate tenant is also a victim of past housing municipalisation and state interventions, as well as of the behaviour of the 'minority' of 'yobs', 'neds', 'problem families', and assorted others from various 'hells' of one kind or another.

It has been widely argued that under New Labour social policy has become increasingly 'criminalised'. While it is important to draw attention to the ways in which a wide range of social policies have become imbued with criminal justice objectives, nonetheless it is crucial that we recognise that social policy has long been intertwined with practices of social control. Further, in suggesting that social policy has been criminalised, we must not project a view of social policy 'itself' as being intrinsically 'pure' or 'soft' but also as coercive. In this respect we need only point again to the activities of generations of housing managers and the housing management systems that worked to regulate tenants in estates across the country. Together with other policies directed at council estates, there is a generalised process of social engineering taking place in New Labour's Britain. Council estates were largely the product of past (and now classed as failed) processes of such engineering. In the contemporary phase there is a much more explicit, and much tougher, policy that is effectively about managing those deemed 'dangerous' classes in their disorderly places which, for New Labour, predominantly refers to Britain's council estates, the 4,000 estates whose current state for Blair "shames us as a nation" (Schaefer, 1998). This is about establishing a new moral order in which the 'good community' and orderly behaviour can be generated. Urban policies today have more focus on crime and community safety, in the process working to bring marginalised people and places into the economic mainstream. To return to an earlier theme of this chapter, in the emerging *hyper*-regulation of council estates and their residents we can see New Labour's multiple strategies of respectabilisation, responsibilisation, and re-moralisation at work. Such estates have to be made 'sustainable', where order, respect, and responsibility prevail.

The inhabitants of council estates continue to generate the capacity for informal mechanisms of social control. Ways of governing from the bottom up often conflict with top-down policy-making strategies that work to prescribe particular patterns of living while regulating others. As Burney (2005) has argued, a key feature of government rhetoric is that poor communities "have somehow lost the ability to deal with bad behaviour" (p 56). However, such sentiments also influence other areas of government thinking that such communities show little ability to cope with 'modern' life. Against this view we argue that the potential for resistance, for fighting against the odds, and for developing coping strategies, is all too evident in poor communities and in council estates across Britain. However, it is this very capacity that continues to reinforce the problematisation of council estates as 'problem' places.

Part III
Communities in control of (dis)order

In this final section we turn to examine the practice of securing an urban renaissance in its multifaceted forms and effects. Here we gather contributions that throw light on the impacts of these initiatives on the communities they touch, as well as the broader social politics that has emerged around concerns with disorder, policing, anti-social behaviour, and a wider renewal agenda that is so often co-present with these initiatives. The preceding chapters have prepared the ground for this final and most extensive section by exploring the theoretical and conceptual assumptions that lie at the heart of current agendas of safe and sustainable communities and the policy programmes and practices that are instigated to pursue such aims. In this section these underpinnings are elaborated via closer investigations within communities, neighbourhoods, and cities to help bring focus and clarity to the ways in which crime has become interlinked with processes of urban and community renewal.

In this section community, as *the* focal point for policy, is understood in two key senses. First, it signifies an emphasis on the local and neighbourhood scale that points towards concrete places and geographical locales. As we said in the introductory chapter (see Chapter One), area-based initiatives have been part of urban renewal processes for some decades now, and yet now the links between community and the delivery of renewal have been asserted as inseparable as is evidenced through the strong reliance on engaging with localities in recent programmes that include yet extend way beyond the flagship New Deal for Communities or Crime and Disorder Reduction Partnerships. Such reliance on this scale, then, can be explained only with reference to the second element of 'community' in current policy agendas, namely that concerning the social processes, networks, and their resources within these localities. In this respect many of the contributions here highlight the growing importance assigned by urban and criminal justice policies that have recast the role of community: as agent of change and control, as a means of securing success in processes of regeneration, and as a key output of policy itself – groups of people with responsibility and acting to ensure order in their neighbourhoods.

The emphasis on community has ultimately ended up as perhaps the most fundamental element of New Labour's approach to disorder and regeneration. Policy-maker understandings of the residential neighbourhood and community networks within them have marked the distinctive approach of New Labour to its diagnosis of the critical scale at which such problems are experienced and, therefore, at which services and initiatives should be aimed. However, a key problem for many local residents in this age of empowerment is the emphasis on responsibility that has come in tandem with these rights. As we see in these contributions, a key difficulty for residents in areas suffering disorder lies in responding to an agenda which, at least in part, seeks their involvement as substitutes for officially sanctioned policing duties.

The lack of sympathy with the concerns of fearful local residents found in such programmes has thus perpetuated the air of unwilling subjects unimpressed by a call to get involved and to deal with local problems. The impression of such solutions parachuted in, without sensitivity to local conditions or the profound difficulties of engagement with these communitarian calls to arms, has been marked. Not the least of these has been an unwillingness to understand how potential reprisals have had a paralysing effect on fearful communities who nevertheless aspire to see official agencies of control manage the problems in their neighbourhoods (Atkinson & Flint, 2004). In this section these difficult issues are interrogated in more depth as we take a look at the various facets of regeneration and renewal programmes that are now so deeply linked to community policing, to the control of demanding and disorderly behaviour, and to the control of night-time economies, among others.

As Stenson and Raco have both discussed earlier in this volume (see Chapters Two and Three, respectively) the role of community has been twofold under New Labour. First, cast as responsible agent it has been asserted that community is duty-bound in its intervention into local problems. Second, community has been located as a key mechanism by which policy implementation can be achieved. In other words, we have been asked to believe that community participation and action is required in order for policy to be successful. These twin roles of responsibility and action have raised the stakes by suggesting that communities will be given support insofar as they demonstrate engagement with the agenda currently on offer. Not getting involved is seen as the malaise of disorganised and intransigent populations, unwilling to remedy their problems. Community now figures more prominently than ever in the policy process in relation to consultation, development, participation, and evaluation. The devolution of regeneration programmes and a rhetoric of participation and planning in the delivery of services can be seen as a radical and important step-change in policy methodology in relation to crime, disorder and renewal. It is in the role of community that we see the fundamental linkages between these previously discrete areas of policy formulation and implementation.

While early attempts at the control of disorder, such as Neighbourhood Watch under the Conservative government, introduced the concept of active citizens, New Labour has successfully embedded 'community' in its reworking of state/society relationships, as indicated in the new 'Respect' agenda. Its understanding of 'community' is central to such a reworking under which the tendency to regard community as comprised of 'decent, hardworking individuals' has been replaced by the notion of a diverse and yet somehow connected society. The fault lines in this logic are not hard to spot – while society has not perhaps become the aggregate of individuals in the way that Thatcher suggested, it is nevertheless more atomised, fluid, and differentially cohesive than the kind of society that emerged in the post-war period. Into this complex social milieu the political appeal to the ideals of community, reciprocity, and confidence in local intervention has been significantly impaired. This is felt acutely in those particular locales characterised by danger and risk, and it is into these spaces that demands for integration, enforcement, and intolerance of deviance have fallen flat.

To return to some of themes of the earlier chapters, these changes in the governance of disorder have not only involved the empowerment and bolstering of the rights of specific communities. The unrolling of this agenda has also encumbered and disciplined those, often marginalised, voices by conscripting them into the role of key catalyst whereby their involvement is necessary to improving their local situation. If they do not 'step up' to this role it is likely that any failure will be marked down as further intransigence, rather than any failure in the policy architecture being built in these spaces of relative and continued fear. This disconnection between a 'middle England' majority whose neighbourhoods were seen as unproblematic and these aberrant spaces of a disenfranchised and socially excluded minority were now seen as critical to a moral agenda in which citizens were seen as necessarily active, in order to be recognised as units with rights. Perhaps the most alarming aspect of these exhortations has been the sense of a double-standard through which those with least and suffering most have been required to present themselves for intervention in order to achieve the kinds of environmental amenity and social order that middle England has taken for granted as an inalienable right.

Such differentially expressed rights and responsibilities have set up a geography within which the logical explanation of neighbourhoods experiencing higher levels of crime and disorder is to be found in the neglect and apathy of their residents. If only they would get involved, runs the Blairite and successive Home Secretary rhetoric, these places could be reclaimed from a disorderly fraction whose criminality has held hostage respectable local citizens and prevented them from accessing their full rights to local calm and order. The final section of this volume highlights most of all how these projects which have reworked citizen–state relationships have been translated into neighbourhoods and communities, often dogged by complex politics, the onerous requirements of evaluation, and the ways in which apparently noble local communities have often turned out to present narrow and reactionary agendas.

This section has been assembled with the aim of enquiring, not about some monolithic notion of *community*, but about the diverse work of *communities* in their roles within the day-to-day work of securing an urban renaissance. For this purpose, the ensuing chapters provide detailed, searching, and empirically grounded pieces of research into practices at this often fragmented local level. They point to the importance with which a sense of sustainability needs to be more than a further fad in a self reinventing and media conscious government machine, and that there may be some reason for optimism in how a more holistic and less partial regeneration/disorder agenda might be worked out. And yet the assessments provided in this section also call for a cautious reading and assessment of such initial confidence. As the fault lines of local community politics and broad diversity of opinions and identities emerge, these policies in practice appear less polished or intuitively engaged with those groups they aspire to help.

Given the importance assigned to new and reconfigured policing initiatives, the first three chapters in this section deal explicitly with a range of agencies and initiatives in the public and private sectors. Paskell starts the section (Chapter Nine) by presenting findings from a long-term study of deprived neighbourhoods and the impact the establishment of police community support officers (CSOs) has for the regeneration agendas in these communities. This is followed by Flint and Smithson (Chapter Ten), who, again concentrating on residential neighbourhoods in two British cities, investigate the involvement of public police in the control of localised anti-social behaviour. They contrast different strategic approaches: dispersal of young people in one place and the establishment of a highly visible patrol force in the other place to ask questions over the involvement of different communities in shaping local policing agendas.

Questions over the kind of communities being drawn into the

policing agenda, both as subject and objects, are taken up by the three final chapters in this section, Smith (Chapter Eleven) introduces the kind of emerging private policing performed by night-club bouncers in a central city setting. He asks pertinent questions over the extent to which a 'post-industrial' regeneration agenda focused on a night-time economy driven by alcohol is, in fact, generating many of the kinds of disorder targeted by traditional forms of policing. Hubbard and his colleagues (Chapter Twelve) meanwhile complement Smith's argument by introducing a community that commonly only enters debates of policing and community safety as perpetrators of crime: women and men engaged in street prostitution. Their chapter, alongside the final contribution by Hermer and MacGregor (Chapter Thirteen), challenges the notion of community as a narrowly defined entity and furthermore amplifies the importance of examining the tendencies of urban policy to criminalise and marginalise groups such as young people, in this case street prostitutes and beggars in urban spaces. As with many of the contributions in this volume the chapters in this section persist in challenging current policy agendas based on such criminalisation, even while publicly aspiring to reduce exclusion and ameliorate social injustice.

NINE

Community–police relations: support officers in low-income neighbourhoods

Caroline Paskell

Local policing levels have been a matter of public concern for decades, but the combination of a move to car-based patrolling, year-on-year declines in police numbers, and the growth of private security provision made the relative absence of street policing a priority issue as Labour took office in 1997. Not only was this lack of visible local policing seen as increasing the risk of crime but also as facilitating problems of anti-social behaviour and environmental disorder. Such 'lower-level' issues of noise, vandalism, graffiti, and fly-tipping were gaining public attention as problems that could hamper quality of life and an area's success, especially low-income areas that typically experience above-average rates of crime and disorder.[1] This chapter considers one response to these simultaneous demands to focus on lower-level problems and to increase the local police presence: the introduction of police community support officers (CSOs).

From early in its first administration, New Labour acknowledged that tackling environmental disorder and anti-social behaviour would be central to its ambitious plan for local regeneration. Thus its neighbourhood renewal strategy, intended to 'narrow the gap' between deprived areas and the national average (SEU, 2001b), emphasised the need for local monitoring and low-level enforcement in order to ensure local environmental quality and a sense of safety. Separately, but simultaneously, the government initiated a process of police reform. This came to encompass a refocusing on local or 'neighbourhood' policing as government and senior police recognised the influence of lesser crimes and disorder on public understandings of crime levels (Millie & Herrington, 2005). The police reform, combined with plans to improve local order and police concerns at the growth of private patrols, led to the creation of CSOs. Introduced to England and Wales by the 2002 Police Reform Act, these uniformed civilian support staff provide a high-visibility local presence, supporting police and enhancing local quality of life. They have two core functions: addressing lower-level crime and disorder, and "providing reassurance to the communities they serve".[2] However, their powers are very limited[3] and so there are questions over how effective they can be as a deterrent or 'reassurance'.

This chapter outlines the development, introduction, and character of this policing initiative. Drawing on research for a longitudinal study of 12 low-income areas in England and Wales,[4] the chapter details how CSOs interact with police, staff, and residents. Specifically, it considers the role of CSOs at the police–community interface, assessing whether they can reassure or deter, given their limited powers, and whether they fulfil other functions within the neighbourhood. The chapter has three parts. Firstly, it charts the development of CSOs. Secondly, it reviews the national roll-out, showing their ostensibly quick uptake, but noting objections and police forces' differing interest. Thirdly, it assesses what the study reveals about the role of CSOs in local policing, drawing on police, warden, staff, and resident perspectives. The chapter concludes by discussing how CSOs could contribute to the regeneration of low-income areas.

Origins and development

This section situates the development of the CSO alongside two key pressures to which police were responding: the emphasis on local monitoring, and the growth of non-police patrols and security provision.

Local policing: a role for police?

From 1993 until 2000, police numbers fell year-on-year, and the number of police 'on the beat' fell further as car patrols and response work increased (Blair, 2003). This reinforced public concern with policing levels and prompted a re-evaluation of the local presence of the police. Police concern was not with numbers per se, but with how agencies such as security firms were occupying the local arena (Crawford, Lister, Blackburn, & Burnett, 2005). Then Deputy Metropolitan Police Commissioner Ian Blair was particularly vocal. His proposal of police-checked private patrols was rejected, but the question in his speech 'Where do the police fit into policing?' remained unanswered (Blair, 1998).

Police-backed policing alternatives received little government attention[5] until 2001 when Home Secretary Jack Straw proposed that police use security firms for extra patrols. Although direct substitution was sidelined (changed to an emphasis on "building partnerships to ensure safer and more secure communities" [Charles Clarke MP, Home Office Minister, *Hansard*, 2001]), discussion over how police should respond to the growth of civilian patrols had been reignited. Furthermore, the broader issue of local policing had itself become more notable, receiving attention as the government worked to improve local quality of life and area conditions.

Not just cleaner and greener, but safer too

Labour came to power emphasising the need to improve people's lives and their surroundings. These efforts focused on 'narrowing the gap' between areas with average conditions and those with the worst conditions (SEU, 2001b), but the broader aim was to enhance quality of life overall: physical conditions; crime, disorder and anti-social behaviour; and perceptions of local safety (ODPM, 2002). Noting that minor signs of disorder undermine quality of life, the government emphasised local monitoring and low-level enforcement in both its 'neighbourhood renewal' strategy and broader 'cleaner, safer, greener' plans (ODPM, 2002).

The earliest action was taken by the Office of the Deputy Prime Minister, opting for wardens as a "high-visibility, uniformed, semi-official presence".[6] The Office gave 245 warden schemes £91 million from 2000-06, supporting others through its Neighbourhood Warden Unit and regional warden resource centres. Crucially for the police, the Office of the Deputy Prime Minister intended wardens not only to make areas cleaner and greener but also safer. The Association of Chief Police Officers (ACPO) welcomed wardens as 'helping community safety' but the introduction of another front-line service "to deter crime and tackle anti-social behaviour, creating a greater feeling of security and confidence among residents" (NRU, 2002, p 3) again called into question what local role the police performed (McLaughlin, 2005).

Local policing: the development of the CSO

In reappraising the local police role, Her Majesty's Inspectorate of Constabulary asserted that the police had to become more visible, accessible, and familiar to those they served (HMIC, 2002), but research conducted into the 'reassurance gap' suggested that this would be insufficient (Innes & Fielding, 2002). This research investigated the gap between public ideas of crime trends (as increasing) and actual trends (decreasing).[7] It found that some crimes or disorders prompt disproportionate levels of concern among residents, and therefore proposed that local police focus on tackling these 'signal crimes' to reassure the public (Innes, Hayden, Lowe, Mackenzie, Roberts, & Twyman, 2004). The pilot studies of 'reassurance policing' conducted in 2002 and 2003/04 convinced the police and the government that this more locally engaged form of policing should be adopted more broadly (see Home Office, 2006b).

Yet neither reassurance policing nor demands for increased monitoring of low-level disorder could be staffed by police. Numbers were rising with 1,349 extra police recruited in 2000/01 and 3,992 (3.1%) in 2001/02, but officers could not focus on the low-level monitoring and enforcement of minor crimes or signal disorders given their concern with serious offences. Recognising that local policing needed this, the Home Office and ACPO developed a role for uniformed but non-commissioned support staff, addressing issues officers could not prioritise, and boosting local police presence.[8]

The proposal was carried into the Police Reform Act: to designate civilians as CSOs,[9] that is, as uniformed, patrol-based staff with limited enforcement powers. Unlike special constables they would not have full powers and, unlike the police, would only have powers at work; furthermore, although this and subsequent Acts[10] outlined powers, each force decided which to grant. These are now standardised (Home Office, 2005b) but there was great disparity in 2005 in how the CSOs were empowered, as there was in their uptake overall.

A mixed reception for CSOs: national deployment

The deployment of CSOs was driven by the Home Office, with £41 million funding in 2002, £50 million funding in 2004 for 1,600 CSOs (Home Office, 2004a), and plans to recruit 18,500 more in 2006-08 (Home Office, 2004b). The 2004 funding was specifically for 'neighbourhood policing' teams providing "dedicated, visible, accessible and responsive" local policing (Home Office, 2005a, p 2; 2004c). Neighbourhood policing developed from the National Reassurance Policing Programme, adopting its methods of local engagement, working in partnership, and targeting signal crimes (Innes, 2005) but providing neighbourhoods with a minimum of four CSOs, two police constables (PCs), and a sergeant who would not be diverted elsewhere except in emergencies – a significant numerical increase on previous forms of 'community policing' and one that was intended to allow even closer and more flexible engagement with the local area.

Most CSOs in this study arrived with neighbourhood policing, but others predated it. The Metropolitan Police Service employed CSOs in September 2002; from early 2003, 26 forces did so; by December 2003, 39 of the 43 area-based forces had CSOs;[11] and in late 2004, all 43 applied for neighbourhood policing funding. Figure 9.1 shows the rapid rise in numbers, from 300 to 3,500 in a year and 6,300 by mid-2005 (when this research was conducted). A total of 24,000 CSOs are planned by early 2008 (Home Office, 2005a). Home Office Minister Hazel Blears asserted that the 43 forces having applied for the fund "illustrat[es] the police service's support for CSOs and the important contribution they make to fight crime and strengthen links with the local community to increase public reassurance" (Home Office, 2004a). Yet the take-up of CSOs was not as enthusiastic as the figures suggest.

Of the 39 forces with CSOs by September 2004, seven had 20 or fewer, only six had over 100, and most had around 50 (Home Office, 2004e). Even with neighbourhood policing funds most employed fewer than 30 CSOs (Home Office, 2004d). Uptake was limited by management capacity, office space, and doubts. The support of the ACPO (ACPO, 2005) was not echoed across the service. Johnston's (2005, 2006) study of CSO implementation in the Metropolitan Police Service highlights police doubts over what CSOs could offer.

Figure 9.1: Number of CSOs employed in England and Wales (2002–05)

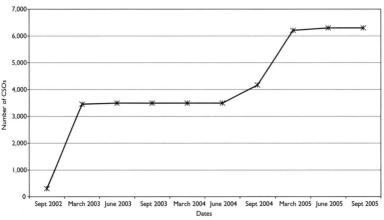

Sources: Home Office (2004a, 2004e, 2005c)

Reservations were expressed by the Police Federation whose magazine carried articles objecting to spending on ancillary staff rather than officers, asserting that CSOs would have neither the skills nor training to cope with conflict, concerned at unclear distinctions between the police and CSOs and arguing that CSOs would be hampered by their limited powers (Police Federation, 2004). Even senior police officers were reticent, as shown by the few powers chief police officers chose to grant. No forces took up all 13 sets of initial powers; one of the six forces trialling 'force in detaining a suspect' later withdrew it (despite a positive evaluation; see Singer, 2004); and at least one force granted no powers at all.

The role of CSOs in local policing: evidence from low-income areas

The 12 study areas

The research drawn on in this chapter examines diverse low-income areas and provides insights into whether these reservations were justified, or whether the CSOs were able to offer support both to the police and to the local communities they served. The research is from a study of 12 areas, 11 in England, one in Wales.[12] The study has tracked the dynamics of decline and renewal since 1999, to document how and why low-income areas change. The study uses interviews, extended visits, documents, and quantitative data on demography, crime, education, health, and so on. Each research phase has a focus: 2003/04, the physical environment (Paskell & Power, 2005); and 2004/05, the social environment and community safety, in particular wardens, CSOs, and neighbourhood policing.

CSO deployment in the study areas: a mixed picture

Deployment was highly varied across the study areas. CSOs came to most with the roll-out of neighbourhood policing in early 2005. Yet Hackney had CSOs from late 2002, Redcar from early 2003, while three areas did not have CSOs until mid-2005 and two had no CSOs. In the 10 areas with CSOs the powers varied, in number and form (Table 9.1). None had full powers but Leeds' CSOs had most of the commonly designated powers, while Knowsley's had none. Nor did those with most powers necessarily have extensive ones: Caerphilly CSOs had almost twice as many powers as Nottingham's or Blackburn's but only the latter two could issue fixed penalty notices or detain. In all areas, however, powers were among the least extensive, focused on lesser anti-social behaviour or youth disorder (Box 9.1).

Table 9.1: Powers available to CSOs[13] and powers designated within the study areas

Selected powers that can be designated to CSOs		Birmingham	Blackburn	Caerphilly	Hackney	Knowsley	Leeds	Newcastle	Nottingham	Redcar	Sheffield
Environmental	To remove abandoned vehicles	✓	✓	✓			✓			✓	
	To issue fixed penalty notices for littering	✓			✓		✓		✓	✓	✓
	To issue fixed penalty notices for dog fouling	✓			✓		✓	✓	✓	✓	✓
	To issue fixed penalty notices for graffiti and fly-posting	✓			✓		✓		✓	✓	✓
Transport	To stop cycles				✓		✓				✓
	To carry out road checks	✓			✓		✓				
	To stop vehicles for testing				✓		✓				
	To seize vehicles used to cause alarm							✓		✓	✓
	To issue fixed penalty notices for cycling on a footpath		✓		✓			✓	✓		
	To direct traffic for escorting abnormal loads										
Alcohol & Tobacco	To seize tobacco from a person aged under 16	✓	✓	✓			✓	✓		✓	✓
	To require persons aged under 18 to surrender alcohol	✓	✓	✓			✓	✓		✓	✓
	To require people in designated places to surrender alcohol	✓	✓				✓		✓		
ASB	To issue penalty notices for disorder				✓			✓			✓
	To require name and address for anti-social behaviour	✓	✓	✓	✓		✓	✓	✓	✓	✓
	To disperse groups and remove persons under 16 [to home]				✓						
Enforcement	To enforce byelaws										
	To issue fixed penalty notices for truancy				✓				✓		
	To detain [until police arrive on the scene]		✓	✓	✓		✓				
	To use reasonable force [to detain]						✓				
	To require name and address for relevant offences			✓	✓		✓		✓		
	To use reasonable force to prevent detained person [leaving]										
	To [take] children in contravention of curfew notices [home]				✓						
Security	To enforce cordoned areas				✓		✓				
	To stop and search in authorised areas										
	To enter and search premises [to prevent harm occurring]		✓					✓		✓	
TOTAL (of 26 most commonly designated powers)		6	8	12	9	0	15	8	7	10	6

Box 9.1: Powers most commonly designated within the study areas

- Power to require name and address for anti-social behaviour (11 areas)
- Power to seize tobacco from a person aged under 16 (7 areas)
- Power to require persons aged under 18 to surrender alcohol (7 areas)
- Power to issue fixed penalty notices for dog fouling (7 areas)
- Power to issue fixed penalty notices for graffiti and fly-posting (6 areas)
- Power to issue fixed penalty notices for littering (6 areas)

A further disparity between areas reflected a more fundamental difference in how CSOs work. Some CSOs were used to tackle 'hot spots', supporting police across wide areas; others served local areas (most, but not all, residential: see Crawford, Blackburn, Lister, & Shepherd, 2005). 'Itinerant' CSOs are used to help police with specific events or free police for other action. 'Local' CSOs focus on patrolling ("They have targets of about 90 per cent patrol time", sergeant) but also attend meetings and events. Initially, CSOs worked across large areas so most places received only sporadic provision. However, with the roll-out of 'neighbourhood policing', more were employed to serve specific areas, and some itinerant CSOs re-focused on neighbourhoods. By mid-2005, all but two (Birmingham and Sheffield) of the 10 areas had dedicated CSOs. Not all were in neighbourhood policing teams but all worked with the aim of providing visible local policing:

> "We've had [CSOs] here for 18 months, but for the first year or so they were used on a fairly ad hoc basis – they didn't have specific areas, they just got sent to problem areas week by week…. Now we're one of the pilot areas in the force for neighbourhood policing." (CSO sergeant)

The role of 'local' CSOs

CSOs are intended both to tackle disorder and to 'reassure the communities they serve'. For those sent to hot spots, reassurance follows more from their presence than from any rapport. For local CSOs, however, engaging with residents and staff is a clear aim, in order to reassure, gather information, and raise the profile and 'approachability' of the police.

> "They will be able to seize alcohol, request people's name and address if there's disorder, and issue FPNs [fixed penalty notices] for particular issues … but for me it's just about seeing people you can trust on the streets, breaking down barriers with young people and with the public in general." (sergeant)

One evaluation found that residents and workers develop strong links to CSOs, and see them as a resource for improving local conditions (Home Office, 2005d). In particular, the role of CSOs in liaising between locals and the police facilitates communication: "CSOs are seen as more accessible than police officers by some members of the public who are reporting issues ... and intelligence to them that they would not normally 'trouble' a police officer about" (Home Office, 2005d, p 1). Yet other research has found problems with public understandings of CSOs (Crawford & Lister, 2004). Distinctions between patrol-based staff, such as wardens and CSOs, are blurred (Cooke, 2005) and partnerships can be problematic (Crawford, 2006). Police–CSO relations can also be confusing (Johnston, 2005), as can the form and extent of their powers (Home Office, 2004c). The chapter outlines the discoveries from the research about conflict and confusion around CSOs in the study areas. The research draws on interviews with CSOs, police, wardens, local workers, and residents to illuminate how the CSO dual role of tackling crime and engaging locals was working, and assesses what CSOs can contribute to improving low-income areas.

Central to the local work of CSOs is their relationship with police. All of the constables, sergeants, and inspectors admitted to initial misgivings. Some had seen CSOs as 'policing on the cheap': "I thought they were a way of skirting around the issue of needing more police to deal with changes in society", one sergeant observed. Many had expected them to be a hindrance rather than an asset, expecting them to escalate situations and to require intensive management. Most had also been confused as to the role of CSOs in the policing structure, and had little guidance from their force or the Home Office. In particular, the degree of control given to forces, and local units, was seen as contributing to delays in employing CSOs and confusion in establishing their role:

> "Having an overview document of what [CSOs] are really about would be good, because ... it's a case of learning as you go along ... we know the rules and the regulations for police officers, but not so for [CSOs]." (sergeant)

Yet the introduction of CSOs was smoother than anticipated. There were issues – confusion over CSO roles meant most initially worked 'as and where needed' rather than with clear tasks, worries about the abilities of CSOs lessened but concern at their limited training continued, and some stations had space problems; but overall CSOs were viewed as an asset. As stations evolved core CSO duties and as neighbourhood policing provided clearer roles, their contribution to policing was better defined and more valued.

> "My objections weren't justified at all, because although police do this work, the [CSOs'] role as support can really provide great benefits." (sergeant)

"He's my other half, there to support everything I do. We're a team." (police officer)

Nevertheless, exactly what form of asset varied. All CSOs patrolled, attended local meetings, and reported problems to agencies, but differed in their autonomy, priorities, partnerships, and responsibility. Some police still doubted whether CSOs had sufficient training to do more than patrol: "I'm not sure how well-informed they'll be with only four weeks' training" (sergeant). Such police accompanied CSOs in meetings, but elsewhere police were represented by the support officers. Having CSOs represent the police at meetings was highlighted as a particular advantage because the police could maintain a public profile (and gain insights from CSOs) while focusing on more serious problems. Where this was not in operation, it was a clear objective: "I want to see the [police] CSOs building up their community knowledge even more, so that they're the ones to go to TRA meetings and community events" (sergeant).

Significantly, in the six areas that had had CSOs for over a year, the police had started to entrust them with extra duties: report writing, delivering target-hardening projects, and even conducting enquiries after minor incidents. In most cases the police tasked CSOs because they had extra time; one sergeant noted that CSOs can visit all houses when making enquiries and so not identify 'grasses'. But others explained that they gave particular CSOs much more demanding work, emphasising that tasking "is determined by the individual's competence, much more than for police officers" (sergeant). Across all eight areas, however, the police had come to value CSOs for their proximity to the public, not only because their public presence enhanced the police profile, but for the observations they made and information they were given. There was a common view among the police interviewees that CSOs were indeed supplementing local policing in ways that were at least beyond the time limits of officers and, in some areas, also different in kind to the work sworn officers could engage in: "There was some talk at first that [CSOs] were policing on the cheap, but I think that people now have seen they're doing a useful job" (inspector, Caerphilly).

In demarcating their own role and rapport with locals, the CSOs had to negotiate those of the neighbourhood wardens who shared their area and – at first sight – their work. The official line is that wardens "should recognise the great potential that exists for increased partnership working with the police and the benefits that this can bring to their community" (NRU, 2004, p 2), but, having been supported by different departments from the start, there were concerns over wardens and CSOs having to compete for money once central funding ended (Crawford, 2006). Such worries were very much evident, with wardens quick to list their advantages over CSOs as if to validate future funding. Having started earlier, wardens also viewed themselves as the senior agency: in two areas, wardens hoped to manage CSOs, "to better integrate the services". In other areas, wardens saw CSOs as "pointless" (as wardens themselves addressed anti-social behaviour and environmental disorder) and "clueless" (inexperienced, somewhat in limbo). For their part, CSOs saw wardens as unable to tackle potentially conflictual situations:

> "Wardens are good for gathering intelligence, but they can't provide security as such; they end up calling us to disperse groups." (CSO)

Nevertheless, where CSOs had been in some time, they and wardens had evolved an informal division of labour. Both sought to tackle local disorder, but wardens tended to concentrate on engagement and CSOs on enforcement. Wardens saw their advantage as being distinct from the police, so they emphasised this, working to build rapport with community groups and clusters of young people. CSOs defined themselves as 'tougher' than wardens and so, while they sought to develop links with local people, they maintained a greater distance than wardens did, being less often involved with community projects and more explicit about their boundaries:

> "The kids on the street are on first-name terms with me; I have a joke with them and they know how far they can go. I give them a bit of leeway but then say 'that's far enough'." (CSO)

Police had come to value CSOs for their local links, but CSOs themselves recognised these as more tenuous than for wardens and saw their role as being more one of enforcement. So how did residents and local workers interpret the role of CSOs? Where CSOs had arrived shortly before the visits, interviewees were confused over CSOs' difference to special constables or police. When the role was outlined, most approved in principle but were uncertain what they could achieve given limited powers. Longer-standing CSOs were more widely recognised and respondents were better-informed about their role, yet many were still marginal figures:

"I've met them once but more by accident than design. I'm not really sure who they are." (Youth Offending Team worker)

"I met them last week – I was meeting with [another statutory agency] and the [police] CSOs were just passing." (resident)

"There's the same issue with them of never being seen around except flying about – police in cars and them on bikes." (resident)

Workers and residents who liaised directly with CSOs had clearer understandings of their role, and were typically positive about their contribution. Locals who knew CSOs through projects were broadly supportive: "They're alright. They were involved a lot with the garden project so we got to know them" (resident activist). Workers who gained information or support from CSOs were the most positive. Yet the key factor in relationships with and evaluation of CSOs appeared to be the individual CSO. For example, in liaising closely with agencies and organising a local fun day, one CSO dispelled the negative impressions that his predecessor had engendered, despite having no additional powers and an equally indistinct role:

"We called him the super traffic warden 'cos he'd got no powers. The new one is much better, he comes to the community centre, he's more visible. I still don't know exactly what he does but he's more useful. He works in tandem with the police and the Anti-Social Behaviour Officer. They spot more minor things like fly-tipping and abandoned cars [and let us know]." (housing officer)

Familiarity with the role of CSOs enhanced worker and resident opinions of them, but their limited powers were always seen as problematic. While exact limits on their powers were not common knowledge (indeed the police themselves had little idea which were granted), even people familiar with CSOs saw them as significantly constrained. Specifically, people thought them unable to tackle anti-social behaviour and disorder effectively: "If they're out on patrol and they don't [have the powers] then I don't know what the issue is; maybe it would be money!" (resident). While experienced offenders tended to dismiss CSOs rather than antagonise them, minor offenders and those 'at risk of' offending did taunt CSOs about their limits. But this did not appear to dispirit CSOs:

> "Really it's only an issue with those who are known to the police already, they make it their business to know what [CSOs] can and can't do, but they're definitely the minority." (CSO)

More obvious was young people's disdain, explicit in calls of 'plastic police' in some areas. Yet such derogatory names did not reflect all young opinion; many were aware of the limitations of CSOs, but for some this 'soft' policing offered a chance for more positive relations. A senior school employed a CSO to liaise with students, and elsewhere a youth worker noted how the frequent visits of CSOs to their project were well-regarded by most members. Overall, relations varied ("some are alright with the kids, some not so good, just depends on the CSO" [resident]) but had improved:

> "Young people definitely don't see them as fully-fledged police, which can be a bonus as young people will talk to them, although they still bandy about that call of being 'plastic'. They did have stones thrown but that's not such an issue now because they recognise the kids. Trying to build bridges with young people takes a long time; in part it's down to the CSO, you've got to have the knack of doing the community bit if you're going to get anywhere with it." (sergeant)

Many of the best-informed interviewees, who had witnessed CSOs over longer periods, noted that having the "knack of doing the community bit" was key to CSOs making the most of their position. Generalising guidelines for CSO success – as sergeants asked the researchers to – is difficult given the contextual nature of the work, but it was evident from the sample that the CSO role brings something qualitatively different to local policing, not least because it provides ample time to do the detailed groundwork on which police–community relations are premised. Balancing the tasks of liaising with residents and enforcing standards appears, from the research, to succeed best where CSOs do indeed have an aptitude for weathering the knocks of local public opinion while developing small but significant practical links with staff and residents. On the evidence that was collected, CSOs have a valid durable contribution to make to the difficult work of making police more acceptable to and more successful within the most difficult-to-police neighbourhoods. Furthermore, the evidence suggests a role for CSOs in area renewal.

Conclusion

Overall, the findings indicate broad knowledge of the presence of CSOs, increasing over time along with recognition of CSOs as distinct workers. Knowledge of the role of CSOs appears more patchy, influenced most by whether the respondent has direct contact, and what individual CSOs bring to the role. However, where CSOs were in post for over one year, most interviewees thought they had broadly positive local relations, which reflected well on the police: "I think they improve the image and responsiveness of the police" (housing officer). Even those confused by the role of CSOs or dismissive of their powers favoured them over nothing. Indeed, whether interviewees valued CSOs or would rather have had more police on the street, all saw CSOs as part of a cohort of street-based workers ("the yellow jacket brigade") who were providing increased visible authority:

> "[Police] CSOs have added to the yellow jacket cohort on the street, as also are police, wardens, some council staff and others. These are seen as having a positive and deterrent effect upon youth, and are an attempt to return authority figures to the community." (community worker)

But was there more than this warm (yellow) glow to show for the local presence of CSOs? Looking at those areas where CSOs had served longest, there were indeed significant findings. CSOs, the police and others noted that older people in particular "are supportive of us" (CSO) and reassured by their presence: "I think they do make people feel safer, predominately older people and those who feel vulnerable" (community worker). CSOs were even proving able to engage some young people. Friction that could impede CSO work with police and wardens has faded or been pragmatically overlooked (excepting concern over future funding). Community groups find CSOs especially flexible in responding to their needs. And residents, most importantly, are reported by staff and residents alike to view CSOs as at least a step toward more attentive local policing:

"They're a good idea; it doesn't matter that they're not full police, that won't be a problem as long as we actually see them about." (resident)

The research indicates that quite soon after their national introduction, CSOs were delivering (to a varying and modest degree) on their aims of enhancing local policing and tackling lower-level problems. CSOs were proving able to foster community safety by facilitating local–police relations, reporting from residents to police, and reassuring residents that the police were engaging with local concerns. But more than this, CSOs and the police observed that the role's flexibility particularly suited the 'grassroots' nature of local policing, enabling support officers to access (albeit partially) the local networks and agents through which change occurs and news travels.

This research also suggests that the work of CSOs in building police–resident relations could boost local regeneration efforts, not only through the advantage such closer working can bring in attempting to address environmental disorder that is central to 'narrowing the gap' between 'worst' and average neighbourhoods, but also through the visible engagement of police staff with community projects and neighbourhood renewal initiatives, and through the limits of CSOs.

Crawford's (2006) analysis of wardens posits that CSOs are compromised by their association with the police and so unable to develop the loose ties that foster social cohesion in deprived neighbourhoods, but this was not supported by the evidence. The presence of wardens does tend to steer CSOs towards enforcement, but CSOs also link into local projects and engage residents in positive, supportive relations. In so doing, CSOs are bringing policing back into the resident groups, area networks, local programmes, and streets where regeneration takes place. For the low-income areas of the study, the growth of the 'yellow-jacket brigade', and specifically the bridge to the police that CSOs offer, provides a visible boost to aspirations for neighbourhood renewal and a further resource for achieving it.

It is not only these successful links, however, that can be understood as facilitating local order, communication, and work towards renewal. It is also on the basis of their constrained position that we can see an additional role for CSOs in fostering local regeneration. The very fact that CSO work bridges association with residents and enforcement of law and order constrains its range; CSOs cannot tackle environmental or disorder problems outright, nor can they associate themselves closely with residents' agendas as community development workers can. However, the research indicates that such limitations, while initially hampering acceptance, not only offer a basis for closer liaison with residents than police could achieve but also promote the agency of residents over issues of crime and disorder, crucial to delivering regeneration. It is in recognising the limitations of CSOs, the research suggests, that the police and residents can come to a more realistic view of what neighbourhood policing can offer and what residents need to do.

> "[CSOs] are soft, basically, you don't expect them to resolve the issue, but their presence heightens the support network and fills the vacuum around policing. They can help to tackle the notion of police as a panacea. We're looking for people to vocalise their ownership of the street and community, not to just wait for 'the sheriff' to come in and sort it out. And with CSOs not having full powers, people have to work that bit harder to address the problem. So CSOs can be a tool to help encourage people to stand and fight." (community development worker)

Notes

[1] See Simmons and colleagues (2002) for data around the time of the development of community support officers (CSOs), and Nicholas, Povey, Walker and Kershaw (2005) since.

[2] http://police.homeoffice.gov.uk/community-policing/community-support-officers/?version=4

[3] See Part 1 of Schedule 4 of the 2002 Police Reform Act (HMSO, 2002a).

[4] The Economic and Social Research Council-funded Dynamics of Low-income Areas Study started in 1998.

[5] See Paul Boateng MP, Home Office Minister (*Hansard*, 1999).

[6] 'What are wardens?' (www.neighbourhood.gov.uk/page.asp?id=567, 6/6/05).

[7] As measured by the British Crime Survey, crime has fallen year-on-year since 1995 (Nicholas et al, 2005).

[8] Sir Ian Blair recently commented that, "[the role] is tedious, absolutely necessary and vital, but tedious.... The police officer brings intelligence-generating analysis, value-added skills. [CSOs] bring ability to problem-solve, dealing with very minor issues. It's a long time since police officers wanted to deal with graffiti" (Police magazine, 2005, p 12).

[9] Three other civilians positions were empowered: investigating officers, detention officers, and escort officers (see Schedule 4 of the Police Reform Bill [HMSO, 2002b]).

[10] 2003 Anti-Social Behaviour Act; 2005 Serious Organised Crime and Police Act; 2005 Clean Neighbourhoods and Environment Act.

[11] The British Transport Police have not employed police CSOs, although forces have used theirs on transport.

[12] The study mapped the 3 per cent electoral wards in both 5 per cent with highest rates of work poverty (households with no one of working age in employment, education, or training) and 5 per cent highest on Breadline Britain's Multiple Deprivation Index (Gordon & Pantazis, 1997). Twelve areas (semi-rural, outer-urban, urban and inner-city) were chosen to reflect this geographical distribution (Glennerster, Lupton, Noden, & Power, 1998).

[13] The Home Office (2005e) shows powers that may be designated on CSOs.

TEN

New governance of youth disorder: a study of local initiatives

John Flint and Hannah Smithson

This chapter identifies key characteristics of the evolving governance of youth disorder in the UK, including a focus on youth activities in public space, new legal mechanisms for regulating conduct in residential areas, and reformed models of policing. The chapter provides a comparative evaluation of two local initiatives specifically aimed at reducing anti-social behaviour among groups of young people: a Dispersal Order implemented in Manchester and a social landlord-funded additional policing initiative in Glasgow. The chapter examines the operation of these initiatives, evaluates their impacts on anti-social behaviour and community relations, and explores the perceptions of public agency officers, adult residents, and young people themselves on the impacts of the initiatives. The chapter concludes by linking the findings to wider debates about tackling anti-social behaviour within the new governance of youth disorder in the UK.

Since 1998 the UK government has made tackling anti-social behaviour a key political priority. The 1998 Crime and Disorder Act and the 2003 Anti-Social Behaviour Act introduced new mechanisms including Anti-Social Behaviour Orders (ASBOs), Acceptable Behaviour Contracts (ABCs), Parenting Orders, and Dispersal Orders. The Anti-Social Behaviour Unit was established in the Home Office in 2003 to coordinate the national TOGETHER campaign and in 2005 the Respect Task Force was set up to develop the policy programme addressing anti-social behaviour.

Generational conflicts have a longstanding history and young people "continue to evoke adult condemnation" (Muncie, 2003, p 202). Current political discourse around anti-social behaviour has focused on the problematic conduct of young people in public space. ASBOs may now be applied to children aged over 10, sometimes accompanied by publicity strategies to 'name and shame' individuals (Home Office,

2005f); dispersal and curfew orders have been deployed against teenagers and the government is currently considering the introduction of 'baby ASBOs' that could apply to under-10s. Simultaneously, parental responsibilities for the actions of children have been strengthened through the introduction of Parenting Orders and new proposals to link social housing tenancies to adequate parental supervision (Hennessey, 2005).

Policy background to the new governance of youth disorder

UK anti-social behaviour policy discourse has been characterised by a conflating of problematic behaviour in local communities with the activities of young people. Evidence suggests that the general (adult) population associates anti-social behaviour with young people. Since 1992 the British Crime Survey (BCS) has consistently identified 'young people hanging around' as one of the top three 'big' or 'fairly big' problems in local communities, linked to concerns about graffiti, vandalism, drug use, and rowdiness (Millie et al, 2005).

Policy responses have increased the formal control of young people in public space through new legal mechanisms for regulating their behaviour and increasing the visibility of official authority, restricting the movement and association of young people, and imposing fines or other sanctions on young people or their families. Parenting Orders and parent contracts with schools have resulted in parents being increasingly accountable and subject to sanctions for the behaviour of their children, based around the impact of conduct on 'local communities' (Cleland & Tisdall, 2005).

ASBOs are civil orders that place prohibitions on the conduct of identified individuals and apply across the whole of the UK. They are effective for a minimum of two years and their breach is a criminal offence. The 2002 Police and Criminal Reform Act and 2003 Anti-social Behaviour Act extended the use of ASBOs to 10- to 15-year-olds. While 855 ASBOs were issued nationwide in the 30 months between June 2000 to December 2002, 1,323 were recorded in the 12 months between April 2003 and March 2004, representing a 268 per cent rise, with juveniles the subject of 54 per cent of all ASBOs issued in England and Wales (Campbell, 2002; YJB, 2005).

Dispersal Orders were introduced in Sections 30-6 of the 2003 Anti-social Behaviour Act (and the 2004 Anti-social Behaviour [Scotland] Act), giving the police, working jointly with local authorities, new powers to disperse groups in a designated area that has previously been the site of anti-social behaviour and if delegated officers have reasonable grounds for believing that the presence or behaviour of a group has resulted in, or is likely to result in, a member of the public being harassed, intimidated, alarmed, or distressed. The police can direct individuals congregating in groups of two or more to leave the designated area and exclude them from this area for 24 hours. If an individual is dispersed and returns to the area within this 24-hour period this constitutes a breach of the order and may lead to arrest.

In addition to powers of group dispersal, young people under the age of 16 found unsupervised on the streets within a designated area between the hours of 9pm and 6am may be taken to their place of residence by the police unless there are reasonable grounds for believing that this would cause the young person significant harm. However, this 'curfew' element of Dispersal Orders has been subject to a successful legal challenge, resulting in a ruling that it is illegal for police officers to forcibly escort a young person to their home. It should be noted that the curfew element of the Order did not apply in Scotland and the Orders are yet to be used in Northern Ireland.

Curfews have been criticised on a number of levels, by, among others, Walsh (2002) and Jeffs and Smith (1996), who raise concerns about age discrimination, the criminalisation of previously non-criminal behaviour, oppressive state control, increasing a moral panic about the behaviour of young people, and creating hostile relations between young people and the police. These concerns are not reflected in the take-up of Dispersal Orders, with over 800 implemented since January 2004 (Home Office, 2006a).

The enhanced visibility of an official authority presence in residential areas in the UK has been achieved through increasing the police presence in communities, with record numbers of police officers (now over 140,000) supported by community support officers (CSOs), envisaged to number 24,000 by 2008; and through new neighbourhood policing models that maximise police visibility in order to provide reassurance to local residents (HMIC, 2003; Home Office, 2004d). There is a growing pluralisation of policing functions in residential areas arising from visible patrol activities undertaken by the police, neighbourhood wardens, and private security personnel (Crawford et al, 2005). This mixed economy of security provision has resulted in a diverse network of funding and contractual relationships in which additional visible patrols operational in specified locations are purchased by a growing range of organisations and resident groups, including housing associations (Loader, 2000; Crawford, 2003; Crawford, Lister, & Wall, 2003; Crawford et al, 2005).

Overall these measures represent an increasingly intensive monitoring and regulation of young people's use of public spaces (James & James, 2001) as the welfare orientation of youth policy has become increasingly punitive (Grier & Thomas, 2003; Cleland & Tisdall, 2005). The problematisation and criminalisation of previously non-criminal activities by young people has resulted in young people's citizenship rights being curtailed through the use of ASBOs to prohibit the wearing of certain clothes or mixing with certain friends, and through the use of ASBOs and Dispersal and Curfew Orders (and Exclusion Orders in private shopping centres) to prohibit young people's access to and use of public spaces (Jeffs, 1997; James & James, 2001; Goldson, 2002).

The government's targeting of young people, is set within a wider context focusing on "groups of people at the bottom of the social heap" (Burney, 2005, p 45). The Manchester and Glasgow initiatives are indicative of this approach as both were implemented as local governance solutions to the 'youth problem' within areas of low social economic status subject to wider regeneration programmes. As such, they symbolise the embedding of anti-social behaviour strategies within neighbourhood renewal and management strategies, evidenced by the proposals to 'mainstream' the Respect agenda across all urban regeneration programmes (Home Office, 2006a).

They further reflect the fact that national policies and strategies are interpreted and implemented through the filter of local government structures and the responses and actions of local agencies and practitioners, evident in the differential levels of enthusiasm for, and utilisation of, ASBOs and Dispersal Orders in urban authorities (for example, in the neighbouring cities of Manchester, Leeds, and Sheffield) and leading to diverse priorities and approaches, which are evident in the following case studies.

Research studies: overview and rationale of the two initiatives

Manchester Dispersal Order

The research undertaken in Manchester was part of the wider national evaluation of the New Deal for Communities (NDC) crime theme, one among five other key themes: health, education, employment, housing, and crime. NDC is a government programme that aims to tackle multiple deprivation in some of the most deprived areas within the UK.

A MORI survey carried out in 2004 as part of the NDC national evaluation found that 45 per cent of residents from the Manchester NDC responded that teenagers 'hanging around' on the streets was a serious problem in the area. Youth nuisance has historically been perceived to be a big problem in the area. It was second only to crime in a list of resident priorities in a local survey carried out in 2002. Greater Manchester Police figures indicated a 15 per cent increase in the reporting of youth nuisance-related incidents in the area between 2002 and 2004.

The NDC community safety manager presented the Dispersal Order to the local police and the city council as a means to tackle anti-social behaviour among young people in the NDC area. The Order was implemented within a designated area for a period of three months between 20 September 2004 and 10 January 2005. The local area police team wrote a report for the divisional chief superintendent stating the case for requiring the Order, which included figures for calls made by residents in relation to youth nuisance and 500 signatures from residents in support of the Dispersal Order.

The research study included an analysis of complaints about anti-social behaviour perpetrated by young people recorded by Greater Manchester Police, interviews with police officers, NDC practitioners and young people, a survey distributed among residents and observation of the enforcement of the Order (see Smithson, 2005).

Extra resources to implement the Dispersal Order were provided by Greater Manchester Police including financing transport to police the curfew for under-16s and two police officers working overtime between 7pm and 1am, seven days per week patrolling the designated area and enforcing the Order. The NDC's youth intervention officer occasionally accompanied police officers on area patrols in order to assist officers in dealing with local young people appropriately. The Order was jointly resourced by the police and the Manchester Partnership, with both organisations supplying additional resources to establish enforcement procedures (see Box 10.1).

According to police and NDC practitioners, the policing of the Order resulted in young people being stopped and spoken to without necessarily being dispersed or taken home. Police officers would firstly warn young people that the curfew began at 9pm and would recommend that they return home by that time. During the three-month period 277 young people were stopped and 177 young people were dispersed by being told to split up from their friends if they were in a group of more than two and advised to return home by 9pm. Of those young people aged under 16 who were seen on the streets after 9pm, 96 were escorted home. A total of three arrests were made

Box 10.1: Steps involved in policing and enforcing the Dispersal Order

Two officers patrolled the designated area in a police vehicle from 7pm to 1am. If young people were on the streets they were reminded that the curfew commenced at 9pm for those under the age of 16.

It was at the officers' discretion whether young people in groups of two or more were dispersed.

From 9pm onwards details could be taken of those young people still on the streets. Those under the age of 16 were told to go home. It was at the officers' discretion as to whether or not they accompanied a young person home.

A young person who had been dispersed and had returned to the area within a 24-hour period could be arrested, at the discretion of the officers.

If a young person under the age of 16 continually breached the Order their parents were asked to attend a multiagency Dispersal Order Panel, facilitated by police officers and NDC practitioners to provide parents with information and guidance about the Order.

throughout the duration of the Dispersal Order. An NDC practitioner described how the Order was enforced:

> "There has been a bit of leeway with the officers policing this. When the 9pm curfew starts it's pretty unrealistic with the nature of the young people we work with that they are going to adhere to that. I think officers will generally give a 15 to 30 minute stay of execution where young people can make their way to the bus stops or be picked up or make their way home. After that what we've found the people out after 9.30pm are the ones deliberately staying out. Whether they want to engage in a bit of fun or games with the police or whether it's not been enforced by their parents."

Dispersal Order Panels were set up by the police for young people who frequently breached the requirements of the Order. Letters were sent to parents of the young people who had been dispersed three times or more, requesting them to attend a panel meeting at the police station with their child at which the police advised parents of the 9pm curfew and stressed that they should ensure that their child was indoors by that time. The police gave advice about actions that may follow if children did not adhere to the Order, including the issuing of an ABC and potentially a subsequent ASBO. Parents were also advised that they could lose their tenancies.

The procedures to police and enforce the Order, as illustrated in Box 10.1, lacked consistency. On occasions, liveried police vehicles were not available and unmarked vehicles had to be used, and additional officers were not always available to police the Order due to other commitments in the area. The lack of a specifically allocated pool of officers led to inconsistency in policing the Order arising from the reliance on individual officers' discretion.

Reidvale Community Policing Initiative

The Reidvale Community Policing Initiative began in April 2004, involving a partnership between Reidvale Housing Association and Strathclyde Police whereby the housing association funded overtime payments to police officers to undertake 16 hours of additional high visibility patrols in a small designated area where the association's stock was located. The initiative was funded as a 12-month pilot but has continued since April 2005. The evaluation of the Reidvale Initiative included baseline and final surveys of 181 residents in April 2004 and April 2005, focus groups with adult tenants and young people in April 2004 and April 2005, interviews with housing and police officers and youth workers, and analysis of complaints about anti-social behaviour recorded by Strathclyde Police and Reidvale Housing Association, patrol report sheets completed by police officers, and vandalism records kept by Reidvale Housing Association (see Flint & Kearns, 2005).

The Initiative occurred in response to growing concerns about serious youth disorder in the area and the inadequacy of a local police presence. The additional police patrols were specifically targeted at young people's activities. However, although the principle objectives of the scheme were to reduce anti-social behaviour and to increase residents' feelings of safety and confidence in the police, it was also recognised that improving relations between young people and adults and fostering tolerance was an important element of enhancing a sense of community locally, and the initiative was linked to the provision of youth facilities (including a youth shelter) and the promotion of an awards scheme for young people.

The Initiative operated through the funding of overtime payments to police officers to undertake 16 hours of additional patrolling activity in a designated area of a few streets. Two officers jointly patrolled between 6pm and 10pm on two designated evenings each week. A total of 91 patrols were conducted between April 2004 and 31 March 2005, amounting to 364 additional police hours, with over a third of patrols conducted on Friday evenings. The timing of the patrols was negotiated between the police and housing association, and the housing association gave the police specific instructions about particular streets or premises to focus on. Unlike the Manchester initiative, additional patrolling activity was almost always delivered, with less than 20 hours of police coverage being lost due to cancelled patrols or officers being called outside the designated patrol area. A total of 65 police officers undertook the patrols, although a quarter were conducted by a core of eight community police officers.

The police provided Reidvale Housing Association with detailed report forms for each patrol and a weekly record of complaints received about anti-social behaviour. The majority of patrol activity involved walking or cycling the streets with some visits to youth facilities, commercial premises, and residential properties. During the additional patrols 115 stop-and-searches were carried out and 18 arrests were made, and on a third of patrols groups of young people were dispersed. The concentrated nature of the housing association stock and the designated area meant that a police presence and visibility increased significantly, as a police officer described: "Sometimes on one additional patrol night we will be in a street five or ten times ... whereas on normal shifts we may be lucky to be in that street once."

The residents' surveys showed a 28 per cent increase (to 82 per cent) in the 12 months of the Initiative in the proportion of residents who had seen a community police officer and a 21 per cent increase (to 29 per cent) in the proportion of residents who had spoken to a community police officer. However, only two thirds of respondents were aware of the Policing Initiative and only a third of residents reported perceiving an increase in police presence in the locality during the 12 months of the Initiative (although this was a 21 per cent increase on the previous 12 months).

Impacts of the initiatives

Reducing anti-social behaviour involving young people

Greater Manchester Police figures provided for calls made by residents regarding juvenile nuisance in the Manchester Dispersal Order area were obtained for August to December 2001-04 (Table 10.1).

Figure 10.1 illustrates that calls fluctuated over the three-year period,

Figure 10.1: Calls made regarding juvenile nuisance between August to December 2001–04

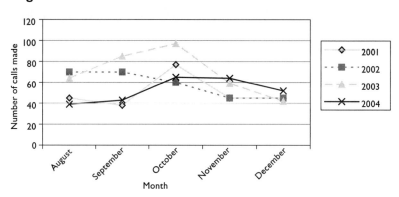

although 2003 experienced higher figures compared with other years. The figure provides evidence of a 'seasonal spike' occurring in the month of October, which police officers and NDC staff attributed to the misuse of fireworks. Comparing the 12-month period of January 2003 to January 2004, figures for 2004 are lower throughout the year until November and December when there is an increased percentage change. The difficulty with comparing 2003/04 figures is that 2003 saw an exceptionally high numbers of calls being made compared with other years. September and October 2003 had the highest number of calls over the three-year period 2001-04.

The figures provided for August–December 2004 demonstrate that prior to the inception of the Dispersal Order, 2004 figures were among the lowest over the three-year period. Conversely, figures for 2004 were highest while the Order was in place. One explanation for this is that the Order could have raised residents' expectations and willingness to contact the police while simultaneously reducing residents' tolerance of youth nuisance. Unfortunately, figures for January 2005 and beyond were not made available. As a result, it is not possible to comment on long-term effects of the Order. The figures are therefore inconclusive about its impact.

Reidvale Community Policing Initiative

A range of evidence suggests that the Policing Initiative led to a considerable reduction in anti-social behaviour and street disorder involving young people in the Reidvale area. Table 10.2 shows the number of complaints received by Strathclyde Police about anti-social

Table 10.1: Number of calls made regarding youth nuisance in East Manchester: January 2003 to January 2004

Number of calls made regarding youth nuisance	2003	2004	% change
January	39	48	+9
February	68	54	−14
March	59	40	−19
April	53	42	−11
May	59	42	−17
June	60	44	−16
July	64	36	−28
August	64	36	−28
September	85	43	−42
October	97	65	−32
November	59	64	+5
December	42	52	+10

Source: Greater Manchester Police

behaviour in the Reidvale area during the 12 months of the Policing Initiative compared to the preceding 12 months. We have classified incidents into *major*, involving serious disturbance including physical and verbal assaults, acts of vandalism, and public drug taking, *nuisance*, including excessive noise, graffiti, and complaints of young people 'hanging about', and *other*, which comprises complaints about adults and neighbour disputes.

The figures reveal that complaints overall fell by 41 per cent over the period of the Initiative. The particular targeting of police patrol

Table 10.2: Complaints about anti-social behaviour in Reidvale: April 2004 to March 2005

	2003-04	2004-05	%
Major incidents	197	106	−46
Nuisance	196	110	−44
Other	39	38	−3
Total	432	254	−41

Source: Strathclyde Police records 1 April 2003 to 29 March 2005

activities towards young people is demonstrated in the fall in complaints of 46 per cent and 44 per cent relating to major incidents and youth nuisance respectively while incidents involving adults and within properties show little change. There were considerable falls for each month during the Initiative compared to the previous 12 months with the exception of September 2004, and the cumulative impact of the Initiative is demonstrated by the 70 per cent fall in complaints in its final three months compared to the monthly situation before the initiative began. Further data provided by Strathclyde Police showed that complaint levels were down a third from the situation two years ago. Reidvale Housing Association also recorded a 35 per cent fall in the number of recorded vandalism records over the course of the initiative compared to the previous 12 months (150 incidents costing £5,631.17 compared to 232 incidents costing £7,796.29). By comparing the dates and times of complaints with logs of additional patrol times it is also possible to show that there were proportionally fewer calls about youth nuisance and street disorder during the times of police patrols (an average of 0.31) than during equivalent days and times when the patrols were not operating (an average of 0.73); and this finding was consistent for each weekday.

Table 10.3 shows that the proportion of residents regarding the activities of young people as big problems in their locality halved by the end of the Initiative and there were considerable reductions in the proportion of residents who believed anti-social behaviour involving young people was getting worse.

However, attributing the fall in anti-social behaviour among young people in Reidvale solely to the Policing Initiative is problematic. According to Strathclyde Police figures, the fall in Reidvale was proportionally the same as two surrounding neighbourhoods (although considerably higher than the most adjacent neighbourhood) and was the same as the proportional fall across the wider East End of Glasgow. On the other hand, these figures also suggest that concerns about the Initiative merely displacing youth disturbance into neighbouring communities may have been unfounded.

Changing relations between the police and young people

Relations between the police and young people were not prioritised either by police officers or NDC practitioners when implementing the Dispersal Order in East Manchester. During patrols, officers referred to themselves humorously as the 'child catchers'. NDC practitioners viewed the Order as being a valuable safety mechanism for young

Table 10.3: Reidvale residents' perceptions of anti-social behaviour involving young people

	2004	2005	% change
Residents reporting 'fairly big' or 'very big' problem (%)			
Rowdy or disrespectful young people	79	33	–46
Teenagers hanging around the streets	79	33	–46
Vandalism	78	32	–46
Graffiti	77	27	–50
Drugs and alcohol	67	38	–29
Residents reporting that problem got worse in the last 12 months (%)			
Rowdy or disrespectful young people	48	6	–42
Teenagers hanging around the street	48	6	–42
Vandalism	43	7	–36
Graffiti	42	7	–35
Drugs and alcohol	40	9	–31
Residents avoiding walking past groups of young people	63	57	–6

Source: Household Surveys April 2004 and April 2005 (*n*=181)

people as it reduced the number who could be out on the streets late at night: "As a safety issue it gets young people off the streets at a reasonable time. It came into effect at the end of September when dark nights and safety issues come to the fore."

However young people reported an increased hostility between themselves and the police as a result of the Order. They spoke at length of the perceived unfairness of the Order and also the inconsistency in the way it was policed:

> "They only go for the kids they don't go after the adults. They think we're easier. We're easier to target aren't we?"

> "Sometimes you might get these nice police officers yeah, who just tell you to move away from the area cos people are asleep, but some knob-heads they'll tell you to fuck off home just get away from the area and if I see you in this area I'll just lock you up."

The 9pm curfew was an issue that produced a great deal of resentment, with young people bemoaning the fact that it was unfair for a police officer to have this authority: "They think they're your mum and dad or summat setting your own curfew up." Young people either stated that the Order had not impacted on their behaviour as they tended to ignore its powers, or argued that it had negative impact on their behaviour due to greater antagonism towards the police: "It made us worse because the police make you angry for making you go home at that time, so when you see em you just annoy them", or "So if they take you home you just go back out again and then you get caught again and you just get into even more trouble."

Young people often contradicted the police officers' and NDC practitioners' perceptions of the Order as a safety mechanism:

> "One day they tell ya to hang about with more people so you're not getting jumped or ought and then the next day they're saying you can't. It's just like saying you're not allowed to have more than two friends."

> "Nah, there's no way that's fair because you see on the news or TV after there's been a rape or murder all you see on the news yeah is if you're going out go with a friend never be on your own, that's one thing I don't understand. The police must want people to be murdered or raped."

A number of young people believed that the Order was unnecessary as they did not congregate in residential areas causing distress to local residents. They explained that they would rather 'hang out' in areas such as parks where there was little adult or police presence. They felt particularly aggrieved that one of the main parks fell within the designated dispersal area, thereby limiting their access to this location: "We go in the parks and then they cordon it all off so then what can we do?".

While the Order increased the contact between police officers and young people, the evidence suggests that this interaction was not beneficial for their relations. From the outset, practitioners missed the opportunity to try and generate more positive encounters between the police and young people. Although NDC practitioners canvassed the opinion of adult residents with respect to implementing the Dispersal Order, nothing similar was carried out with young people in the area. No efforts were made to visit schools and discuss the requirements of the Order and seek feedback from young people regarding the types of diversionary activities they would like to see in the area. The antagonism felt by young people was heightened by the curfew stipulation of the Order restricting legitimate facilities for young people in the area. For example, youth clubs in the area had to close early to ensure that young people were 'off the streets' by 9pm, and no alternative youth diversionary activities were provided.

The Order could also have resulted in a more positive impact on the relations between the police and parents in the area. Advocates of curfews often cite the safety of young people as a justification for their use (see Jeffs & Smith, 1996) although the police did not use this view as a platform for promoting the requirements of the Order. Officers only had contact with those parents who were asked to attend a Dispersal Order Panel meeting to discuss their child persistently breaching the Order. At the panels observed by the researchers, parents were aggrieved by the curfew stipulation of the Order as they believed that 9pm was too early, and most parents stated that they set their children 'curfews' of 10pm, only one hour later than the Order requirement. Parents were also concerned about the repercussions of breaching the Order as a number of them were not fully aware of the powers of the Order and were obviously distressed at the thought of losing their tenancy as a result of the behaviour of their child.

In Glasgow, police officers, housing officers, and youth workers believed that the Initiative had been largely beneficial for relations between the police and young people. The additional time enabled officers to engage with young people in greater depth and to seek longer-term solutions, which crucially also meant challenging adults about their responses to young people, as a community police officer described:

> "Guys in patrol cars are under pressure to sort something out and move on to the next call. We have more time to sort it out and look to longer term solutions, we can speak to a group of kids for five to ten minutes, we have time to listen to the kids...."

The increased regular interaction between police officers and young people also widened encounters to include positive situations, as another police officer described:

> "Officers on the regular shift are responding to complaint calls and are operating in a negative context when there has been a complaint about young people's behaviour. We

are able to speak to kids in a positive context which is very important, we can ask them if they are behaving and praise them when they are."

Police officers believed that these more positive encounters had impacted on general relations between the police and young people in the Reidvale area:

"We've improved relations with young people. I was in [a local youth facility] and kids were shouting my name, kids are starting to like us, kids know who we are and what we are trying to do. There is a perception of fairness. This leads to cooperation, for example kids gave us information about a missing youngster."

Increased encounters and recognition between the police and young people had improved the effectiveness of enforcement activity, as one police officer described: "We know who the young people are now, and where they live. There is no point in them running away." Moreover this increased knowledge enabled the police to engage with parents about their children's behaviour and to negotiate strategies to resolve problematic behaviour before situations escalated, and police officers reported that visiting parents was an increasingly important element of their activities. However, a local youth worker pointed out that young people were more likely to be moved on due to the additional police presence, often on multiple occasions in the same evening and that this bred some resentment towards the police, the continuing adult intolerance, and the lack of 'legitimate' facilities and activities for young people in the area.

Building community relations

The Dispersal Order in Manchester was not particularly effective in terms of building community relations. Nearly half of the residents surveyed had not heard about the Order and therefore were not aware of its powers and the majority of those residents who were aware of the Order responded that it had had little impact on levels of anti-social behaviour among young people. Residents offered several explanations for this outcome, including: young people taking no notice; young people not being the only cause of anti-social behaviour; and ineffective enforcement and sanctions:

> "It does not reduce nowt because when they [the police] leave all the kids come back again playing football until 11[pm]."

> "If children are on the streets whether they are doing something or not, they are children and they shouldn't be made to go home if they are not doing anything wrong."

> "For all the bad things these kids do I don't think they get punished hard enough. If they continue to cause nuisance then the parents should be heavily fined."

The above quotes demonstrate that the Order was not perceived by residents either to be effective in reducing levels of anti-social behaviour or an appropriate method of tackling anti-social behaviour. Intolerance towards young people engaging in legitimate activities such as football could suggest that the Order raised expectations and increased intolerance. Ineffectiveness was also referred to as a result of the discriminatory nature of the Order towards young people who were perceived as 'doing nothing wrong'. The responses from residents illustrate that the community could have been divided over the issue of young people's involvement in anti-social behaviour, with some being intolerant, while others were more sympathetic. It is therefore unsurprising that the Order had little effect on enhancing community relations.

Some residents were very critical of the Order, especially parents of the young people affected by the restrictions of the Order. Some NDC practitioners were of the opinion that residents had a tendency to exaggerate the negative aspects of the Order:

> "We attended a meeting right at the start of the dispersal process and we took questions from a number of residents who said, 'you dispersed my daughter on her own last night she's only 15 you sent her off in an opposite direction to her friends'. It's just nonsense, absolute nonsense. No police officer would ever send two 15-year-old girls off in the opposite direction. I think sometimes people just want to create problems."

Young people are far more likely to become victims of crime than older groups and are usually actively encouraged to socialise in groups of more than two (see Wood, 2004). The concerns of parents were entirely valid and rather than dismissing these concerns as the above quote demonstrates, increased efforts should have been made with parents and young people in order to provide reassurance and alleviate resentment towards the Order.

Police and housing officers and youth workers in Reidvale reported that the Policing Initiative had made little impact on community relations and had not reduced levels of intolerance towards young people. Many complaints were made on the basis of potential anti-social behaviour rather than actual incidents and a continuing lack of acceptance of young people congregating peacefully. There were ongoing problems with serial complainers and cases of inappropriate responses and actions towards young people by adult residents. The police officers further acknowledged that ongoing coverage of 'neds' (delinquent young people, primarily young men) in both local and national media continued to reduce the tolerance of young people and accepted that this led to groups of young people being moved on even when they had nowhere to go. However, these perceptions tended to be framed in terms of providing 'legitimate' formal activities and facilities for young people rather than restating the legitimacy of young people utilising public space peacefully.

Conclusion

These findings raise a number of issues about new mechanisms for governing youth disorder in the UK. The relative success of the Glasgow scheme indicates that local initiatives need to be adequately resourced and enforced consistently. Local initiatives also require an enhanced police presence to be used to foster positive interactions between police officers and young people, and for punitive enforcement action to be balanced with simultaneous action to provide 'legitimate' activities for young people. These findings also suggest that local initiatives require a sensitive dialogue and partnership with young people and parents as well as other residents. It is striking that neither initiative impacted significantly on relations between young people and adults or addressed the ongoing intolerance of young people's presence in public space, even when they are acting in a law-abiding manner.

Much of the hostility of young people in Manchester towards the police arose from the curfew aspect of the Dispersal Order that presupposes that young people's presence in specific locations at certain times is problematic or unacceptable.

The Order is an example of an oppressive mechanism of state control over young people that criminalises previously non-criminal behaviour (Walsh, 2002). The governance of young people's behaviour through the imposition of increasingly punitive measures needs to be viewed in terms of the messages they send out about young people by increasing fear and intolerance and also the degenerative effect they have on relations between young people and those organisations who seek to control them. Within these new governing processes we are witnessing how interpretations of the components of urban renaissance and renewal have resulted in an exclusionary dispersal of marginalised populations in both city centres and, increasingly, in urban residential arenas (Rogers & Coaffee, 2005).

Finally, the focus on neighbourhood-level interventions, premised on new neighbourhood management and governance structures, and the increasing use of mixed economy security patrols by local communities (Crawford et al, 2005; ODPM, 2005h) raises wider issues about equality and scales of intervention in the new governance of youth disorder in the UK. Both the Manchester and Glasgow initiatives were deployed in small defined neighbourhoods. In the Reidvale Initiative, an additional police presence was purchased by tenants, through their housing association, to serve a designated area. It may be argued that tenants in social housing should not be paying twice for adequate policing services. However, the fact that Reidvale residents received an enhanced service not available to other residents in surrounding communities symbolises the concerns about a two-tier provision of public safety mechanisms and the emergence of levels of community safety becoming increasingly linked to the financial and organisational resources that particular communities are able to access to secure additional public and private policing presences (Hope, 2000; Loader, 2000; Boudreau & Keil, 2001). The new governance of youth disorder not only requires a balance between prevention and enforcement and a recognition of the rights as well as responsibilities of young people but also needs to be grounded in a more equitable public policing approach that reduces, rather than exacerbates, security differentials between neighbourhoods.

Acknowledgements

The authors wish to acknowledge the contribution of Ade Kearns who was co-researcher on the Reidvale evaluation and all the residents and practitioners in Glasgow and Manchester who participated in and facilitated the research.

ELEVEN

The night-time economy: exploring tensions between agents of control

Gavin J.D. Smith

Town centres are no longer spaces merely restricted to daytime consumption. Indeed, Britain's night-time economy (NTE) is now worth many millions of pounds annually, and is defined as the attraction of mainly young, upwardly mobile people at night to city centre entertainment 'hot spots' such as bars, clubs, restaurants, casinos, pool and snooker halls, cinemas, and cafes to spend significant sums of money on a range of leisure and social activities (Hobbs et al, 2003). That said, NTE is centred on excessive alcohol consumption in 'vertical drinking' venues with limited seating facilities (Monaghan, 2002; House of Commons and ODPM, 2003). Recent changes associated with the shift from the industrial to post-industrial city – for example, the emergence of flexible working hours, public/private sector partnerships, business entrepreneurship, and a focus on the provision of services as opposed to manufacturing, coupled with a re-orientation of urban governance – has meant that the late-night leisure and entertainment industry now employs vast numbers of workers both enabling and encouraging revellers to eat, drink, and socialise until the early hours on most days of the week (Chatterton, 2002; Hobbs et al, 2003).

While the government's active encouragement of night-time economic growth has, on the one hand, facilitated urban regeneration schemes and been beneficial to local economy, employers, employees and consumers, various social order problems are attached to such changes. These include an increase in late-night alcohol-related violence, rowdiness, noise, drug dealing, vandalism, street fouling and litter dropping, and other offences (Roberts, 2004). In response to such disorder, to regenerate city centres more widely and make the public apparently 'feel safer' in such spaces, strategies such as closed circuit television (CCTV) cameras and their operators have been implemented by various public/private sector authorities, alongside other measures such as Pubwatch and Shopwatch (Norris & Armstrong, 1999). The latter schemes effectively link together various agents of social control such as retail security guards, pub/club door staff, police officers, and CCTV operatives over an intelligence-driven, real-time radio network. Pubwatch also involves the training and registering of city centre door staff by the local authority, with premises paying £200 for the radio system. Signing up to Pubwatch is often compulsory in order to acquire a late night licence, but it has the clear benefit of enabling the city's various bar security personnel to communicate and to exchange and share information directly with one another and particularly with CCTV staff (www.nationalPubwatch.org.uk/). In theory, the Pubwatch partnership would facilitate the prevention of incidents, the apprehension of problematic patrons and offenders, and the maintenance of order.

As the NTE has expanded, stretched police forces have become more reliant on Pubwatch partnerships to effectively become the eyes and ears of the night and the symbolic 'guardians' of public/semi-public space (http://news.bbc.co.uk/1/hi/uk/837408.stm). Despite the importance of their role, little is known about relations between CCTV operatives and pub and club door stewards; this issue forms the main focus of the present chapter. Indeed, the aim is twofold. At a pragmatic level, and using micro sociology, the author seeks to empirically analyse the relationship between CCTV operators and door staff by looking at how the two communicate and interact over the Pubwatch radio network. Theoretical reflection, particularly insight taken from General Systems Theory,[1] then helps explain why various tensions and conflicts between the night watchers might exist.

Crucially, this chapter takes as its general starting point two vital issues that have driven the urban renaissance project, namely, the exponential growth of crime control measures in city centre spaces and how they operate in practice, and the realities of economic revitalisation policies. Indisputably, many of the goals of the urban renaissance project – revitalisation, regeneration, and economic growth – are realised in the NTE. Yet crucial paradoxes lurk here. This kind of economic strategy brings with it a range of disorder behaviours increasingly viewed by government, media, and the general public as one of urban Britain's most challenging social problems. The NTE itself is an ambiguous space simultaneously composed of both regulatory control strategies and deregulatory liberalisation policies. The paradox does not end there. Even the very social and technological measures brought in to pacify and civilise urban spaces and counter the NTE's undesirable face are themselves, as will become obvious, riddled with contradiction.

Night-time economy, urban renaissance, and social disorder

While the NTE in the UK began to flourish in large cities during the early to mid-1990s, the last few years has seen the phenomenon grow exponentially nationwide (Roberts, 2004; Roberts & Eldridge, 2005a). This transformation has occurred within a context of greater liberalisation in alcohol and entertainment licensing laws that allow flexible opening hours for entertainment premises and times when alcohol can be sold (2003 Licensing Act). The NTE has also arisen in conjunction with urban regeneration policies, financial incentives to local authorities from medium and large-scale corporate franchises seeking to take advantage of the late night market, later working hours, and general work and lifestyle changes (Chatterton, 2002; Roberts & Eldridge, 2005b). The government's desire to create truly '24-hour' cities based on their continental cousins, such as Madrid and Paris, has also been influential on the emergence of the UK NTE (Roberts, 2004). According to Hobbs et al (2003), the NTE is based on a commercial, competitive ethic and a hedonistic, carnivalesque cultural dynamic, translating as the rational and instrumental pursuit of advertising, sales, expansion, and profit by business franchises, coupled with their encouragement of individualism and indulgence in crazy and lurid pleasure-seeking activities.

The UK's NTE has its origins in local and national authorities' dogged pursuit of the urban renaissance, a 'policy and practice' project based on the principles of attracting greater numbers of people to live and work in town and city centres, thus promoting tourism and consumption and encouraging economic growth and inward investment. This is thought to create and sustain employment, provide enhanced services through partnerships, and create vibrant and safe city centres along with other such urban regeneration benefits (DETR, 2000; House of Commons and ODPM, 2003). A thriving evening and late night economy is assumed to help extend the vitality and vivacity of a town or city beyond normal working hours, making centres more attractive and harmonious places. This in turn lessens the threat of residential expansion into Greenbelt sites, simultaneously aiding the repopulation and redeveloping of previously run-down or 'no go' inner city areas. Moreover, a thriving NTE means significant contribution to the government treasury via VAT, excise duty, Corporation Tax, Income Tax, and so on (House of Commons and ODPM, 2003).

Attached to Britain's booming NTE is a more ominous side. Although violence has always been closely associated with night-time entertainment industries, recent estimates suggest, for example, that 47% of violent offences are committed while the offender is under the influence of alcohol (PSUCD, 2004). Indeed, alcohol-related crime is costing the UK £20 billion pounds annually (Roberts & Eldridge, 2005a), with Accident and Emergency departments, for example, noticing a significant increase in 999 activity during the early hours of the morning, coinciding with later pub/club opening times (House of Commons and ODPM, 2003). The government is acutely aware that violent crime, associated with the NTE, creates images of city centres as places of disorder and lawlessness, effectively intimidating, alienating, and discouraging certain groups (especially the over-thirties) from using the town centre at night thus contradicting the intended goals mentioned above (PSUCD, 2004; Roberts, 2004).

A raft of evidence-based management literature focusing on 'How to run the NTE effectively' has emerged (for example, GLA, 2002; House of Commons and ODPM, 2003; PSUCD, 2004; Roberts, 2004), alongside the formation of government-endorsed multiagency Crime and Disorder Reduction Partnerships (CDRPs) (1998 Crime and Disorder Act). This discourse, while advocating the continued growth of night-time economies, also broadly promotes a variety of key control measures and 'best practice' for CDRPs to follow and implement, in order to tackle anti-social behaviour (PSUCD, 2004). In particular, the literature advocates the increased installation of relatively unobtrusive, technological systems of surveillance such as CCTV cameras and the formation of Pubwatch partnership schemes (Criminal Justice Research Programme, 2003; 2003 Licensing Act; Roberts, 2004).

Clearly, central players in such partnerships are bar, pub, and club door staff. Some excellent work has been written on the crucial control and social sorting role such actors play in policing the NTE and the various formal and informal rules and strategies these gatekeepers employ to regulate, order, exclude, and discipline a mix of celebratory, inebriated, gendered, decorative, corporeally polluted, and stigmatised bodies (Monaghan, 2002, 2004; Hobbs et al, 2003). Monanghan (2002, 2004) in particular considers the importance of performance, class identity, norm enforcement, status, and hegemonic masculinities to such door work, while also demonstrating the embodied aspects of being a door steward in terms of bodily capital, physical risk taking, power, and the emotional labour such individuals have to constantly display in order to maintain the 'right' image.

Hobbs et al (2003) expertly show how the traditional work tasks of such agents of regulation have transformed (although not their working-class identities) in parallel with new and ever-changing socio-legal, cultural, economic, and political contexts, and the burgeoning NTE's contradictory agendas of both freedom and control. In particular, they outline how the regeneration of post-industrial city centre spaces has occurred within a discourse of 'management' and 'safety', with social control of such areas increasingly being contracted to the commercial sector by the state. However, such private security work is difficult both within a "liminal economy that projects an impression of hedonism devoid of restraint" and a context of mass alcohol consumption and tighter regulation of door supervisors (Monaghan, 2002, p 406). As such, and in neoliberal fashion, a mix of both social and technological control strategies such as CCTV, coupled with loosely amalgamated interagency partnerships, have been formed so as to better police the streets. These have been amalgamated with little thought for how such systems function individually and collectively within pre-existing socio-cultural traditions and the normative frameworks outlined by others in this volume.

While Monaghan and Hobbs et al's work provides rich empirical insight into the job, rules, and practices of the bouncer, they say little about the role of night-watch networks and their interactions within varying occupational cultures. It was in this context and due to the dearth of rich empirical research on the subject, that the present study was conducted in a bid to present both sides of the coin. As Roberts (2004) simply puts it, "There has been no systematic research as yet [on] Pubwatch schemes" (p 31).

Pubwatching in Amnicola[2]

Context

The data presented in this chapter comes from multiple research sites and actors located the length and breadth of the UK; however, one setting in particular, 'Amnicola', forms the basis of much of the subsequent discussion. Amnicola was chosen as it has a particularly thriving NTE, containing numerous places of entertainment all of which are located within a concentrated central zone. Typical of most UK cities, every weekend (and now increasingly midweek) thousands of revellers throng the streets within a short radius of one another. Most of the 'after midnight' nightlife is restricted to three hot spots across the centre, each of which experiences regular public order problems. Recent figures from the town's safety partnership – composed of councillors, senior police officers, and business representatives – show that 50% of all assaults take place in the city centre, with most serious assaults occurring on the streets at night, outside licensed premises or taxi ranks. Perhaps even more significantly, 43% of reported city centre serious assaults occurred between 2am and 3.30am. Moreover, a person is around 12 times more likely to be assaulted in the city centre during the night than anywhere else across the city. Currently, licensing laws mean that bars and pubs in Amnicola generally open until 1am, with clubs licensed to 3am.

Methodological techniques

The principal aim of this empirical research was to ascertain how night-watch systems actually work in practice, unlike much of the current NTE management literature that assumes the effectiveness of Pubwatch. A secondary goal was to provide an account of how both CCTV operators and door staff felt about the other's role.[3] To fulfil both objectives, detailed ethnographic observation was conducted nationwide within various city-watch schemes' operational core, the public space CCTV monitoring site. As this portrayed only the CCTV operatives' perspective, data drawn from the author's current doctoral research was also utilised enabling the NTE views of numerous door staff to be simultaneously juxtaposed.

Pubwatch in Amnicola

Pubwatch schemes can have many different radio wave contributors, although the Amnicola scheme generally has door and CCTV staff as its two principal users.[4] The CCTV operators studied in the research were largely public sector employees, being hired and waged either by the local authority or regional police force. Crucially, the CCTV operatives' official role in Pubwatch, aside from monitoring and operating, in teams of three (although frequently less), around 80 public space CCTV cameras on 10-hour shifts, is to act both as real-time informants to the emergency services and, crucially, as police resource 'gatekeepers'.[5] Thus, should a door steward require a police unit to attend an incident, he or she must relay this request to the CCTV room over the radio network as opposed to directly telephoning the police control centre.[6] Theoretically, CCTV staff should then contact the control centre via internal telephone or by radio informing them that a certain bar has requested a police response, before updating the waiting venue on the control centre's reply or unit's progress. However, in practice, largely due to limited police units, CCTV operators often have to view notified incidents and behaviours in real time on the cameras, before forming personalised risk assessment judgements concerning whether the request requires an immediate response. Thus Pubwatch not only operates with a complex, convoluted communication system, but the hierarchical decision-making structure is, as one can imagine, also a very ambiguous area open to subjective interpretation, bias, and much contestation, especially as the operatives are given little formal training in such critical risk assessment procedures.

Functional adaptation of the system

When fully functional, the Pubwatch system can be an extremely effective mechanism of information exchange and social control, providing night watchers with crucial intelligence, cover, back-up, logistical data, and interactive speed in a range of varying situations. Indeed, as the subsequent examples illustrate, the system is often adapted by its key players to transcend official policy parameters, with door staff often informally and altruistically extending their area of concern beyond their defined professional role and spatial responsibility, in passing over miscellaneous information to the operatives.

Formal and informal system integration

As the following fieldnote extract indicates, it was not uncommon for a door steward to provide CCTV staff with information about those suspected of being potential 'drink drivers':

> Jonah's bar informs a CCTV controller that "a foreign guy just got into his car who looks like he's been drinking. He's in a silver Nissan with a foreign registration plate on HH Street. You might want to check him out".

In this case, the CCTV operative quickly located the man, alerted the control centre, followed the car through the city, and updated the control centre operator regarding the vehicle's whereabouts. Close integration among the four parties involved facilitated the individual's initial identification, tracking, and subsequent capture by a nearby police unit, which then proceeded to breathalyse him. Although in this example the suspected motorist had a negative test result, other drink drivers have been effectively snared in similar ways, something that would be far harder to achieve without the system's proactive information-gathering users, wide geo-spatial reach and sight, and in this case interactional swiftness.

A second example of Pubwatch's usefulness for particular stakeholders is shown in the significant number of times that door stewards used the nearby public space cameras to cover themselves, not only for physical protection but also to quell fallacious liability accusations being made by disgruntled patrons. The following extract from my ethnographic research was a typical episode:

> The Castle Bar doorman asks a CCTV operator to "put your camera on the front entrance as we've got a couple of idiots who are not getting in and are being aggressive with our staff". The operative takes control of the nearest camera, and the image shows four young males, two of whom appear enraged; their friends are currently physically restraining them. The doorman appears to point up towards the camera as if telling the main aggressors that they are being recorded on CCTV, and the two swiftly step back from the doorstaff and entrance. After a few seconds, all four walk away from the bar and continue up the street.

> Clearly in this instance, a potentially conflictual situation is quickly defused using a combination of the Pubwatch radio and CCTV camera network. This scenario is also supported by a door steward's comments: "[CCTV's] such a deterrent for possible confrontations, especially when you come out with: 'Walk away now, you are on camera.' They look, see the camera and go." In terms of the legal protection benefits of the system, one door steward observed:

> "I think in this day and age of sue, sue, sue, [CCTV] is a good thing.... I can recall maybe 8 to 10 times last year the CCTV saved our arses, from people basically just making it up as they went along trying to get some sort of revenge for being ejected from the club."

Another valuable dimension of the Pubwatch radio system in Amnicola was the copious times oblivious CCTV controllers were notified about ongoing public order disturbances by door staff. Indeed, from the numerous incidents that occurred involving physical violence during the observations, door stewards were 82 per cent more likely to spot such episodes first, alerting CCTV operatives to the situation via the radio.[7]

Doorstaff, then, act as crucial 'grounded' informants to the law enforcement authorities, informally policing the streets either by alerting CCTV operators to actual or potential disorder, or by calming situations down – occasionally intervening if circumstances are deemed serious enough. Indeed without their input, it is probable that many serious incidents would go undetected, with a corresponding rise in more sustained attacks and life-threatening injuries.

The Pubwatch system also periodically performs an 'extended' and unintentional health and safety function, as the following fieldnote commentary suggests:

> Bar Glitz doormen inform the CCTV room that ... "a male is leaving our bar who has just told us that he is going to commit suicide". A brief description of the individual is passed to the operatives, including details of his clothing, his "distinctive rucksack and carrier bag" and where he was last spotted.... One operator contacts the control centre, whilst another speedily scans the nearby cameras. Once the man is located, his description is relayed back to Bar Glitz door staff who confirm his identity. He is then skilfully followed on several cameras, whilst the second operator directs the arriving police unit.

The Pubwatch radio link enables the further expansion of a growing, interconnected surveillance web through the constant relaying of 'miscellaneous offences information', which covers misdemeanours as diverse as vehicles and people blocking street and door access, to those effectively practising 'naturism' in the city centre! The following observation further makes the point:

> Supreme nightclub contacts the CCTV room about two young males who have been seen stealing newspapers/ magazines from the front door of a neighbouring newsagent. A description and location of the teenagers is given, and the operatives speedily identify and track them, informing the requested police unit that they are "hiding behind a couple of parked cars, a hundred metres or so further down the street".

However, despite the periodic appearance of informal assistance from door staff over the network, perhaps prompted through a mix of care, boredom, spite, or hope of reciprocal support, crucially, both the CCTV operatives' and door stewards' general perspective of each other and the system itself is less favourable, with relations frequently characterised by tension, role misunderstanding, and conflict.

System dysfunction: conflicting interests and goals among participants

CCTV operators on doorstaff

A central problematic in the system concerns CCTV operatives' role as 'gatekeepers' to severely limited emergency service resources, and their related belief that certain door stewards rely too much on the latter and are not doing their job properly when requesting units. The following examples, taken from observations with CCTV operators, provide empirical evidence of such views:

> "Doormen just think they can just pass everything on to CCTV and we will deal with it. They assume we can just snap our fingers and magic a unit there. They can be a bloody pest."

> A doorman asks a CCTV controller to keep an eye on a male who has been ejected and is now being abusive. The operator "Rogers" the request before saying: "Bouncers can be a pain in the arse. I mean that is their job to take a bit of stick from the punters. Some just come running to us every five minutes saying, He's calling me names and Get my mummy. They should grow up and do what they are paid to do. They're not exactly small guys are they? I mean they're quick to shout on us to get a unit, but they're not so quick to tell us when the boy goes away."[8]

The first response given portrays a misinterpretation and naivety on the part of door staff regarding CCTV operators' lack of deployment power and the police's limited resources, but also suggests that the informal nature and sheer volume of information exchange is impeding operators' ability to meet official performance standards. The second commentary perhaps reflects differing perceptions of risk between the night watchers. Operatives are located in the relative peace and tranquillity of an isolated monitoring facility some distance away from the front-line 'action'. As such, they can neither hear what is being said nor get a 'real', embodied close-up sense of the situation's emotiveness, atmosphere, or potential for danger. Perhaps power issues are also pertinent here, in that the door stewards appear, in both scenarios, to be 'instructing' the operatives.

A second major source of frustration for the operatives is door stewards' regular lack of clarity, both in radio transmissions and subsequent descriptions of suspects. It is not uncommon for operatives to shout "Oh shut up" and other expressions of frustration off air in response to certain door stewards' requests and general conversations regarding those who are either too drunk or young for entry: "Settle down, we can't hear you shouting like that" (CCTV operator in response to a doorman's message).

A third cause of annoyance is doorstaff's general attitude toward the CCTV operatives' messages and regular failure to answer what operators believe to be important radio calls. The following fieldnote extract demonstrates the point:

> The police controller wants CCTV staff to contact Supreme via Pubwatch regarding an earlier incident which occurred at their front entrance. The operative contacts the venue, "CCTV to Supreme", four times before receiving a response. "Supreme are useless at responding to calls at closing time. They're too busy chatting to listen or respond to their radio. It's a different story when they need help, though."

Many of the issues identified here amount to a perceived absence of radio etiquette on the part of door staff, brought about by the relative lack of training the latter receive on how to communicate effectively with one another and use the radio link properly: "Most of the doormen haven't been trained properly on how to use the radio, they just shout and scream down it. Too often they don't listen and jump over the top of you and interrupt transmissions." At a deeper level, it may also have something to do with the creation of a sense of physical separation, distanciation, and anonymity that a radio handset can induce in its users. As one operative explained:

> "They just don't know who we are and since they can't see us, and don't actually work for the police like us, I don't think they bother to make an effort. They just shout into the radio all the time. It's probably got something to do with the fact that we're both always changing shifts, so you never really get to know one another, we're probably just a bodiless camera or voice at the end of a radio really."

Two further factors that led operatives to view their NTE colleagues unfavourably, concern previous history and negative attitudes regarding the way in which door stewards operate. On the first point, it is not uncommon for CCTV operators to have previously captured footage that has either shown a door steward in a bad light or even resulted in his or her being charged with assault. The following comments, made from a CCTV operative, provide further insight into the importance of past history and the ways in which ideologies are constructed and shared among the operators, which relocate system 'failure' onto other groups:

> "The door staff at Pickwicks are a bunch of gits. We got a call over the Pubwatch radio the other day telling us that a male had just been seriously assaulted and his assailants were making their way up HH Street toward JJ Street junction.... The bouncer gave a description and we picked the two up as they turned onto JJ Street, just idly walking along the road in no hurry towards Pickwicks. However, after a short discussion with a couple of bouncers at the Pickwicks door, they suddenly started running down JJ Street at full speed where we lost them. By the time the requested police unit arrived, they'd completely disappeared. It's obvious Pickwicks had tipped them off. I'll sure remember that next time they're screaming for a unit. Really pissed me off."

The following comments perfectly capture the disillusionment shown towards public houses' and nightclubs' operating procedures in general, and door staff in particular:

> The Armoury asks an operative to "keep an eye on four males we've just ejected. They're far too drunk and have been abusive to staff". The operator "Rogers" the request before stating off air: "I don't know what they expect us to do about it. I mean they shouldn't have given the boys so much drink in the first place. They're happy to take their money off them, but when they start causing a problem they just pass the buck on to us."

> "I think most of the trouble at weekends is down to bouncers not letting people get in for stupid reasons; they [door stewards] end up causing so many fights outside 'cos

they've [the revellers] got nowhere to go and naturally they're pissed off."

Doorstaff on CCTV operators

While on the whole, door stewards were largely supportive of the existence of CCTV cameras per se, feelings toward their controllers were – perhaps unsurprisingly – far from complimentary, with the second comment below even depicting CCTV watchers as a threat:

> "I am not a big fan of CCTV operators ... 'cos they sit on their fucking arses all day and night watching monitors and ignoring calls, thinking only of what sarcastic fucking answer they can use when the next poor fucker calls in saying that they need assistance."

> "On the basis of what was shown on the city centre CCTV, both myself and my colleague were arrested on suspicion of Actual Bodily Harm. It seems the cameras caught us in the bottom left-hand corner of their coverage and saw what they construed as an unnecessarily violent attack.... Thought CCTV was meant to help us do our jobs, not hinder us...."

Most door staff criticism is levelled at three main areas: CCTV operatives' perceived slowness to react to incidents and lengthy police response times; the operatives' supposed blasé attitude and failure to do their job properly; and their alleged inability to spot ongoing incidents. The first of these is brought out in the following criticisms:

> "The oh so common CCTV response when requesting a unit is – 'sorry they are all busy, you'll have to wait'. Wait, fucking wait.... The average response time is about half an hour."

> "Incident Friday night ... police unit requested. Twenty minutes later police unit requested again, as despite CCTV saying one on its way, still none had appeared. Ten minutes later, CCTV informed us no units were available! Thirty minutes waiting time on a Friday evening and no unit arrives! Great service!"

Relations between police officers and door staff have also been strained lately, due to increasing random police licensing checks. Several door staff were upset with the police's negative attitude towards them, the number of visits made to check door staff badges (one quoted as many as four separate visits), the perceived 'pointless' questioning – for example, are you busy tonight, how many bar staff are working, how many glass collectors – and their frequent blocking of doorways causing disruption. Many door stewards could not understand why the police could perform numerous door checks, yet were unable to attend urgent calls rapidly.

The second area drawing condemnation is illustrated by the following comments from a range of door stewards:

> "Early last night on CCTV, The Rose asks for a unit 'cos a bunch of yobs were shooting at them with an air rifle. One window had already been shot out. CCTV replied: 'We will see what we can do, we are busy just now....' Hang on a moment, this is a firearm problem and they are too fucking busy!"

> "Classic quote from last night – The Crown: 'Crown to CCTV; can we have a unit ASAP?' CCTV: 'What's the problem?' The Crown: 'You have your camera on our door, you can see what the problem is.' Why waste time when they can see what's going on? Just get the bloody unit to attend."

> "Throughout this incident though, CCTV were fantastic deploying not two, not three, but zero patrols to assist us, despite giving them enough information to write a book with!! Not only that, when asked did they get any of the incident on tape, they said they could see doormen diving for cover but didn't see anything else. Surely as a trained camera operator, if you see doormen standing still one second then diving flat on the floor you would spin the camera round and look, or am I just expecting too much??"

These remarks indicate a belief on the part of door staff that CCTV operators fail to take their calls seriously, deliberately ask obtuse questions in order to provoke and avoid doing any work, and possess a misguided view of nightlife reality. These views may emerge from deeper sociological factors concerning contrasting workplace priorities and cultures and differing placements within a spatial control hierarchy, door staff occupying the lowest position and operators a distanced, 'resource controlling' rank above.

Doorstaff are also highly critical of the operatives' ability to monitor and spot incidents:

> "At least CCTV in your neck of the woods picks up things like that. They're pretty piss poor here.... They see fuck all."

> "We had a bit of a scrap that the CCTV operators actually fucking noticed, con-fucking-gratulations to them for once."

Due to the disembodied nature of communication over the radio network, coupled with a desire to form friendships, solidarity, and a shared workplace culture, some door staff create and construct crude and derisive operative caricatures of those whose attitudes, operating procedures, and mannerisms are distinctive, also relaying previous memorable 'run-ins' over the airwaves:

> "But I'll tell you what else rips my shit, the operator who seems to be permanently suffering from weapons grade PMT."

> "Is it not RRRRRRRRRRRRRRRoger...?? I'm sure the woman's related to Tony the Tiger. I reckon she fancies me. She must watch me on the camera all the time, that's why response times are so shit."

> "The guy you can't understand, like he's had one too many whiskies...."

Indeed, some door stewards have effectively been banned from using the Pubwatch radio handset after making unsavoury comments on air: "We were told by quite a few coppers that we were 'not liked within the police fraternity.' Calls were ignored by CCTV, door staff were arrested without reason.... I now have no respect for the police or CCTV." This example is interesting as it presents insight into a perceived unequal distribution of power within the surveillance web.

Despite the above comments, some door staff understand the pressures operatives face and remain positive about the relationship: "As for CCTV, there have been one or two occasions where they have indeed been helpful." Others feel response problems emanate from a lack of police funding, leaving forces understaffed and unable to deal with the sheer scale and volume of disorder associated with the NTE: "In their defence, they [CCTV operators] do pass it [information/unit requests] nine times out of ten straight to the control room, but it is the control room that demands they find out what is going on so they can send enough resources or not send at all as they ain't got any units clear."

Making sense of the 'night network'

Systemic role conflict and interpersonal conflict

In its present state, Amnicola's Pubwatch scheme is characterised by two forms of conflict explained by a range of interrelated sociological factors. On one level, there is deep-seated role conflict plaguing the functioning of the system, emerging largely from two distinct, very different workplace cultures and control organisations being thrust together in a neoliberal style partnership. While on the surface the principal structural aim of both agencies is the maintenance of order, the two groups possess contrasting roles and remits in achieving this end. Indeed, the interactional, day-to-day configuration of Pubwatch is riddled with ambiguity, negotiation, rule bending, and divergent politics of control. Largely as a result of night guardians being separate, public/private sector employees with differing identities, levels of accountability, tasks, priorities, and spatial responsibilities, 'subsystem' goals often oppositional and conflictual in nature are overlooked when the two are carelessly fused together.

At a secondary level, actual working relations between CCTV operators and door staff are often hampered by a form of interpersonal conflict, mainly emanating as a result of misunderstandings regarding job parameters and a lack of trust in one another's accounts and definitions of situations. This has been largely facilitated due to previous negative interactions – especially regarding door staff's perceived negative attitude toward their 'partners' and dependence on resources and, from a door steward's point of view, lengthy response times, unequal hierarchical positioning, and CCTV operatives' reliance, despite their relative distanciation, on subjective decision making regarding risk and resources based on purely visual and mediated stimuli. It can also be added that situation has arisen from a dearth in joint socialisation events, antagonistic views, and attitudes regarding one another's ability to do the job and communicate effectively coupled with a general lack of adequate resources.

Pubwatch as a social system

Amnicola's Pubwatch scheme is a phenomenon that can be usefully located and explored with reference to General Systems Theory. While the goal of this particular system is public order, miscellaneous political, economic, environmental, socio-cultural, and emotive factors – such as the complex interplay between humans, technology, and inadequate resources, coupled with pressurised, anonymised communication and differing spatial boundaries and interpretations of 'priority' over a distanciated time-space network – are, paradoxically, creating a form of profound conflict and dysfunction within the system itself, undermining operational efficacy. Indeed, far from being a rationalised system of stability and effectiveness, Pubwatch can be as unpredictable as those it seeks to control.

Within their very own workplace cultures, Pubwatch users continually exchanging 'negative feedback' regarding one another's competence, are seriously undermining cohesion and overall system equilibrium. That said, the system is by no means 'closed' and determined, with differing operatives and door staff sharing alternative and ever-changing opinions regarding one another, according to the various situations and contexts they find themselves within. So, for example, perhaps a speedy police response to a call from a door steward in trouble may alter the latter's views on CCTV personnel, while a polite and courteous acknowledgment of an operator's assistance in moving a camera, will be appreciated and remembered by the operatives. Similarly, new door personnel may be treated with a fresh and neutral approach by CCTV staff. In other words, by no means is the Pubwatch system necessarily fixed, and there can be both positive and negative scenarios occurring and metamorphosing simultaneously, which will have a direct impact on the scheme's general day-to-day and future operation. Social change and dynamism is very important here.

Even taking into account the above and recognising that the scheme sporadically integrates as an effective system of control, 'full functionality' is still some way off. Indeed, perhaps the very notion is idealistic. The realism of the scenario appears far greyer in colour, with seemingly disparate human individuals and groups, often following very different sub-goals and from backgrounds as varied as the identities and experiences they carry, being thrust together in a melting pot of hedonism, tension, violence, alcohol and drug abuse, confusion, and adrenalin. At times, the job for both parties can be a very difficult and lonely experience. Perhaps it is not surprising, then, that the two carry very similar views of one another, each misunderstanding and blaming the other as a way of forming distinctive workplace cultures and coping with the constant unpleasantness and unpredictability of the work they do. Indeed maybe the aberrant and pressurised nature of such a system simply destines it to failure? Certainly one could be forgiven for concluding that social systems are perhaps more open than many of their advocates make out, and that the structural autonomy of such macro-networks can be significantly compromised by individual actors, agency, negotiation, and the general environment within which they are embedded.

Conclusion

Through its micro focus, empirical light has been shed on a crucial and hitherto under-researched aspect of the NTE, namely the relationship between CCTV operators and door staff across a Pubwatch scheme. As described, Pubwatch can function, both formally and informally, as an effective structural mechanism of information exchange, crime prevention/detection, and social control. The system, however, remains beset with micro agency–created tensions, conflict and dysfunctionality, largely emerging from the interaction of separate and distinct workplace cultures. Neither CCTV operators nor door staff hold each other in particularly high regard, with daily working relations strained at best. The impact and implications such dissentions may have on the efficacy of policing the streets at night are significant, especially in a political-economic climate of limited police resources and increasing reliance being placed on CCTV systems, their operators, and public/private sector security partnerships.

The very social order pressures – for example, spatial overcrowding, drunkenness, and unruly behaviour – created by the NTE and thrust on social control agencies, coupled with a general lack of investment in crime control resources, will continue to undermine policing effectiveness and put further strain on the system. While the technology is in place for relative spatial control, the actors and mechanisms required to realise such a scenario are steeped in humanness, cultural dynamics, and emotiveness. Ultimately, too much dependence is being uncritically placed in social control partnerships without due attention being given to the dynamics of such partnerships, the development of training programmes and the securing of greater cooperation and socio-cultural professional workings.

This chapter has indicated that a central facet of urban renaissance, the emphasis on NTE development and growth, has created significant tensions between attempts to encourage young people to city centres at night to spend money, and their subsequent control via security partnerships in the public and private sectors. In particular, it has focused on the practice of one such policy measure of the NTE, namely Pubwatch. It has been shown that such a response may produce quite mixed results, with operational integration often seeming precarious. All of this may lead to the conclusion that regeneration, within the NTE and central city spaces more generally, may lead to further strategies of social control and spatial management being developed and introduced, precisely in order to overcome current limitations in existing measures and the negative behavioural overspill stemming from attempts to promote a hedonistic economy which, paradoxically, is both enabling and constraining.

Notes

[1] An approach centred on the examination and understanding of the logic behind, and varied contextual relationships between, the many aspects and components of a 'social system' (Ritzer, 2000).

[2] To protect the anonymity of all those researched, names, locations, and identities used in this chapter are fictitious.

[3] This is an important issue, as it will provide insight into whether the system is integrated and cohesive, or underpinned by separation and dysfunction arising through the micro-interactions of the two sets of key players.

[4] Pubwatch radio handsets, while on the same channel, operate on differing frequencies. Thus when premises call, their venue name usually appears on an LCD screen on the CCTV operators' desk so that the latter know who is calling them and where to direct the cameras. However, pubs and clubs regularly forget to register their radio units at the start of the evening, meaning that their names abstractly appear as 'Club 1, 2' etc. Some operators do not know where the pubs are anyway, regardless of whether their name appears on the screen.

[5] CCTV operatives are not gatekeepers to the fire and ambulance services, and cannot telephone them at door staff's request.

[6] Door staff and premise managers generally telephone the police control room only in an absolute emergency (usually when CCTV operatives are dealing with another premises or have told staff they will have a prolonged wait for a unit), as the number of telephoned police

call-outs is recorded, and is a crucial factor that the licensing board committee considers when reviewing renewal licences. Too many 999 call-outs may result in an establishment's licence being revoked. CCTV operators have no control over police deployment; staff in the police control centre administer all directives to officers on the ground.

[7] Perhaps this finding is unsurprising given that Amnicola's door staff outnumber CCTV operators by around 50 to 1, possessing an extra 150 pairs of eyes with which to scan the surrounding streets. Also, operatives are often short-staffed or busy monitoring, recording, and reviewing other incidents.

[8] Operatives must often judge whether or not to contact the control room, based on either the message relayed or distanciated 'readings' of situations. Most of the operators have worked in the job for years, so have effectively become behavioural experts. They also are acutely aware of limited police resources. It would be interesting to see whether newer employees, without the experiential expertise, would feel more pressured to contact the control centre and how long it would be before the dominant 'deal with it yourselves' mentality develops.

TWELVE

Prostitution, gentrification, and the limits of neighbourhood space

Phil Hubbard, Rosie Campbell, Maggie O'Neill, Jane Pitcher, and Jane Scoular

Conceived as a series of policies intended to bring people back into cities, urban renaissance offers a new vision of environmentally sustainable, socially balanced, and aesthetically inspired urban regeneration. While clearly informed by New Labour's specific concerns about active citizenship, social inclusion, and community participation, urban renaissance has nonetheless been identified as following a well-tested and *global* model of urban regeneration reliant on the rolling out of the 'gentrification frontier' (Lees, 2003b; Atkinson, 2004; Atkinson & Bridge, 2005). In essence, the suggestion here is that the Urban Task Force and subsequent urban White Paper promote a model of regeneration that idealises middle-class lifestyles, and hence encourages the middle classes to move 'back to the city'. In practical terms, however, the cash-starved state seems unprepared to intervene significantly in central city property markets, meaning this model of middle-class led regeneration is reliant on investment by private developers keen to exploit the gap between current and potential ground rent.

Local authorities lacking the financial means (or imagination) to revitalise areas of urban blight and disinvestment thus aim to serve up the central city as an unmissable investment opportunity for developers, believing an injection of capital is necessary to prevent a net outflow of consumers, businesses, and residents from city centres bedevilled by images of anti-social behaviour, drunken yobbery, second-class shopping, and unemployment (Baeten, 2002). Often, this requires local authorities to take steps to tame urban 'disorder', pioneering new techniques and technologies of 'policing' designed to promote consumer-led revitalisation. In some instances, this has involved the extension of private property rights to public space, with new agents of social control (for example, city centre guardians) seeking to maintain the civility of the streets through innovative forms of policing (Belina & Helms, 2003; Raco, 2003). Simultaneously, demands for reassurance policing has encouraged many communities to be more active in seeking partnership solutions to crime and disorder issues, with community watch and neighbourhood warden schemes now widespread (Crawford, 1998; Sagar, 2004).

Imposing a particular form of order on the streets is thus often depicted as the precursor of a benign form of civic renaissance. However, critical voices have stressed this is often about the imposition of middle-class consumerist values, and is actually about the displacement of those 'Others' who threaten consumer-led regeneration. On this basis, commentators such as Lees (2003b) argue that discourses of 'urban renaissance' have allowed gentrification to become established as UK urban policy. Given the involvement of corporate developers who target middle-class consumers, policies encouraging a UK-style urban renaissance thus appear in keeping with Smith's (2002) description of 'third-wave' or corporate-led gentrification rather than one led by 'marginal' gentrifiers. This is not to say the residents attracted 'back' to the city are drawn exclusively from the ranks of the mobile and affluent, but the majority are young individuals, couples, and families who have the purchasing power necessary to buy into a mode of metropolitan living which re-imagines city centres as 'theatres of consumption' (Zukin, 1995). As Smith (1996) notes, these gentrifiers characteristically identify themselves as streetwise citizens, and claim to be attracted to the city centre because it offers a contrast to the staid mores of suburban living. Yet, simultaneously, this population seems remarkably anxious about certain 'Other' populations, whom they regard as an un-aesthetic presence in 'their' urban space. This suggests a close connection between urban renaissance and urban *revanchism* – a process whereby the middle classes seek to exclude those users of urban space who trouble them. Hence, the impact of urban renaissance on 'minority' groups such as buskers, skateboarders, the homeless, beggars, leafleters, teenagers, and street entertainers has been widely noted (MacLeod & Ward, 2002; Rogers & Coaffee, 2005).

Another group whose occupation of urban space is being challenged by processes of urban renaissance in the UK, yet whose spatial exclusion has been less frequently acknowleged, is that of street sex workers. Historically, strategies of policing in the UK, coupled with the opposition of wealthier and more articulate citizens to street prostitution, have conspired to push sex work towards inner-city districts (Hubbard, 1999). In many such areas, street sex work has been regarded as part of the local scene and, despite occasional campaigns of opposition, has largely been accepted by populations who have been either unconcerned or insufficiently articulate to voice opposition. Yet an influx of more affluent homeowners surprised to find themselves sharing their community space with sex workers (and their clients) has in many instances acted as the impetus to more prolonged and high-profile campaigns of exclusion (see, for example, Bondi, 1998). Recognising this tendency, in one Scottish city, councillors have gone so far as to order housebuilders redeveloping warehousing into luxury flats to warn potential buyers street prostitution occurs in the vicinity (*The Scotsman*, 14 September 2005, p 4).

The seeming incompatibility of street prostitution with urban gentrification poses some important questions about the limits of urban renaissance. Sex work has been an established part of the street scene in many UK cities for decades, and it is frequently the case that sex workers live in the neighbourhoods where they work. Even in cases where they do not, they contribute to the local economy and may be welcomed by publicans, cafe owners, and shopkeepers. Further, their social relationships and friendships with others in the neighbourhood may be longstanding. Yet, as a marginalised and relatively muted group it appears they are rarely – if ever – consulted in the processes of renewing community spaces that is a critical part of New Labour's policies for urban renaissance. In this respect, it is interesting that recent Home Office (2006c) recommendations suggest that community conferencing is vital to address issues of local concern in relation to sex work, but do not list sex workers as key participants. Elsewhere, the same document argues that sex work markets need to be disrupted, arguing "we fail our communities if we simply accept the existence of street prostitution" (Home Office, 2006c, p 13) – the implication being that sex work is antithetical to the cultivation of community. In this sense, while some forms of corporatised adult entertainment are tacitly encouraged by the local state (Hubbard, 2004), street sex workers appear to be lumped together with those 'Other' populations "displaced and excluded from the reconstruction and re-imagining of urban spaces by an idealized white middle class hegemonic notion of urbanity" (Hall & Hubbard, 1998, p 110), and are highly unlikely to be consulted in plans to redesign and regenerate urban space. Indeed, in North America, where processes of gentrification are arguably more entrenched, it has been repeatedly demonstrated not only that gentrifiers are active in opposing sex work, but that the removal of commercial sex work from neighbourhoods is regarded by authorities as a necessary precursor to gentrification (Larsen, 1992; Kerkin 2003; Sanchez, 2004).

However, in the UK in particular there has been a distinct lack

'purify' middle class areas

of research on the attitudes of different communities to sex work. Beginning by recognising that some residential communities and businesses are more tolerant of sex work than others, our research thus explored the differentiated landscapes of sex work in five residential areas undergoing regeneration in England and Scotland. Drawing on focus groups and interviews with residents and local stakeholders, including street-based sex workers, in the remainder of this chapter we thus explore the degrees of tolerance extant in different locales and seek to identify why street sex work is regarded as more of a problem in some regenerating areas than others. In doing so, we seek to question whether the forms of difference personified by sex workers can be accommodated in revitalised city spaces that are aesthetically pleasing, culturally convivial, and socially inclusive – and in so doing, raise serious concerns about the elasticity of the concept of 'public' space as well as the limits of the putative urban renaissance.

Community responses to sex work

Given it is necessary to locate conflicts between residents and sex workers in specific locales, our research focused on how residential streets in neighbourhoods characterised as areas of female street sex work are used and shared. The aim of this study was to assess the range of community responses to street sex work, investigating why some communities have mobilised to 'reclaim' the streets by excluding sex workers, while other residents exhibit greater tolerance. The report draws on a detailed study of street sex work in five cities in England and Scotland carried out between July 2004 and September 2005 (Pitcher, Campbell, Hubbard, O'Neill, & Scoular, 2006). The project involved fieldwork in five major provincial British cities in neighbourhoods with an established history of street sex work. To protect the anonymity of respondents, these areas were identified in the research as Eastside, Westside, Southside, Riverside, and Central (the last having two areas of street sex work, referred to here as Central City and Central South). In each area, our research included interviews with project staff and volunteers working with street sex workers; interviews and discussions with staff in public services, including the police, local authority, and drug treatment agencies; attendance and observation at meetings, including local prostitution forums, police liaison meetings, and community meetings; observation of sex work project activities, including outreach sessions; five focus groups with agency representatives and four with community representatives; interviews with 36 sex working women; and interviews with 69 residents, community, and business representatives (further details of the methods and approach are provided in Pitcher et al, 2006).

Our study therefore took into account a wide range of views about street sex work, allowing us to explore the local inflection of national policy agendas and variations in community responses to sex work. Nonetheless, it is important to note that all five were inner-city areas with diverse populations and pockets of deprivation. Traditionally, it has been noted that street sex work tends to cluster in deprived inner-city environments where residents do not feel a strong attachment to place and have little incentive to complain about behaviour that they regard as detrimental to residential amenity (Hubbard, 1999). However, there may be other reasons for such clustering, and it is important to stress that residents in all our areas claimed to possess strong levels of attachment to their locale. Yet none of the areas could be characterised as a unified community, being fractured along ethnic, age, and class lines in a number of distinctive ways. For example, Eastside had a large (and growing) student population, while recently arrived refugees seeking asylum were further increasing the diversity of the Central South, Eastside, and Southside areas.

Although our case-study areas exhibited relative social deprivation, residents typically stated quality of life in their area was no worse than elsewhere in their respective city. However, a large majority were able to identify issues that impinged negatively on their quality of life. Furthermore, the issues raised across the study areas tended to be remarkably similar, with anti-social behaviour, environmental quality, quality of housing, and lack of local facilities and shops identified as main priorities. Yet it was crime that appeared the overwhelming concern for the respondents, and while burglary and car crime concerned many, safety on the streets was perceived to be the most significant issue. Most were able to recount anecdotes where local residents had been attacked indiscriminately. Further, in both Central South and Southside there was also much concern articulated about gun crime and gang culture. Few interviewed had direct experience of crime (with some notable exceptions). As such, it is fear of crime rather than crime per se that appeared to constitute the major quality of life issue in the study areas.

This relates significantly to the issue of anti-social behaviour, which most seemed to be associated with young people on the streets at night. For example, several local stakeholders suggested complaints about, for instance, people playing football in the street were symptomatic of an increasingly intolerant attitude in society, but, from the other perspective, it was clear that some residents felt unable to go onto the streets at night because they believed that drug use, street drinking, and 'yobbish' behaviour perpetrated by young people had created a more dangerous atmosphere on the streets. Public drinking in particular was identified as a major issue by stakeholders, not least in Central City where a street drinking ban had been introduced to reduce 'intimidating' public consumption of alcohol.

The question as to whether soliciting and kerb-crawling should be considered as criminal or anti-social behaviour was raised by several respondents given both activities are technically illegal. Yet for many, sex work was considered a separate issue that was not a priority in quality of life terms. Indeed, many residents suggested sex work did not unduly concern them because "most of it is during the night-time when it can't be seen" (male resident, Eastside). The suggestion here is that most soliciting and kerb-crawling was carried out in a relatively unobtrusive manner, with few negative consequences for local residents. Nevertheless, displays of sexual activity were a major concern for some:

> "I think it's one thing to go to work and know that it's gone on but it's cleaned up and you don't see it. I think it's another thing actually to have to face it when you open your door ... and there would be a couple ... they would be having sex in the porch or in their front garden or something and it just, nobody would want, you know that's, I think that's unacceptable anyway and I would understand anybody not wanting that." (agency representative, Southside)

Likewise, the visible legacy of sex work, in terms of the 'detritus' often encountered in areas of street sex work activity, was a significant issue for many. Business owners in particular reported having to clean up detritus that they assumed had been left by sex workers: "We had to pick up their condoms and any paraphernalia that they had left lying about which included sanitary towels, toilet paper" (business representative, Riverside). The explicit connection made here between sex work and forms of bodily waste is significant, not least because exclusionary fears often feed on images of bodily impurity (Sibley, 1995).

Beyond these directly perceptible nuisances, it appeared the media labelling of specific neighbourhoods as areas of prostitution meant at least some of the respondents felt it needed to be eradicated:

> "It gives the area a bad reputation. It isn't the local people who are indulging in these kind of activities, but we're stuck with that label at the end of the day." (resident, Eastside)

Related to this anxiety about labelling was the perception that sex work attracts criminal elements. This view was underlined by a councillor in Riverside who suggested "we have mugging and things like that but we've found that if we get rid of the prostitute we get rid of a lot of this…. I don't know what the correlation is, but certainly if we reduce the number of women on the street we seem to see a correlation in the reduction of burglaries, muggings, robberies". In all cases, the idea sex work forms part of a street scene in which drugs, crime, and alcohol entwine thus exercised a powerful influence on relations between sex workers, residents, and local agencies, although there was also some acknowledgement that drug dealing went on independently of the sex work scene:

> "If I was to remove prostitution, would I remove the drugs problem? No, is the first answer…. I think what you've got with prostitutes … is the people who have an overt need to obtain drugs rapidly. They have very serious addiction levels. And they need to be close to their suppliers. So if you have a historic red light area and you are a supplier of drugs it makes sense to put your market as close to the people who need it as possible." (police representative, Southside)

In the Central area, there was a differentiation between the beats: in Central South, there was seen to be an overlap between sex and drug markets, whereas in the Central City area there was perceived to be a separation between the two. Previous research has suggested drugs and street sex markets may often coexist, but that the nature of the relationship between drug use and street sex work is a complex one (May, Edmunds, & Hough, 1999). Hence, reductions in street sex work are not always accompanied by declines in drug dealing and other crimes. In fact, the opposite may often be true, as the presence of sex workers can enhance levels of street surveillance. Moreover, the presence of street prostitution is often associated with heightened levels of police surveillance, which may drop if workers move elsewhere: in one of our interviews, a policeman stressed that while residents in areas of street sex work often demand more policing, the area is already the most policed in the city because of the presence of sex work (police representative, Riverside).

Community safety and the 'nuisance' of sex work

As the previous section has shown, residents may express opposition to sex work because of fears of crime, detritus such as discarded condoms, or the amount of traffic attracted to an area. Yet our interviews suggested perhaps the most pressing concern was that it impinged negatively on the use of public space:

> "Well it's the fact that local communities couldn't walk through the park at night. You couldn't take a short cut. It was the condoms there in the morning. The needles and just the fact that those public open spaces became no-go areas, during the day as well as during the night." (agency representative, Southside)

While this implies there are close connections between people's avoidance of particular spaces and their perception that such spaces are unclean, these anxieties were closely related to fears of crime. Public parks and alleyways understood to be used for street prostitution were thus avoided by particular groups because of associations with "prostitutes and drug takers and pimps" (resident, Westside). In the case of Eastside, for example, local nursery staff stopped taking children to a local park because of the fears of parents. Notably, some residents also reported avoiding pseudo-public spaces at night (including stairwells, drying areas, car parks, and porches), as well as abandoned places such as building sites, disused garages, and car parks.

For the majority of residents, however, sex work did not create 'no-go' areas, but encouraged the adoption of *selective* strategies of avoidance (Pitcher et al, 2006). For example, one resident suggested she was not worried when walking around the area when "dressed for work" but had become aware that when going out at night she was not dressed "so very differently" from sex workers on the beat and thus tended to catch taxis rather than waiting at bus stops where she felt "vulnerable". In such instances, adoption of avoidance strategies prompted a mix of emotions:

> "I feel slightly uncomfortable and a bit angry because I feel it's kind of ... my lifestyle's being impinged on in a way I don't want it to be.... Not feeling comfortable in my own space and public space as it were. Not feeling you have some ownership of it any more.... It's mainly because of the kerb-crawling and the cars. I think it makes you feel

very uncomfortable, especially as a woman walking about late at night by yourself." (resident, Southside)

Characteristically, men expressed less anxiety about walking the streets at night, and not all claimed to understand why some female residents found it so problematic:

> "I don't understand how you could be very intimidated by a punter stopping for you, but at the end of the day no one should really have to deal with that if they don't want to. I think of it … like building sites and stuff … some women will just be really, really upset and intimidated and walk miles out of their way to avoid getting shouted at by the builders." (resident, Westside)

Conversely, many men reported they always drove female members of their household around rather than let them walk around the neighbourhood after dark. Again, this was not necessarily justified in terms of concern for their safety, but because they had been previously placed in situations where they felt profoundly uncomfortable (as one Riverside resident claimed, "I don't feel physically threatened but yes it's uncomfortable so why should I have that imposed on me?"). Against this, one female resident claimed she felt 'safer' knowing there were sex workers in the neighbourhood, as she felt they would draw unwelcome attention away from her.

In noting these gendered fears of public spaces, it is important to emphasise that sex workers likewise regard many public spaces as dangerous, and exercise similar discretion in their choice of working beats. Further, some were sympathetic to those local residents who complained about their presence (as one Riverside sex worker put it, "I wouldn't want it going on outside my house"). In some instances, particularly where mediation had occurred, there was some evidence that workers were aware of particular community concerns, and were sometimes willing to change their working practices. This was certainly the case in Eastside, where the primary school had become a focal point for anxiety when some workers began soliciting near the school gates at times when guardians were dropping off and collecting children. After some complaints, and mediation by the local sex work outreach project, the majority of workers subsequently avoided this area. Likewise in Riverside, soliciting around a school had provoked considerable complaints, triggering the installation of new fencing and CCTV systems designed to displace street soliciting.

Such episodes emphasise that the *public visibility* of sex work was the most significant issue for many residents, with a frequently expressed concern being that local children see street sex workers and parents have to explain what they are doing. For instance, one Riverside resident claimed sex work could co-exist with residential space, "but not in front of a house with three children in it and, you know, and the kid wants to go out for an ice cream … that's not bringing the kids up nicely" (resident, Riverside). Likewise, several Central South residents spoke of the reactions of friends and visitors to the area who were not aware of the area's use for street sex work, and the need to 'explain away' the activities of the street workers. It was this anxiety about the sights of sex work, coupled with the real and imagined fears about crime, that appeared most important in encouraging some respondents to talk of the need for 'the community' to claim back their public space from sex workers. Here, it was significant that sex workers were almost unanimously identified as outsiders, 'Others', who had no place in the community, and were not 'local girls'.

Such efforts to 'reclaim' space from sex workers took different forms in the case study areas. In Westside, groups of residents (organised through residents' associations) had regularly completed patrols where they would note car registration numbers of kerb-crawlers, and seek to move workers on:

> "It's usually three or four residents who go round … we've usually got mobile phone numbers and if we do see a worker we ring the police officer or text the police officer and say there's something happening on this particular corner or in this particular place…. So it's really keeping a watch…. We're not enforcing stuff." (resident, Westside)

Over the course of three years, such patrols were acknowledged to have had considerable success in displacing sex workers, although the relationship between the Street Watch initiative and organisations providing support to sex workers had been tense on occasions. This was also the case in Riverside where less formalised patrols had been instrumental in displacing sex workers from a long-established area of street soliciting.

Similar tendencies towards displacement were also apparent when public spaces deemed to provide suitable settings for soliciting and transacting were modified (following the precepts of situational crime prevention). In the case studies, such measures included gating; the installation of CCTV systems; the removal of foliage; the demolition of public toilet blocks and disused buildings used by sex workers; and the removal of street furniture (in particular, benches and phone boxes). Evidence for the success of such 'target hardening' measures was mixed, and while some proclaimed that measures (such as gating off a mosque car park in Eastside) had had an instant and positive effect, the more normal outcome appeared to have been local displacement, with sex work moving from one area to another nearby location.

Moreover, the cumulative effect of target hardening was perceived by some to have made local public space much less comfortable and convivial. For instance, local shopkeepers in Central petitioned to remove benches and a phone box used by sex workers and 'street drinkers', yet their removal means these facilities are now not available to others. Likewise, landscaping a park in Eastside so that it was more open was claimed to have made the park safer for children, but had made the park less attractive overall ("and if it doesn't look nice people get, people are not going to use it" – resident, Eastside). As such, intolerance of sex work appeared to have been implicated in the declining quality of public space in our study areas, and while steps taken to 'target harden' specific public spaces provided some reassurance to affected populations, they appear of questionable long-term impact.

Sex work in the context of regeneration

In most of the case study areas, the overall amount of street sex work was perceived to be diminishing. While changing working practices (such as the increasing use of mobile phones among sex workers) may be considered significant, most stakeholders believed that the main reason for the decline was stricter enforcement, typically in response to types of community action noted above, as well as persistent lobbying of police and politicians. The influx of new resident groups was considered as highly significant in this regard, with social transformation deemed the most important factor shaping sex work markets:

> "Sex work has declined because of the type of people who have moved into the area. When we moved here there was a presence of prostitutes on street corners. As more young professionals moved in there was pressure from the residents on the police and council and they more or less eradicated it....There are now only a couple around. They are on their last legs...." (resident, Central South)

In Southside and Westside this form of gentrification had been gradual and piecemeal, although in Central, Eastside, and Riverside it had been encouraged as part of major local authority regeneration initiatives. In such instances, existing warehousing, factory, and housing units had made way for new apartments and housing blocks, often attracting young, single workers rather than families. This was recognised to have had dramatic impacts on the social character of the local community. For instance, in Riverside, the new entrants were generally characterised as young professionals who had little time to participate in local affairs (and it is significant such groups were under-represented in the focus groups and interviews). One respondent who had been resident in the Riverside area for some years stated, "Nobody quite knows who these people are because none of us have ever met them" (community representative, Riverside). Another suggested that the influx of young working populations fundamentally changed the nature of local life: "There's no time for other people or to sit down and have a talk" (community group representative, Riverside). This accords with the wider literature on gentrification, which suggests that it often causes social polarisation and displacement rather than promoting social cohesion (Atkinson, 2004).

While gentrifiers appeared to play a minimal role in community affairs, crucially it was noted that new entrants were prone to complain about activities they regarded as anti-social, and, even if they bypassed established resident and community groups, were often able to get something done about them:

> "For thirty years [part of Riverside] has been living inside a cloud of hydrogen sulphite which is the smell of rotten eggs ... coming from the sewage works. Well over the last three years and because of the kinds of people who've moved in, people have been able to articulate their anger in a more structured way and as a result ... we've managed to put [company name] into a corner and they are now being forced legally to get rid of the smell." (resident, Riverside)

Academic commentators have suggested gentrifiers often have a vested interest in displacing anti-social elements as they wish to enhance property prices in an area; moreover, they are often effective in mobilising longer-term residents to raise complaints about issues (Larsen, 1992). Residents, agencies, and the police confirmed this was the case in several of the study areas. For example, in Riverside, the decline in sex work was seen to be directly related to the lobbying of new entrants:

> "Local residents ... that have been there for a far longer period of time [did not get] anywhere near the sort of response from local services that the new people who have moved in ... appeared to have been given. So while [prostitution] is not a big issue on the agenda across the city as a whole in this particular area it's become a very big issue." (resident, Riverside)

Hence, in Riverside, regeneration was seen to be the major factor encouraging the displacement of sex work from a zone where it was tacitly tolerated by the authorities to another part of the district. As well as generating a new series of complaints from residents in the affected area, such displacement was seen to have profoundly negative effects for service provision, making it harder to maintain meaningful connections between sex workers, service providers, and the local community.

It is here that some of the contradictions of contemporary prostitution policy are thrown into sharp relief. On the one hand, prostitution is recognised as an inevitable part of the urban scene, with recent Home Office proposals suggesting that sex workers are vulnerable individuals who need to be supported through appropriate social services. On the other hand, they are positioned as a threat from whom the community needs protecting. For example, the Home Office's (2006c) advocation of community conferencing hints that sex workers might begin to be better represented in community life; yet in the same document there is a countervailing argument for stricter enforcement of kerb-crawling and soliciting legislation – "taking every opportunity to reduce the opportunity for sex work markets to flourish" (p 13). Further, the "hugely distressing" nuisances of "harassment from kerb-crawlers, prostitution and drug-related litter ... public sex acts and the general degradation of areas used for street prostitution" are also spelt out (p 13). In policy terms, therefore, it is incorrect to suggest street sex workers represent a group subject to a simple 'clearance politics': rather, we need to remain mindful of the new institutional arrangements that have emerged to support, discipline, and re-educate those "marginalised or dispossessed by the neoliberalism of the 1980s" (Peck & Tickell, 2002, p 389; see also O'Malley, 2000; Scoular & O'Neill, 2006). Moreover, it is crucial to explore the way these contradictory tendencies are played out according to local contingencies, not least the complaints about anti-social behaviour that emanate from specific residential groups in particular neighbourhoods.

Conclusion

The studies in five British cities suggest there are a multitude of tensions that may arise in areas of street sex working. Irrespective of whether these tensions are a result of the 'real' nuisances caused by sex workers and their clients, or a general unease about the presence of sex work in particular locales, the result is a differentiated landscape of tolerance (Pitcher et al, 2006). Hence, it is possible to find a spectrum of views about prostitution within specific communities, with large numbers of residents actually appearing highly ambivalent about the presence of sex workers in their communities. However, it appears there is now less tolerance evident in areas of street sex work than was the case in previous decades, with gentrification a significant factor in the gradual displacement of sex workers from many long-established street-beats. In the case study locations, it was thus notable that more or less-developed processes of gentrification were prevalent in those areas least tolerant of prostitution. In contrast, there was greater tolerance evident when sex workers lived as well as worked in the area, with longevity of residence improving the degree of communication between residents and sex workers.

In this respect, the social disruption caused by gentrification may pre-empt and provoke concerted campaigns of enforcement and exclusion. This accords with the generally made observation that gentrification relies on the prioritisation of a particular middle-class vision of urbanity that excludes certain forms of difference (Atkinson, 2004). In this instance, middle-class codes of sexual and social comportment regard sex work as an unacceptable (and nuisance-causing) dimension of urban life. There are of course tensions here, and it is notable that gentrifiers' privileging of particular forms of night-time activity may, in some instances, tacitly encourage the development of "up-market (and off-street) adult entertainment centres" (Hubbard, 2004, p 683).

Lees (2003a) argues that urban renaissance initiatives have been remarkably ambivalent about diversity – promoting inclusion at the same time as pandering to local complaints of those who equate difference with nuisance. In policy terms, there is thus a need to recognise that 'urban renaissance' cannot be a renaissance for all unless gentrifiers adapt to some of the local practices and understandings of who belongs in a particular neighbourhood.

Here, the current debate around questions of conviviality is suggestive of some of the issues at stake. Conviviality is a term that stresses the importance of cultural respect and dialogue, and it contrasts with the agenda of multiculturalism that emphasises respect for cultural difference without resolving the problem of communication between cultures. It may also be contrasted with those versions of cosmopolitanism that suggest cultural difference will ultimately disappear through inter-ethnic mixture and hybridisation (Keith, 2005). In the UK, New Labour favour the former, and have sought to criminalise expressions of religious and ethnic hatred without addressing the question as to how such antipathy might be dissipated. Thrift (2005) goes so far as to suggest that social conflict emerges from different populations being asked to subscribe to notions of citizenship, community, or shared order that they regard as fundamentally flawed. Rather then seeking to challenge these political visions by building alternative categories of inclusion and exclusion that make rights-based claims on the state, Thrift (2005) argues a more credible and effective form of politics is simply to encourage differently situated individuals to develop rules of placed conduct through negotiation. Conviviality, therefore, is about a living-together of different cultures in public space: something that may require new urban spaces where dialogue between strangers is the norm, and not the exception. Whether such conviviality can ever be fostered in areas of street sex work remains to be seen.

Acknowledgements

This chapter draws on research ('Living and working in areas of street sex work') generously funded by the Joseph Rowntree Foundation as part of their Public Space Programme.

THIRTEEN

Urban renaissance and the contested legality of begging in Scotland

Joe Hermer and David MacGregor

Programmes and visions of urban regeneration and beautification, present in many of the most affluent cities in the world, have raised serious questions about social exclusion, citizenship, and the plight of the urban poor. A common feature of the politics of this movement is a crackdown on so-called 'aggressive beggars' and others types of disorderly people. Indeed, demands for removal of people begging from city pavements have become a tired cliche of urban politics today.[1] Unlike in England and Wales and in North American cities such as Toronto or New York, Scottish cities, in forging their own urban renaissance, are without one of the main tools of 'cleaning up the streets'. Since 1991, begging in Scotland has been legal, a situation that has not sat well with officials in cities such as Glasgow, Edinburgh, and Aberdeen who have argued that those begging are a serious public threat that requires the police to be armed with vagrancy-type law.

This chapter offers an analysis of the campaign to re-criminalise begging by City of Edinburgh officials in the late 1990s, and the response of the then Scottish office. In arguing for a new begging offence, Edinburgh officials exercised familiar tropes in depicting those begging as a public menace: vague appeals to public safety and 'community', the protection of tourist and consumer dollars, and aspirations for a 'world class', cosmopolitan city where visitors are not distracted by unpleasant reminders of poverty and social inequality (Helms, forthcoming).[2] What is notable about this case, is how the response of the then Scottish Office (now the Scottish Executive) represented an unusually tolerant position when compared to other jurisdictions: citing a number of legal and practical concerns the Scottish Executive declined to allow Edinburgh to promote a begging byelaw, a position that has been reiterated in more general terms earlier this

)06) to the City of Aberdeen that argued that a criminal offence
:ded to deal with the presence of those begging.

egin by briefly examining how anti-begging ordinances, as an
~~~ of a much wider 'criminalisation of urban policy', effectively
reduce the homeless to the status of 'bare life'. Laws that target visibly
disadvantaged people such as new 'public space' ordinances usually
include bans on public sleeping and restrictions on panhandling
(Feldman, 2004, p 2). We use the province of Ontario, in Canada's Safe
Streets Act as an example of exclusionary legislation that thrusts the
poor into a zone where conventional civil protections are inoperative
and opportunities for legitimate political engagement sharply curtailed.
With this example in place, we then explore in some detail the highly
contentious and unsuccessful campaign to re-criminalise begging
in Edinburgh, paying particular attention to difficulties involved in
drafting an offence, and the reasons advanced against the case of making
begging illegal again.

'Bare life' in Ontario

Never especially tolerant of the disadvantaged, the progressive
conservative government of Ontario implemented the 2006 Safe
Streets Act in response to a perceived invasion of 'squeegee kids' and
the increasing presence of people begging on the streets of Toronto
and other urban centres.[3] As we detail below, the law constructed a
stereotype of the aggressive beggar portraying the indigent person as
a foul-mouthed, potentially violent transgressor of civility on public
pavements. The Ontario legislation illustrates a pathology in modern
democratic societies whereby certain categories of citizens are cast
outside the normal framework of politics and law, and propelled
into a netherworld of 'bare life'. This pathology of modern urban
governance is usefully analysed in Feldman's *Citizens without shelter*
(2004). Legislation targeting the homeless, Feldman (2004) argues,
exemplifies the distinction between 'bare life' and citizenship.[4] The
state itself constructs "relations of hierarchy, exclusion and identity/
difference ... hitherto traced to culture or society" (p 15). Feldman
refers here to Italian philosopher Giorgio Agamben's interpretation of
homo sacer: he "who may be killed and yet not sacrificed" – "a being
whose exclusion is the very means by which the law constitutes itself"
(Willis, 2006, p 128).

Agamben's notion of 'bare life' (*la nuda vita*) (1998) returns to the
dual Greek terms for life: "*zoe*, which expressed the simple fact of living
common to all living beings, and *bios*, which indicated the form or way

of living proper to an individual or a group" (Enns, 2004, p 9). Diane Enns (2004) points out that Agamben's concept mirrors "Aristotle's distinction between mere life and the good life; between private life and the public life of the polis where justice arises from the human community's capacity to reflect on what is best and necessary for the common good" (2004, pp 9-10).

From this perspective, legal sovereignty is founded on distinguishing mere human existence – 'bare life' – from the polis. As Agamben (1998) puts it, "he who has been banned is not, in fact, simply set outside the law and made indifferent to it but rather 'abandoned' by it" (p 28). Those without a home, and reduced to squalid conditions of life lived in public spaces alone, are beyond the realm of political rights. They take on the status, notes Enns (2004), of "the occupied body: the individual stripped of political and human rights, reduced to a bare existence, who sometimes turns to self-sacrifice in the name of revolt... " (p 2). Enduring an existence narrowed to bare life the homeless are liable to be assessed and judged as either 'deserving' or 'undeserving poor'. Events in Ontario and other Anglo-American jurisdictions reveal the oscillation of these terms, their dialectical movement in which a person defined as 'deserving' may shortly be transformed into someone 'undeserving' (see Johnston and Mooney, Chapter Eight, this volume). The way out of this cycle, Feldman (2004) counsels, is to view the homeless as part of a pluralising political society that would "nurture political practices that run across the distinction between bare life and the political" (p 21).

The pathological cycle of deserving versus undeserving poor is vividly illustrated by the genesis of Ontario's Safe Streets Act. Tolerated in the early 1990s as innovative merchandisers of their own labour, squeegee kids in Toronto and other Ontario cities became highly unpopular as political winds shifted under the right-wing Mike Harris government, elected in 1995. The Harris 'Common Sense Revolution' earned much electoral goodwill when it passed the 1999 Safe Streets Act prohibiting many squeegee cleaners and panhandlers from city curbsides, but critics suggested the Act resembled 19th-century vagrancy laws that punished and imprisoned the poor.

The Safe Streets Act is extraordinarily detailed and specific but also opaque and overly broad. Two main sections of the Act ban 'aggressive begging' and prohibit soliciting to a 'captive audience'. The Act's definition of *soliciting* is especially far-reaching:

> ... 'solicit' means to request, in person, the immediate
> provision of money or another thing of value, regardless

of whether consideration is offered or provided in return, using the spoken, written or printed work, a gesture or other means. (Section 1)

Within this definition of solicit, the Act bans a wide range of conduct in a broad range of spaces to the extent that in many circumstances simply looking poor, and thus in need, in public space invites police intervention.[5]

Civil liberties groups and homeless advocates hoped the new Ontario Liberal government, elected in 2003, would repeal the Safe Streets Act. Expectations were dashed in 2005 when the Liberals supported a private member's bill that would amend the Safe Streets Act "to recognize the fund-raising activities of legitimate charities and non-profit organizations". Although the government acknowledged the unwieldy character of the Safe Streets Act, its response was to re-enforce the authority of legislation that they had, in opposition, condemned as an attack on the poor and vulnerable.[6] The Liberals were, however, sensitive to arguments from established charity organisations (that is, those formally registered as such under the Federal Taxation Act) that Section 3(2) of the Act – that forbids curbside solicitation – interfered with benevolent fund-raising activities. Legislators pointed, for example, to volunteer firefighters' efforts on behalf of Muscular Dystrophy, which featured campaigners blocking small town roadsides for collections deposited in a firefighter's boot – the so-called 'boot toll'.[7] Disgruntled motorists complained to the police, who found themselves compelled to apply the law. Muscular Dystrophy and other charities across the province, such as the Boy Scouts, contended that the Safe Streets Act reduced their funding by hundreds of thousands of dollars.

The Amendment, which makes it legal for registered charities to importune on the roadway, potentially renders the Safe Streets Act more vulnerable to court challenge. According to lawyers who argued against its validity before the Ontario Court of Appeal, "it has the effect of outlawing one class of speech, asking for money for oneself, while allowing another, asking for money for others" (Rusk, 2006a). Proponents of eight street people charged under the Act contend that instead of getting rid of its aura of status offence the Amendment to the Safe Streets Act reinforces discrimination "against the poor as a class of people" (Rusk, 2006b,) in its particular phrasing. In point of fact, the defects in the Ontario law follow a pattern also identified, as we will show, by the Scottish Office: that criminal law already exists to prohibit the categories of obstreperous conduct outlawed by the provincial Safe Streets Act; the Act discriminates against individuals on the basis of social status, and violates ordinary human rights; the law is founded on an extreme characterisation of indigent people emerging from an intolerant and retributive political climate.

The Ontario experience reflects a perverse standard now familiar in jurisdictions across North America where the homeless, confined under the category of 'bare life', have no access to enforce legal rights of citizenship. Feldman (2004), for example, contrasts two federal cases involving political protest. In one case, where a New York City tenants' group built a tent city as a symbolic dissent against a rental increase, the court ruled that their protest was protected as a form of free speech. In the second case, homeless activists in Washington, DC constructed a campsite to protest homelessness but their action, which violated camping regulations, was deemed not to be a form of protected expression. "It is worth noting the irony of these two cases read together. They permit housed citizens to engage in symbolic public sleeping to protest their *potential* homelessness but prevent homeless citizens from occupying a tent city to protest their *actual* homelessness" (Feldman, 2004, p 141). It is in this context of defective legal regimes constructed to regulate the visibly poor in many 'world class' cities that we turn to the Edinburgh case.

The Edinburgh case[8]

Originally extended to Scotland in 1871, the 1824 English Vagrancy Act was repealed by Scottish authorities in 1982. Local burgh acts in Scotland, which usually contained a begging section, were abolished in 1991 as part of the reorganisation of local government law (Edinburgh, 1998a). The lack of criminal sanction for begging has been a point of contention for local officials in Scottish cities, who, influenced by the Town Centre Management movement, have called for re-criminalisation to get those begging off the streets.

Media coverage ignited the campaign in Edinburgh to re-criminalise begging when *The Scotsman* newspaper (edited by arch-Conservative Andrew Neil) and the *Edinburgh Evening News* ran stories in 1996 critical of visibly indigent beggars and street drinkers. Conservative City Councillor Lindsay Walls subsequently wrote to the Scottish Office urging the reintroduction of the vagrancy laws to deal with 'aggressive beggars' and argued that a long-suffering public appeared to be threatened by beggars in the streets who were also described as 'chancers' receiving enhanced benefits from the state. James Douglas-Hamilton, the then Minister of State responsible for criminal law in Scotland, responded to Mr Walls by first pointing out that being 'drunk and incapable' was an offence under Section 50 of the 1982 Civic Government (Scotland) Act,[9] and that since 1993 provisions had been introduced to allow local councils to introduce city centre byelaws to ban street drinking.[10] The specific issue of begging, the Minister commented, was more complex and involved "moral and social, as well as legal issues to consider" (Douglas-Hamilton, 1996, p 1). The Minister pointed out that those who do indeed "extort money with menaces" were subject to a "very flexible" common law offence of "breach of peace" that addresses behaviour that threatens, intimidates or alarms (Douglas-Hamilton, 1996, pp 1-2). In addition, those who are begging under 'false or fraudulent pretence' could possibly be charged with the common law offence of fraud.[11] Otherwise, the Minister argued, those begging who do not obstruct the highway, or commit breach of the peace, or commit fraud at common law are not in fact committing any criminal offence. "You urge the reintroduction of the Vagrancy Acts," the Minister wrote to Councillor Walls,

> by which I take it you mean the old local offences of the burgh acts which made it an offence to beg. I am not persuaded that this is justifiable. No one would argue that begging is welcomed. But to rule that beggars should be treated as criminals, even where their behaviour does nothing to cause alarm, would categorise those who may be genuinely deserving of charity in a way which many people would find it difficult to agree to. (Douglas-Hamilton, 1996, p 2)

The admission by a State Minister, that some of those begging are genuinely needy, and that public opinion in part reflects this perception, strongly contrasts to the near hysterical discourse of many public officials in England and North America that those begging are all frauds and harbingers of disorder and urban decline.

Begging once again emerged as a public issue in the summer of 1997 when the *Evening News* and *The Scotsman* launched a sustained campaign to re-criminalise begging through the enactment of a local byelaw (McBeth, 1997).[12] Addressing the Edinburgh Book Festival Andrew Neil remarked that "beggars are turning Scotland's capital into the biggest urinal in the United Kingdom" (Lister, 1997). The Labour-led council refused to recommend a no-begging byelaw, and with the support of the Liberal Democrats, instructed the Urban Regeneration Sub-Committee to study the issue of begging as part of the wider issue of 'social exclusion' (Edinburgh, 1997a, 1997b). The issue of re-criminalising begging was effectively sidelined for the next seven months until the Policy and Resource Committee released their report *Managing Edinburgh's city centre* on 28 May 1998.

Remarkably, the report viewed begging as the most important threat to Edinburgh's "healthy economic future"; the presence of beggars received more attention in the report than changes that would take place with the introduction of the new Scottish Parliament. The report began by noting that the enabling power for a byelaw appeared in principle to exist in a provision of the 1973 Local Government (Scotland) Act.[13] Any proposed begging byelaw would have to be 'promoted' to the Secretary of State, who may hold a public inquiry into the matter before deciding if the byelaw would be confirmed (Edinburgh, 1998a). The main theme of the legal issues report was the discussion of the 'possible contents' of a begging byelaw, of the possible ways in which city lawyers could draft a specific begging encounter that could constitute a criminal offence.

The report suggested two versions of a possible byelaw. 'Version A' attempted to reintroduce the burgh offence of 'collecting alms' and contains language similar to the Safe Streets Act. 'Version B' constructs a crime called 'aggressive begging'. According to Version A of the byelaw:

> Any person who in a public place begs or acts in any way for the purpose of inducing the giving of money or money's worth shall be guilty of an offence. (Edinburgh, 1998a, p 3).

While Version A focuses on the thing potentially given and taken, Version B shifts the emphasis to the conduct of the importuner:

> Any person who in any public place in the course of begging or acting in any way for the purpose of inducing the giving of money or money's worth behaves in a threatening or aggressive way or adopts a threatening or aggressive manner shall be guilty of an offence. (Edinburgh, 1998a, p 4).

The report discussed in some detail the significant obstacles facing the promotion of both byelaw versions. Most generally, the Secretary of State would have to be convinced of the necessity of creating a new criminal offence – especially after the old burgh laws were not deemed significant enough to be preserved.

Version B posed serious difficulties in this regard, most notably in how the activity of 'aggressive begging' (which remained undefined) could already, as was earlier pointed out by the Minister of State to Councillor Walls, be dealt with as a common law breach of peace. The informal opinion of the Scottish Office on this matter, requested by the City Council solicitor (Bain, 1997), was that "The offence of breach of the peace does provide a means of addressing the problem of those who threaten, intimidate, alarm, and make a deliberate nuisance of themselves to the obvious annoyance of members of the public" (Baxter, 1997). In addition, the police opposed Version B of the byelaw, citing the fact that 'aggressive' forms of begging can be dealt as breaches of peace under common law. The report noted that, in prosecuting 'aggressive begging' offences, police officers would "have to have evidence of aggressive or threatening behaviour in much the same way as they would to justify a charge of breach of peace" (Edinburgh, 1998a, p 7).[14] The strongest blow against the 'aggressive' Version B was the "clearly inimical" view taken by the authorities responsible for criminal prosecutions: the Lord Advocate's position was that the current criminal law was adequate to deal with 'aggressive' begging (Edinburgh, 1998a, p 8).

Indeed, if 'aggressive begging' was so similar to the offence of breach of peace, and was such a problem to pedestrians in the city centre, why did the police not use this power to crack down on 'aggressive beggars'? Remarkably, 'breach of peace' was not even included in a summary of crime statistics appended to the report, which, on the whole, reported a decrease in the level of reported crime in the city centre since 1991 (Edinburgh, 1998b). It does seem curious that, considering the constant and sustained emphasis on the problem of 'aggressive begging', the police seemingly did little to curtail this behaviour with what they themselves admitted was effective criminal legislation.

The police did express 'qualified support' for Version A of the byelaw that created a new criminal offence of begging (Edinburgh, 1998a, p 7), recast with a novel ingredient, namely the verb 'induce': "Any person who in a public place begs or acts in any way for the purpose of inducing the giving of money or money's worth, and fails to desist on being requested to do so by a Constable in uniform, shall be guilty of an offence" (Edinburgh, 1998a, p 6). However, this version – as the report conceded – could be used to criminalise "street performers who invite contributions" (Edinburgh, 1998a, p 5). For city officials, however, street performers "invite" the giving of a "contribution", while beggars "induce the giving" of "money or money's worth". The distinction apparently relies on a different conception of the subjectivity of the passer-by when importuned: the busker exists in a realm of invitation and consent where the passer-by can exercise choice, while the beggar does not 'invite' but rather 'induces' the passer-by, as an act of persuasion. Nevertheless, the proposed offence of acting "in any way for the purpose of inducing the giving of money or money's worth" is a perfect description of both busking and street collections.

"There is a clear risk," stated the report, "that such an exemption [for busking] would result in begging activities being continued to be conducted under the guise of street performers even by persons totally unskilled in any performing art" (Edinburgh, 1998a, p 6). In addition, Version A faced further problems as raised in a council solicitor's letter to the Scottish Office:

> I do, to some extent, apologise for raising this issue, but I am fairly convinced that if it is not canvassed by me at this stage, it is almost certain to be raised by bodies which hold an opinion that any byelaws associated with the prohibition or curtailment of begging are unacceptable from the unnecessary interference with civil liberties. (Bain, 1997)

Specifically, the solicitor was concerned that a byelaw that criminalised begging per se could be challenged in relation to the European Convention on Human Rights and could be considered incompatible with two articles of the Convention: Article 10^{15} that enshrines a right of freedom of expression, and Article 14^{16} that states that the rights and freedoms set forth in the convention are to be secured without discrimination on various grounds including status and property. "Since arguably any byelaw," the solicitor suggested,

> ... relating to begging might be regarded as focusing on persons who might be bereft of property or, alternatively, focusing on persons because of their particular "status" there might also be an issue here of incompatibility between byelaws and the freedoms set out in the convention. (Bain, 1997)

Reminding the council that they would be expected to take out their own legal advice as part of the byelaw promotion process, the Scottish Office responded that:

> The only thoughts we have to offer at this point are that byelaws to prohibit begging, of a kind which would otherwise not involve an offence under criminal law, might, as you suggest, be challenged on the grounds they violated

> Article 14 or Article 10. There would seem to be a strong
> risk of violating Article 14 unless the byelaws distinguished
> between different groups, but if the byelaws prohibited the
> simple act of asking for alms, then there may be a significant
> risk of violating Article 10. Of course this is an informal
> view. (Baxter, 1998)

Surprised by the tone of the report which, according to one Labour official, exhibited an 'obsession' with begging, the Labour group declined to follow the recommendation to promote a byelaw, and instead passed a motion to support a 'City Centre Summer Initiative' with a policing initiative that would target 'anti-social behaviour' (Edinburgh, 1998c). The Labour-led council blocked attempts to re-criminalise begging by invoking a specific notion of 'anti-social behaviour' that could be addressed within a new political emphasis on 'social exclusion'. That such reframing along the lines of anti-social behaviour may be problematic in its own right is clearly spelled out in a number of other contributions to this volume, notably by Flint and Smithson (Chapter Ten) and by Millie (Chapter Seven).

Conclusion

In 2005 officials in the City of Aberdeen, citing beggars as a blight on the city centre and a threat to the public, requested that the Scottish Executive allow them to promote a begging byelaw.[16] The Scottish Justice Department rejected the request: "Scottish Executive policy is," wrote a policy advisor to Aberdeen Councillor Greig,

> ... that in general, byelaws should not duplicate existing
> offence provisions. Aggressive begging is already addressed
> by common law (breach of the peace) and by statute (section
> 53 of the Civic Government Act and Anti-Social behaviour
> etc [Scotland] Act 2004). In particular, the 2004 Act provides
> police and local authorities with a range of powers to deal
> with intimidating behaviour. (Cossar, 2006)

The response goes on to state that a "multi-agency approach, such as the one you describe in your letter is considered to be a positive way of dealing with street begging and associated problems", and underlined the value of the Scottish anti-social behaviour legislation (Cossar, 2006). It is interesting to note that in replying to Aberdeen the Justice Department pointed to the City of Edinburgh Council as engaging a multi-agency approach, (including the use of Anti-Social Behaviour Orders), that Aberdeen should emulate. Almost 10 years after refusing to allow Edinburgh to promote a byelaw, it appears that the Scottish Office will continue to block the re-criminalisation of begging. This position is particularly striking, not only in comparison with North American jurisdictions like Toronto, but also given the contrast with England and Wales, where the 1824 Vagrancy Act has been resuscitated and integrated into Criminal Justice reforms, as part of a retributive and often hysterical fight against the beggar as anti-social bogey. In continuing to reject calls for re-criminalisation, the Scottish Executive has resisted one of the most overt tools used to force the visibly poor on public streets into the realm of bare life – to an existence outside the polis. In doing so, the Scottish Executive, in a sound and responsible position, recognised four major flaws – brought to the surface in this chapter – that make anti-begging ordinances 'bad law' in being impractical and discriminatory tools: (1) that adequate criminal law already exists to deal with genuine threats to public safety; (2) that as demonstrated by the near identical character of begging, busking, and registered charity collections anti-begging law is inherently capricious, over-broad, and discriminatory as it inevitably requires enforcement that would hinge on a person's status and/or appearance; (3) that significant human rights issues are raised; and (4) that public feeling and opinion about those begging encompasses a wide range of reactions (including sympathy) that cannot simply be reduced to hysterical characterisations of fear and alarm.

The lack of criminal sanction denied to local city officials in Scotland will, for the time being, frustrate one of the main instruments that other jurisdictions use to mount overtly punitive policing programmes. Only time will tell if other strategies will be configured, in the evolving use of ASBOs, to satisfy a politically expedient and intolerant view of visibly poor people, one that endangers a vital aspect of citizenship: the provision of a "'space for engagement' within which the public (or various publics) comes to recognize themselves" (Mitchell, 2005, p 85). We would suggest that urban renaissance strategies, if they are to be a reflection of an ethos of inclusion, must resist further pushing the visibly poor into a zone of 'bare life', into an existence outside the normal relations of the polis. The refusal of the Scottish Executive to re-criminalise begging stands as an important and enlightened example of this resistance.

Notes

[1] The crackdown on begging now extends beyond the homeless to those who actually do the giving. Las Vegas recently became the first city to ban feeding 'the indigent', although the rule is restricted to public parks. "Las Vegas officials said the ordinance was not aimed at casual handouts from good Samaritans. Instead, they said it would be enforced against people ... whose regular offerings ... have lured the homeless to parks and have led to complaints by residents about crime, public drunkenness and litter" (Archibold, 2006).

[2] Similar issues in Glasgow are explored by Belina and Helms (2003). "Begging, especially aggressive begging," they write, "again became a heated issue for Glasgow when in Spring 2001 the Lockwood Report on city-centre retailing claimed that aggressive begging acted as brake on Glasgow's economic success" (p 16).

[3] Unlike in Edinburgh, where the proposed anti-begging byelaw would constitute an offence of criminal law, the Ontario Safe Streets Act is a non-criminal provincial offence.

[4] The concept of 'bare life' is developed in Feldman (2004, pp 15-24). Susan Willis (2006) provides an interesting discussion of Agamben's notion of bare life in relation to so-called terrorist prisoners held by the US in Guantanamo Bay. This theme is also taken up in Agamben (2005).

[5] For a detailed discussion of the Safe Streets Act see Hermer and Mosher (2002).

[6] Bill 58, Safe Streets Statute Law Amendment Act, 2005 (www.ontla. on.ca/library/bills/381/58381.htm).

[7] See, for example, the testimony of the London Professional Firefighters Association to the Standing Committee on Regulations and Bills, Legislative Assembly of Ontario (www.ontla.on.ca/hansard/committee_debates/38_parl/session1/regsbills/T013.htm#P205_38035).

[8] This section draws on the analysis of Hermer (forthcoming).

[9] Section 50 (1) reads: "Any person who, while not in the care or protection of a suitable person, is, in a public place, drunk and incapable of taking care of himself shall be guilty of an offence and liable, on summary conviction, to a fine not exceeding £50".

[10] The model byelaw was approved after pilot projects in Dundee, Motherwell, and Galashiels. The most notable deployment of this byelaw has been in the city of Glasgow (Douglas-Hamilton, 1996).

[11] "That route may not often be taken," comments the Minister, "but it remains a longstop, and the possibility that it may be resorted to does, I think, have an effect in curbing the more blatant claims of those who do beg" (Douglas-Hamilton, 1996, p 2).

[12] For example, 'Capital's beggar's needy or greedy?' (McBeth, 1997).

[13] Section 201 gives the council powers to "make byelaws for the good rule and government of the whole or any part of their area, as the case may be, and for the prevention and suppression of nuisances" (Edinburgh, 1998d, p 3).

[14] Edinburgh, 1998d, p 7. The report adds, "I am not certain whether case law precedent in relation to breach of peace could be cited in a prosecution for 'aggressive begging' contrary to byelaws" (Edinburgh, 1998d, p 5).

[15] Article 10 reads:

1. "Everyone has the right to freedom of expression. This right shall include freedom to hold opinions and to receive and impart information and ideas without interference by public authority and regardless of frontiers. This Article shall not prevent states from requiring the licensing of broadcasting, television or cinema enterprises."

2. "The exercise of these freedoms, since it carries with it duties and responsibilities, may be subject to such formalities, conditions, restrictions or penalties as are prescribed by law and are necessary in a democratic society, in the interests of national security, territorial integrity or public safety, for the prevention of disorder or crime, for the protection of health or morals, for the protection of the reputation or rights of others, for preventing the disclosure of information received in confidence, or for maintaining the authority and impartiality of the judiciary."

[16] Article 14 reads:

1. "The enjoyment of the rights and freedoms set forth in this Convention shall be secured without discrimination on any ground such as sex, race, colour, language, religion, political or other opinion, national or social origin, association with a national minority, property, birth or other status." See Gomien, David and Leo (1996) for a general discussion of the Convention articles.

[17] See Aberdeen City Council (2004) for the strategy developed by the council to deal with street beggars.

FOURTEEN

Conclusion: British urbanism at a crossroads

Gesa Helms and Rowland Atkinson

We started this volume with the observation that urban policy, like social policy before it, has become criminalised in the processes of viewing regeneration as closely linked to a broader and populist 'disorder' agenda. Such specific views on regeneration have been promoted not only by a punitive central government but also at a local level where the neoliberalisation of urban governance, in particular through new models of management and working practices, has been established. As the various chapters have shown, a reading of the criminal justice, anti-social behaviour, and urban agendas and attempts to revitalise neighbourhoods and central cities are now deeply entwined areas of public policy intervention. What we see now is the buttressing of policy in both fields by reference to each other as the disorder agenda seeks out places and communities damaged by or deficient in their control of crime and as explicit urban regeneration policies construe policing, disorder, and citizen engagement as the central hallmarks of effective control. In short, it no longer makes sense to treat these concerns as separable fields of policy, just as citizens see those linkages operating in local arenas on a daily basis.

In the first part of this collection we saw how policies dealing with crime control and urban regeneration are increasingly intertwined from a conceptual perspective. In particular the emphasis by New Labour on joined-up policy, while conferring new legitimacy on such policies, also had the effect of imbuing urban regeneration programmes with a strong criminal justice agenda, thus effectively criminalising urban policy. Here the chapters from Stenson, Raco, and Hancock (Chapters Two and Four respectively) moved beyond an initial analysis of policy initiatives and opened up the ways in which state–society relations are being reconfigured in the interlinking of urban, social, and criminal justice policies. In all of these contributions we see a strongly critical interpretation of the value of such a turn in policy making as an emphasis on 'active communities' and citizens has been undermined by an emphasis on strategies of policing and empowerment that have operated in punitive ways – actively excluding those very constituencies most in need of help and social inclusion. It is ironic that, while celebrating the need for rights and charters supporting the role and duties of citizens that the New Labour project has seen a growing economic splintering of its cities as income-based segregation has grown, urban unrest has been amplified by racial tensions, and excluded groups have been kept at the margins of civil society.

Stenson has drawn out the importance of taking seriously those "frames, or imaginaries of interpretation" (p 24) that try to impose orderly visions on the city and the tensions that exist in relation to a city's creative energies. In so doing, his argument chimes with David Pinder's (2005) recent work on urban visions, and it is with this eye on the underlying rationalities and reasoning that Stenson has turned to a critique of the key technologies by which current government tries to promote security and control crime. The everyday and commonsense appearance of many of these 'community security techniques' need to be unpacked and questioned so that we, as academics, commentators, and analysts, get a closer grip on ongoing policy and the kinds of punitive, or controlling, practices that it has tended to produce. Providing a conceptual bridge between visions of control and regeneration and its everyday pragmatic practices, Stenson's opening comments provided a framework for the ensuing chapters. These governmentalities were explored further by Mike Raco in relation to one of central government's key urban policy programmes, the sustainable communities agenda, by examining the role of planning for the provision of not only new, more sustainable communities, but along with them, new kinds of citizens. The rights and, in particular, the responsibilities of urban inhabitants have gained pronounced attention and emphasis under the current government. Hancock continued by asking questions over power and legitimacy in local politics by questioning the basis of several of its assumptions and asks, provocatively, whether much of the crime that is found in urban Britain may not be indeed a product of urban regeneration policies themselves. These limitations, so she argued, exist precisely because regeneration policies are so closely interconnected with the criminal justice agenda that it more often criminalises and excludes, rather than aiding, those it touches.

These three chapters further developed our opening remarks regarding the necessity of exploring in more detail how this confluence of neoliberalism and paternalism is being constructed and applied at the intersection of urban policy, criminal justice, and social policy.

This process has been predicated on the production of new tools and techniques of governance that were held to 'work' through the joining up of crime control with urban policy, itself partially the result of a rhetoric, of 'rights and responsibilities', that stemmed from a desire for populism. This interlinking of departmental responsibilities in a broader 'neoliberal' framework that continued to celebrate the orientation of earlier waves of Thatcherite market preferences has created notions of an empowered citizenry while at the same time pushing away those who fail to join a broader community seeking vengeance on the causes of disorder. Furthermore, however, these policies are, above all, projects and strategies, and therefore their success or failure is very much dependent on their implementation or, more accurately, their being put to work. Here the chapters have developed a set of analytical tools for studying the conditions of contemporary British social and public policy, even while their emphasis is clearly on urban policy and social disorder. These policy projects have reorganised the way in which British cities function and have produced new geographies of risk, relative inclusion, and devices through which some kind of uneasy settlement and social order might be engineered.

There has been a strongly critical tone throughout many of the chapters. In grappling with the implications of the embedding of punitive criminal justice approaches within regeneration policies this has also highlighted the extent to which there has been a fragmentation of departmental portfolios, and also a conflict resulting from such fragmentation. One example of this is the tension between the desire to liberalise drinking laws, on the one hand, and the attempt on the other to control the results of an exuberant and disorderly night-time economy of young revellers in British city centres. Another has been the emphasis on community as a resource for tackling anti-social behaviour while popular media and politicians have often described poorer areas as the containers of problematic people. For some ministers the emergence of such disorder can be linked to the inability of already fearful and deprived communities to take charge of such problems. Throughout the contributions to this collection there has been criticism of these tensions as well as an enquiry into the underpinnings of current policy and the ways in which the broader New Labour project has tended to combine efforts to tackle regeneration with crime and disorder.

Governmentality, urban security and safety

Understanding current policy developments through the lens of the Foucauldian notion of governmentality has been a common conceptual thread, both in this volume and for other commentators writing on crime, disorder, and the control of anti-social behaviour. The interest of such a focus has been twofold. Firstly, it reflects current disciplinary debates in criminology, social policy, geography, and wider urban studies on the explanatory value offered by such an account of institutional and social relationships. Secondly, and as we have argued before in this volume, such an explicit envisioning of social relations is right at the heart of New Labour's own project of modernisation. This project has been a keynote of the administration and it has fed closely into the kind of paternalism that was directed at excluded and deprived communities that were seen not only as the particular victims of earlier economic restructuring and problems of disorder, but also as groups containing those deviant bodies and actions to which both local residents and law enforcement needed to direct urgent attention. Here, the multidisciplinary perspectives brought together in this collection has been key to exploring further the implications and consequences of such policy and practice without remaining solely focused on one of its elements.

Among all of this it is important not to forget those other dimensions of power and control intrinsic to government (and intentionally we are harking back to this concept rather than *governance*). In this volume the contributions from Hancock as well as from Johnston and Mooney are explicit in this, with the former demonstrating how 'primary definers' (Coleman et al, 2005) are able to shape *apparently* successful crime control agendas, pursued in turn by government agencies who are keen to meet their community participation goals. As a consequence, Hancock sees a process of power relations at work whereby: "'Inclusion' policies and communitarian discourses conceal the way class divisions are reconfiguring and obscure the manner in which power relations are defended in the contemporary city" (Hancock, Chapter Four, this volume, p 64). Such understanding of power relations in the contemporary city is taken up later on in the volume by Hubbard and his colleagues (Chapter Twelve) and Hermer and MacGregor (Chapter Thirteen) whose two chapters pinpoint the exclusionary processes at play with two of the most contentious activities in urban public space: the former in relation to street prostitution, the latter in relation to begging.

The reorganisation of governance has been manifold, in particular in relation to the creation of new government organisations, internal restructuring of ministries, and service section at central and local levels but also in terms of quangos (quasi-autonomous non-governmental organisations) and public–private partnerships. These reorganisations above all point to the central role played by government at different scales (nationally and below). That the various reorganisations have in many cases removed the democratic accountability of public sector agencies, most notably of quangos as well as public–private partnerships is a key problematic here (Newburn, 2001; Coleman, 2004a). This has meant that even while an agenda has been promoted celebrating the new rights of citizens to be free from crime and to live in more inclusive communities, the experience on the ground and in neglected neighbourhoods remains to be one of unaccountable organisations with stark influence on the daily lives of residents in these spaces, for example in relation to urban night-time economies or large-scale housing and regeneration projects such as pathfinder programmes or New Deal for Communities (NDC). Here we continue to find models of governance created under Thatcherite principles involving a property-led renaissance (particularly now in the North of England) and that, far from seeking empowerment and participation, now seek to displace those communities in favour of more 'diverse' resident bases as a recipe for longer-term sustainability. Indeed, we can concur with Clarke and Glendinning (2002) in their assessment on how central government's mistrust of local government organisations has led to far-reaching attempts to regulate local democratically accountable processes through centrally controlled ones:

> ... we think it is worth considering how the changing processes of governance involve the remaking of state power and its extension through new means.... This perspective enables us to view New Labour's compulsory partnerships as an attempt to recruit subordinate partners into the project of "modernising" government. (p 46)

All of this echoes the contribution of Raco who sets out the implications of the sustainable communities agenda for a sense of community and civility modelled on active citizens capable and willing to engage with the moralising tone of these policy prescriptions. The significance of such citizen engagement should not be understated since, just as the power of the New Labour ideology reaches a plateau and perhaps falls away, the institutional remains of the administration and its popular approach to searching for social injustice and solutions to social problems will likely be continued in future. This is not only because this approach did, in fact, provide some effective working models in practice, but also because the continuing thread running through much of what has been discussed in this volume is the interaction of a market orientation to solving those problems that are, in many cases, the fallout of earlier liaisons with such solutions. In other words, there is little reason to fear or hope that partnerships, the reinforced exclusion of young people, and deviant others will either be disconnected from a broader agenda of urban renewal or that the kind of neoliberal market-based solutions to such places and communities will be erased by any incoming administration. So embedded is the logic of market property relations, responsibility, wealth, and the spur to success, such practices will likely remain in place for some time yet. Finally, the fight for ascendancy and political dominance in a broader discourse of fear, terror, and crime will continue to mark out the policy wares of political parties keen to capitalise on the continued need for salvation from many of these problems.

The acknowledgement of state power is crucial to an understanding of the kinds of transformations we have witnessed over the past decade. Such power continues to be asserted, primarily through the police as a key enforcement agency, which cannot be bypassed in discussions of urban regeneration and crime control. The ways in which such state power has been reorganised over the past 25 years has been discussed at different points here, with Stenson outlining the broader frame reference and Hancock offering insights into the reworking of local power in relation to community. Paskell (Chapter Nine), on the other hand, explored the extension of public police services through community support officers whose presence reconfigures not only social interaction on urban streets but also the institutional governance of policing and social control. Such an organisational perspective does equip us with an important corrective to governmentality.

A city-wide urban renaissance?

A key critique levelled at the urban renaissance White Paper was that, in championing design-led central city revitalisation, while this blueprint might act as a vehicle for a successful repositioning of many cities, in fact many parts and constituencies within the city would be left out. Writers like Lees (2003b), as we have already shown, saw this as a gentrifiers' manifesto, welcoming the well-heeled and perhaps benignly neglecting the low-income. Indeed, this promotion of the central city over and above residential and more peripheral urban quarters has been part of urban regeneration for quite some time, as for example earlier arguments over an emerging dual city (Marcuse, 1989; Mooney & Danson, 1997) demonstrated. As the social exclusion agenda, led by the Prime Minister, targeted a neighbourhood poverty agenda, there was perhaps some balance in the attempt to include residential and peripheralised poverty with the kind of vision that emerged from the urban renaissance documentation. However, tensions did and still do remain. For example, it is clear that the most recent emphasis in urban policy circles is with the iconic spaces of central cities and the role that these might have in attracting investment. This has also led to a similar emphasis on these spaces as being critical to ensuring safety for users and consumers of the lifestyle opportunities opened up by these spaces. Nevertheless, novel initiatives like neighbourhood wardens have also opened up possibilities for strengthening areas with low social trust, even while running the gauntlet of anti-'grassing' cultures and existing formal police networks.

Perhaps there is increased optimism for the generation of a deeper urban renaissance, one that delivers greater security and social equity. Here, the creation of sustainable communities may counter such a critique of the urban renaissance White Paper. With this framework the focus has been moved to 'ordinary' urban residential neighbourhoods – similar to Johnstone and MacLeod's argument in relation to the housing pathfinder programme, which, through a combination of demolition, renovating, and incentives for private developers, focused on the physical remodelling of a small number of the worst-affected housing areas in England and Wales. In so doing, this framework may be seen as a more holistic model of urban regeneration, and as such it argues to bring together central city and residential neighbourhoods to approach concerns of urban development in a more integrative manner.

There have, of course, been numerous initiatives and programmes for failing and problem communities ever since urban decay moved to the attention of policy makers (arguably as early as the first sanitation and slum clearance programmes in Victorian cities). Most of these have been in the past, and are indeed increasingly under current government, again, framed as area-based initiatives. A focus on urban areas of multiple deprivation by the Social Exclusion Unit or indeed Health Action Zones, Employment Zones, the Scottish Social Inclusion Partnerships or the biggest area-based initiative under New Labour, the NDCs, has been a key scale for the delivery of public policy. Targeting for need geographically is seen here as vital for solving problems. Yet, as Imrie and Raco (2003) argue, it also serves in pathologising and stigmatising further particular social groups and their needs. Indeed Hall (1997) has gone so far as to state that such an area-based and inward-looking approach of regeneration in the context of peripheral housing schemes presents "a limited and unbalanced approach to estate regeneration.

Such policies have failed to tackle many of the root causes of estate decline" (p 885).

Analytically, such a perspective that takes into account the whole city seems commonsense and necessary if the breadth and depth of urban change is the object of investigation. Amin and Graham's (1997) account of 'The ordinary city' provides an important epistemological corrective for understanding the normality of city life that is not merely taking place either in the city centre or in particular (problem) neighbourhoods. It is with such a view across the city that the urban can be understood as "the co-presence of multiple spaces, multiple times and multiple webs of relations, tying local sites, subjects and fragments into globalizing networks of economic, social and cultural change" (Amin & Graham, 1997, p 417f). One of us has argued against the compartmentalisation of different parts of the city, as particular image and marketing campaigns try to do by separating out the new, successful city centre spaces which hiding the seemingly old and unregenerated. Examining daily patterns of work/leisure and movement across the city of not only service sector workers and shoppers but also of homeless people and outreach service users, Helms (forthcoming) argues that

> ... it appears that the dual city is much more permeable than it has commonly been discussed to be, an argument which has been made repeatedly as a critique of the dual city thesis. But, more important in relation to the theme of imagineering, something of an 'unhiding' has here taken place. (p 120)

Such unhiding can, as Katz (2001) argues, provide an important epistemological perspective of understanding the uneven development of urban change and its tendency to obscure not only social reproduction but also particular spaces and people from the view of onlookers.

The sustainable communities agenda does in some way refocus policy attention to different urban neighbourhoods across the whole city and as such attempts to overcome the spatial selectivity of previous programmes designed to merely address problem areas. It does so mainly by arguing that sustainable communities are necessary for creating good conditions for business – as the recent Scottish *Regeneration policy statement* (Scottish Executive, 2006, p 2) emphasises: "We [Scotland] are open for business". Similarly, we can find renewed interest in cities per se (be they vital or resurgent) (Cheshire, 2006), this interest presents the recent version of the need to reposition cities within inter-urban competition as Harvey argued almost 20 years ago. Increasingly, such competition also takes place on a local, or even neighbourhood scale with increasing competition, most notably for out-of-town shopping and leisure complexes, within different parts of the city. It is with these recent turns and modifications that the current inititative takes up themes of competition and (uneven) development expressed in the urban renaissance and earlier urban programmes, and it is with these programmes and their adaptation that neoliberalism is being produced in practice. It is with such continued attempts to re-order urban spaces in light of their competitiveness and with the aim of making them, as well as the whole city, more competitive, that sustainable communities indeed present little more than a continuation of previous urban policies.

Yet, where sustainable communities can be seen as a move towards a holistic policy formulation is that it brings together, even more so than previous urban policy documents such as the urban renaissance report, urban policy and the criminal justice systems. It does so with its assemblage of a communitarian, and as such paternalistic, view on social relations that concentrate on a narrow notion of community, joined up with visions for a market-led housing renewal. As Johnston and Mooney (Chapter Eight) emphasise, however, many of these programmes actively construct problem families and problem neighbourhoods. In this context the idea of sustainable communities presents what is essentially a familiar story in which a deserving poor are distinguished from the undeserving, and victims of urban restructuring are blamed for their own misery.

Playing politics with urban fears

Out of all these discussions it is particularly clear that an emerging politics of behaviour (Field, 2003) and a moralisation of city life have become central elements of not only the traditional law and order agenda but also the way in which the good, and therefore regenerated, community might be assessed. The apparent endpoint within these discussions is of what Field has called responsibilised citizens, tenants, and residents – groups of people capable of setting the parameters of acceptable behaviour in neighbourhood contexts. The clear driver of this would seem to be a fear of disconnected individuals and groups, unplugged from local labour markets and, in some cases, distant from the imagined norms of the good British citizen. It is no coincidence, then, that these debates have filtered into broader debates about citizenship tests, home-grown terrorism, neighbourhood decline, and crime.

What Furedi (2005) has called a politics of fear is now an accepted daily part of media discourses and treatments of cities, just as much as it is with non-spatialised understandings of fear of crime or law and order in general. Yet, by putting under the microscope ever more minute forms of behaviour and codes of civility there is a danger that pandering to the narrowness of community needs in fact amplifies these fears and is relayed through broader media circuits. As fears about paedophiles have shown, mob rule in local contexts can produce further anxiety that is often spatialised in its construction of dangerous places and groups. Just as many neighbourhoods have been stigmatised by association with crime, by adverse media treatment, and by concentrations of social rented housing, so too would such a politics of conduct potentially exaggerate the kind of criminal and disordering malaise and its causes. There is a real danger in this kind of sound-bite culture of a growing condemnatory tone to political rhetoric and to practice-based solutions that seek more to be tough than to resolve many such problems. Here the tendency for police officers to put out good news rather than bad rings somewhat true.

As writers like Young (1999) have convincingly argued, the criminalisation of incivility has been produced by a simplistic model of society that gathers solutions and evidence in order to generate 'what works'. Of course the result of this is a dramatic intransigence on the part of deprived and disconnected communities to be disciplined and to adopt mainstream codes of conduct, lifestyles, and aspirations. This is the fatal mistake of much policy rhetoric on urban problems and on concentrated poverty in particular, since it confuses the short-term attempts to remedy such problems with the reality – the social detritus and exclusion created by an unequal society that tends to become concentrated together not necessarily out of choice, but through necessity and a housing system that operates through bidding in a private market or is allocated on the basis of dire need. We continue to be left with these areas – resistant to a hundred years of urban policy in some cases – because the social reality of these urban contexts cannot be addressed by simplistic solutions and platitudes, Rather there is a need not only for social engagement and efforts at inclusion, but also the diminution of media machines that support populist sound-bite understandings and simplified solutions that continue to fail us and, critically, leave us less safe as a result.

Outlook: towards a deep renaissance?

Crime, disorder, and the future quality of our towns and cities are firmly linked together. These relationships have matured under a modernising government keen to see connections between disparate policy problems and subsequent interventions. While central government has set the tone and pace of many of these changes, local government has been equally forceful in implementing programmes wherein commonsense linkages between disorder, economic development, and quality of life are seen as inextricably linked. The resulting and generally punitive agenda that has emerged has largely focused on anti-social behaviour and generalised disorder as the key questions that need to be resolved. In these lay theories of regeneration the connection between revitalisation and sowing seeds of confidence, local empowerment, intermediaries, and agents of order, as well as reinforced traditional methods of policing, have emerged as the central intersection of contemporary policy making. As international events have moved on since we started editing this collection we have found ever stronger connections between a widening 'war on terror' and the micro-conditions of neighbourhoods and urban spaces that have been cast as the breeding grounds for disaffection and resistance. In this sense it would seem that the way in which city futures and public intervention are cast will be fundamentally affected by the continuing linkages made between how we run, improve, and serve local communities and a much broader politics of conduct and citizenship.

In gathering these essays we became ever more convinced that the way in which cities have been seen as sites of disaffection, economic malaise, and exclusion have spurred some of the strongest and deepest of interventions. These have been designed to reform, mould, and otherwise discipline those who are seen as being outside a community of respectable citizens. The complex social systems and pathways of causation that have led to many of these problems are often difficult to trace and yet many of our contributors have shown how an uneven approach, the criminalisation of the already excluded, a populist politics, and, ultimately, a judgemental and punitive series of policy efforts have often exacerbated such problems. None of this is to say that strands of the government's various efforts have not been effective or, indeed, welcomed by many communities. Rather, the hope of many of these communities is likely to be let down by the political realities of media machines and a public politics that continues to condemn rather than to understand and that leaves higher-income households apart from these communities and insulated them from their problems.

In conclusion we would suggest that while regeneration, policing, and disorder have become an explicit and interlinked policy agenda, the roots of such connections go deep into British urban history. For this reason, and others we have sketched here, it seems unlikely that future attempts at remaking, revitalising, and otherwise rebuilding British cities will turn away from the value of tracing out these connections. In the move from a concern with 'renaissance' to 'sustainability' the shifting watchwords of government machines belie a continued relationship with much older fundamentals – including the market orientation towards service delivery. This appears to imply a new kind of vengeful urbanism as communities who can withdraw only to articulate the need for the remote control and punishment of those that make them feel afraid. Meanwhile, those trapped in social housing or distant from economic opportunity are likely to continue to be bypassed by the new opportunities of a growing economy, vilified in ritualised media investigations and subject to new rules of conduct and required engagement. These double-standards seem unlikely to be subject to scrutiny in the kind of urban politics being played out where short memories and self-interest remain critical. Just as regional centres and urban spaces are playing a revitalised role in the British economy and have been lifted by arts and other creative enterprises it would seem that many of these benefits have continued to accrue for affluent newcomers and existing higher-income households. Such improvements appear, then, as a rather superficial renaissance and one geared towards gentrifiers rather than costly welfare dependents. If such shallowness has often appeared a hallmark of media-hungry sound-bite politics we might only express the hope for more analysis, public critique, and informed assessment in order that a deeper and more socially equitable renaissance is achieved in the future as well as one that delivers safety for more than a select citizenry.

References

Aberdeen City Council (2004) 'Street Begging Report', Report of Community Services Committee, 14 September, ref: csc5abx\hc\2.

ACPO (Association of Chief Police Officers) (2005) *Guidance on police community support officers (PCSOs)* (rev edn), London: ACPO of England, Wales and Northern Ireland.

Agamben, G. (1998) *Homo sacer: Sovereign power and bare life*, Stanford, CA: Stanford University Press.

Agamben, G. (2005) *States of exclusion*, Chicago, IL: University of Chicago Press.

Allan, C. (2003) *Fair justice? The Bradford disturbances, the sentencing and the impact*, Bradford: FAIR.

Amin, A. and Graham, S. (1997) 'The ordinary city', *Transactions Institute of British Geographers*, no 22, pp 411-29.

Amin, A., Massey, D. and Thrift, N. (2000) *Cities for the many not the few*, Bristol: The Policy Press.

Archibold, R (2006) 'Please don't feed homeless in parks, Las Vegas says in ordinance', *New York Times*, p A1, 28 July,

Armstrong, K. (2001) *The battle for God: Fundamentalism in Judaism, Christianity and Islam*, London: HarperCollins.

Atkinson, R. (2003) 'Domestication by cappuccino or a revenge on urban space? Control and empowerment in the management of public spaces', *Urban Studies*, vol 40, no 9, pp 1211-45.

Atkinson, R. (2004) 'The evidence on the impact of gentrification: new lessons for the urban renaissance?', *European Journal of Housing Policy*, vol 4, no 1, pp 107-31.

Atkinson, R. (2006) 'Padding the bunker: strategies of middle-class disaffiliation and colonisation in the city', *Urban Studies*, vol 43, no 4, pp 819-32.

Atkinson, R. and Bridge, G. (2005) *Gentrification in a global perspective*, London: Routledge.

Atkinson, R. and Flint, J. (2002) *Neighbourhood boundaries, social disorganisation and social exclusion*, Colchester: ESRC Data Archive.

Atkinson, R. and Flint, J. (2004) 'Order born of chaos? The capacity for informal social control in disempowered and "disorganised" neighbourhoods', *Policy & Politics*, vol 32, no 3, pp 333-50.

Atkinson, R., Blandy, S., Flint, J. and Lister, D. (2005) 'Gated cities of today? Barricaded residential development in England', *Town Planning Review*, vol 76, no 4, pp 417-37.

Baeten, G. (2002) 'Hypochondriac geographies of the city and the new urban dystopia: coming to terms with the other city', *City*, vol 6, no 1, pp 103-15.

Bain (1997) Letter dated 15 December from Edward Bain, Council Solicitor, City of Edinburgh Council to M. Baxter, Home Department, Scottish Office, ref: EB/JW.

Ball, K. and Webster, F. (eds) (2003) *The intensification of surveillance: Crime, terrorism and warfare in the information age*, London: Pluto Press.

Bannister, J., Fyfe, N. and Kearns, A. (2006) 'Respectable or respectful? (In)civility and the city', *Urban Studies*, vol 43, nos 5/6, pp 919-37.

Baxter (1997) Letter dated 29 September from M. Baxter, Home Department, Scottish Office to Edward Bain, Council Solicitor, City of Edinburgh Council, ref: HPK0021097.

Baxter (1998) Letter dated 4 February from M. Baxter, Home Department, Scottish Office to Edward Bain, Council Solicitor, City of Edinburgh Council, ref: HPK00102.028.

BBC Online (2006) *Fight crime, cleaners told* (www.bbc.co.uk/news, 17/05/06).

Beck, U. (2002) 'The terrorist threat: world risk society revisited', *Theory, Culture and Society*, vol 19, no 4, pp 39-55.

Belina, B. and Helms, G. (2003) 'Zero tolerance for the industrial past and other threats: policing and urban entrepreneurialism in Britain and Germany', *Urban Studies*, vol 40, no 9, pp 1845-67.

BIBIC (British Institute for Brain Injured Children) (2005) *Ain't misbehavin': Young people with learning and communication difficulties and anti-social behaviour*, November, Campaign Update, Bridgwater: BIBIC.

Blair, I. (1998) 'The governance of security: Where do the police fit into policing?', Paper presented at the Association of Chief Police Officers Annual Conference, National Exhibition Centre, Birmingham, 16 July.

Blair, I. (2003) 'Surprise news: policing works: a new model of patrol', Paper presented at In Search of Security: International Conference on Policing and Security, Montreal, Canada (www.met.police.uk/campaigns/policingworks.htm, 6/06/05).

Blair, T. (1997) 'Welfare reform: giving people the will to win', Speech delivered at the Aylesbury Estate, Southwark, London, 2 June.

Blair, T. (2001) 'Improving your local environment', Speech at Groundwork UK Seminar, Fairfield Hall, Croydon, 24 April.

Blair, T. (2002) 'New Labour and community', *Renewal*, vol 12, no 2, pp 9-14.

Blair, T. (2004) 'A new consensus on law and order', Speech by the Prime Minister at the launch of the Home Office and Criminal Justice System strategic plans, 19 July, London: Cabinet Office.

Blair, T. (2006a) 'PM's *Respect Action Plan* launch speech' (www.number10.gov.uk\output\Page8898.as, 9/01/07).

Blair, T. (2006b) Speech by the Prime Minister at the launch of the *Respect Action Plan*, 10 January, London: Cabinet Office.

Blair, T. (2006c) Speech to the Scottish Labour Party Conference, Aviemore, 24 February.

Blakely, E. J. and Snyder, M. G. (1999) *Fortress America: Gated communities in the United States*, Washington, DC: The Brookings Institution.

Blunkett, D. (1999) 'The welfare society', Speech to Demos, London: Demos, 19 May.

BMA (British Medical Association) (2006) *Child and adolescent mental health: A guide for healthcare professionals*, London: BMA Board of Science.

Boal, F.W. (1975) 'Belfast 1980: a segregated city?', *Graticule*, Department of Geography, Queen's University of Belfast Press.

Boddy, M. and Parkinson, M. (eds) (2004) *City matters: Competitiveness, cohesion and urban governance*, Bristol: The Policy Press.

Bondi, L. (1998) 'Sexing the city', in R. Fincher and J. Jacobs (eds) *Cities of difference*, New York: Guilford.

Boudreau, J. and Keil, R. (2001) 'Seceding from responsibility? Secession movements in Los Angeles', *Urban Studies*, vol 38, no 10, pp 1701-31.

Brown, A. (2004) 'Anti-social behaviour, crime control and social control', *Howard Journal of Criminal Justice*, vol 43, no 2, pp 203-11.

BSIA (British Security Industry Association) (2005) 'Industry statistics' (www.bsia.co.uk, 12/06/05).

Buonfino, A. and Mulgan, G. (2006) *Porcupines in winter: The pleasures and pains of living together in modern Britain*, London: The Young Foundation.

Burke, R.H. (1998) 'A contextualisation of zero tolerance policing strategies', in R.H. Burke (ed) *Zero tolerance policing*, Cambridge: Perpetuity Press.

Burney, E. (2005) *Making people behave: Anti-social behaviour, politics and policy*, Cullompton: Willan Publishing.

Bursik, R. J. (1988) 'Social disorganization and theories of crime and delinquency', *Criminology*, no 26, pp 519-51.

Cameron, S.C. and Coaffee, J. (2005) 'Art, gentrification and regeneration – from artist as pioneer to public arts', *European Journal of Housing Policy*, vol 5, no 1, pp 39-58.

Campbell, B. (1993) *Goliath: Britain's dangerous places*, London: Virago.

Campbell, D. (1982) *War plan UK*, London: Burnett Books.

Campbell, S. (2002) *A review of Anti-Social Behaviour Orders*, London: Home Office.

CDP (Community Development Project) (1973) *The National Community Development Project: Inter-project report*, London: CDP Intelligence Unit.

Champion, T. and Fisher, T. (2004) 'Migration, residential preferences and the changing environment of cities', in M. Boddy and M. Parkinson (eds) *City matters: Competitiveness, cohesion and urban governance*, Bristol: The Policy Press, pp 111-28.

Chatterton, P. (2002) 'Governing nightlife: profit, fun and (dis)order in the contemporary city', *Entertainment Law*, vol 1, no 2, pp 23-49.

Cheshire, P (2006) 'Resurgent cities, urban myths and policy hubris: what we need to know', *Urban Studies*, vol 8, no 43, pp 1231-46.

Clarke, C. (2005a) 'We will reinforce a culture of respect', Speech by the Home Secretary to the Labour Party Conference, Brighton, 27 September.

Clarke, C. (2005b) 'Foreword', in *Neighbourhood policing*, London: The Stationery Office.

Clarke, J. and Glendinning, C. (2002) 'Partnership and the remaking of welfare governance', in C. Glendinning, M. Powell and K. Rummery (eds) *Partnerships, New Labour and the governance of welfare*, Bristol: The Policy Press, pp 33-50.

Clarke, R. and Mayhew, P (eds) (1980) *Designing out crime*, London: HMSO.

Cleland, A. and Tisdall, K. (2005) 'The challenge of anti-social behaviour: new relationships between the state, children and parents', *Journal of Law, Policy and the Family*, vol 19, no 3, pp 395-420.

Coaffee, J. (2003a) *Terrorism, risk and the city*, Aldershot: Ashgate.

Coaffee, J. (2003b) 'Morphing the counter-terrorist response: beating the bombers in London's financial heart', *Knowledge, Technology and Power*, vol 16, no 2, pp 63-83.

Coaffee, J. (2004) 'Rings of steel, rings of concrete and rings of confidence: designing out terrorism in central London pre and post 9/11', *International Journal of Urban and Regional Research*, vol 28, no 1, pp 201-11.

Cohen, S. (1972) *Folk devils and moral panics: The creation of Mods and Rockers*, London: MacGibbon & Kee.

Cohen, S. (1979) 'Community control: a new utopia', *New Society*, pp 609-11, 15 March.

Cohen, S. (1985) *Visions of social control*, Cambridge: Polity Press.

Cohen, S. (2002) *Folk devils and moral panics* (3rd edn), London and New York, NY: Routledge.

Cole, I. and Nevin, B. (2004) *The road to renewal: The early development of the Housing Market Renewal Programme in England*, York: Joseph Rowntree Foundation.

Coleman, R. (2004a) *Reclaiming the streets: Surveillance, social control and the city*, Cullompton: Willan Publishing.

Coleman, R. (2004b) 'Watching the degenerate: street camera surveillance and regeneration', *Local Economy*, no 19, pp 199-211.

Coleman, R. and Sim, J. (2000) 'You'll never walk alone: CCTC surveillance, order and neo-liberal rule in Liverpool city centre', *British Journal of Sociology*, no 51, pp 623-39.

Coleman, R. and Sim, J. (2002) 'Power, politics and partnerships: the state of crime prevention on Merseyside', in G. Hughes and A. Edwards (eds) *Crime control and community: The new politics of public safety*, Cullompton: Willan Publishing.

Coleman, R. and Sim, J. (2005) 'Contemporary statecraft and the "punitive obsession": a critique of the new penology thesis', in J. Pratt, D. Brown, M. Brown, S. Hallsworth and W. Morrison (eds) *The new punitiveness: Trends, theories, perspectives*, Cullompton: Willan Publishing.

Coleman, R., Tombs, S. and Whyte, D. (2005) 'Capital, crime control and statecraft in the entrepreneurial city', *Urban Studies*, vol 42, no 13, pp 2511-30.

Coligan, N. (2006) 'Residents' fury as YMCA shelter plan is approved', *Liverpool Echo* (http://icliverpool.icnetwork.co.uk/0100news/0100regionalnews/tm_method=full%26objectid=16598950%26sit eid=50061-name_page.html, 18 January).

Collins, M. (2004) *The likes of us: A biography of the white working class*, London: Granta.

Commission on Social Justice (1994) *Social justice: Strategies for national renewal*, London: Vintage.

Cooke, C.A. (2005) 'Issues concerning visibility and reassurance provided by the new "policing family"', *Journal of Community and Applied Social Psychology*, no 15, pp 229-40.

Cossar (2006) Letter dated 10 January from Anna Cossar, Policy Advisor, Justice Department, Criminal Law Division, Scottish Executive to Councillor Martin Greig, Chair Safer Aberdeen Task Group, ref: CPA/1/16.

Counsell, D., Haughton, G, Allmendinger, P. and Vigar, G. (2003) 'New directions in UK strategic planning: from development plans to spatial development strategies', *Town and Country Planning*, no 72, pp 15-19.

Cowans, J. and Sparks, L. (2003) 'JRF consultation response to ODPM on the *Planning policy guidance note 3: Housing – Influencing the size, type and affordability of housing*, Prepared by Julie Cowans in collaboration with Les Sparks, October 2003' (www.jrf.org.uk/knowledge/responses/docs/influencingthesizeofhousing.asp, October).

Crawford, A. (1997) *The local governance of crime, appeals to community and partnership*, Oxford: Clarendon Press/London: Longman.

Crawford, A. (1998) *Crime prevention and community safety: Politics, policies, and practices*, London: Longman.

Crawford, A. (2003) '"Contractual governance" of deviant behaviour', *Journal of Law and Society*, vol 30, no 4, pp 479-505.

Crawford, A. (2006) '"Fixing broken promises?": neighbourhood wardens and social capital', *Urban Studies*, vol 43, nos 5/6, pp 957-76.

Crawford, A. and Lister, S. (2004) *The extended policing family: Visible patrols in residential areas*, York: Joseph Rowntree Foundation.

Crawford, A., Lister, S. and Wall, D. (2003) *Great expectations: Contracted policing in New Earswick*, York: Joseph Rowntree Foundation.

Crawford, A., Blackburn, S., Lister, S. and Shepherd, P. (2005) *Patrolling with a purpose: An evaluation of police community support officers in Leeds and Bradford City Centres*, Leeds: CCJS Press, School of Law, University of Leeds.

Crawford, A., Lister, S., Blackburn, S. and Burnett, J. (2005) *Plural policing: The mixed economy of visible patrols in England and Wales*, Bristol: The Policy Press.

CRESR (Centre for Regional, Economic and Social Research) (2005) *New Deal for Communities 2001-05: An interim evaluation*, London: ODPM.

Cresswell, T. (2001) 'The production of mobilities', *New Formations*, no 43, pp 11-25.

Criminal Justice Research Programme (2003) *Research Findings No 68 – Liquor licensing and public disorder: Review of literature on the impact of licensing and other controls, and audit of local initiatives*, Edinburgh: Scottish Executive.

Crosland, A. (1956) *The future of socialism*, London: Cape.

Crowther, C. (2004) 'Over-policing and under-policing social exclusion', in R. Hopkins-Burke (ed) *Hard cop, soft cop: Dilemmas and debates in contemporary policing*, Cullompton: Willan Publishing, pp 54-68.

Cullen, J.B. and Levitt, S.D. (1999) 'Crime, urban flight and the consequences for cities', *The Review of Economics and Statistics*, vol 81, no 2, pp 159-69.

Cummins, D. (2005) 'Introduction', in C.O'Malley and S.Waiton, *Who's antisocial? New Labour and the politics of antisocial behaviour*, Occasional Paper no 2, London: Institute of Ideas.

Currie, E. (2002) 'Social crime prevention strategies in a market society', in E. McLaughlin, J. Muncie and G. Hughes (eds) *Criminological perspectives: Essential readings* (2nd edn), London: Sage Publications.

Dabinett, G., Lawless, P., Rhodes, J. and Tyler, P. (2001) *A review of the evidence base for regeneration policy and practice*, London: DETR.

Damer, S. (1989) *From Moorepark to 'Wine Alley': The rise and fall of a Glasgow housing scheme*, Edinburgh: Edinburgh University Press.

Danziger, N. (1996) *Danziger's Britain: A journey to the edge*, London: HarperCollins.

Davies, N. (1997) *Dark heart: The shocking truth about hidden Britain*, London: Chatto & Windus.

Davis, M. (1990) *City of quartz: Excavating the future in Los Angeles*, London: Verso.

Dear, M. (2000) *The postmodern urban condition*, Oxford: Blackwell.

Dear, M. and Flusty, S. (1998) 'Postmodern urbanism', *Annals of the Association of American Geographers*, vol 88, no 1, pp 50-72.

DEFRA (Department for Environment, Food and Rural Affairs) (2005) *Securing the future: Delivering the UK sustainable development strategy*, London: DEFRA.

de Lint, W. and Virta, S. (2004) 'Security in ambiguity: towards a radical security politics', *Theoretical Criminology*, vol 8, no 4, pp 4564-89.

Dench, G. (1986) *Minorities in the open society: Prisoners of ambivalence*, London: Routledge & Kegan Paul.

DETR (Department of the Environment, Transport and the Regions) (1999a) *Towards an urban renaissance* (www.regeneration.detlr.gov.uk/utf/renais/1.htm, 31/10/01).

DETR (1999b) *A better quality of life: A strategy for sustainable development for the UK*, London: The Stationery Office.

DETR (2000) *Our towns and cities – The future: Delivering an urban renaissance*, London: The Stationery Office.

Dodd, T., Nicholas, S., Povey, D. and Walker, A. (2004) *Crime in England and Wales 2003/04*, Home Office Statistical Bulletin, London: Home Office.

Donnison, D. (1995) 'Crime and urban policy: a strategic approach to crime and insecurity', in C. Fijnaut, J. Goethals and I. Walgrave (eds) *Changes in society, crime and criminal justice in Europe*, The Hague: Kluwer.

Douglas-Hamilton (1996) Letter dated 29 August from Minister of State James Douglas-Hamilton, Scottish Office, to Councillor J. L. Walls, City of Edinburgh Council, ref: RB24086.

Eames, M. and Adebowale, M. (eds) (2002) *Sustainable development and social inclusion: Towards an integrated approach to research*, York: Joseph Rowntree Foundation/York Publishing Services.

Edinburgh (1997a) Item no 13, City of Edinburgh Council, Economic Development Committee, Urban Regeneration Sub-Committee, Social Exclusion.

Edinburgh (1997b) Item no 8.7, City of Edinburgh Council, Motion, Social Exclusion.

Edinburgh (1998a) 'Proposed byeLaw – legal issues', City of Edinburgh Council, Prepared by the Director of Corporate Services, 21 May, ref:5EB03540.

Edinburgh (1998b) Appendix 5 'Crime and incident trends', City of Edinburgh Council, Strategic Policy 0092/SP/IF.

Edinburgh (1998c) Item 7.6 – 'City centre inter-agency stage 1', Meeting of Full Council, Thursday 28 May.

Edinburgh (1998d) *Managing Edinburgh's city centre*, 28 May.

Edwards, A. (2005) 'Governance', in E. McLaughlin and J. Muncie (eds) *The Sage dictionary of criminology* (2nd edn), London: Sage Publications.

Enns, D. (2004) 'Bare life and the occupied body', *Theory & Event*, no 7, p 3.

Ericson, R. and Haggerty, D. (1997) *Policing the risk society*, Oxford: Clarendon Press.

Esping-Andersen, G. (1990) *The three worlds of welfare capitalism*, Cambridge: Polity.

Etzioni, A. (1993) *The spirit of community*, New York, NY: Crown Publishing.

Etzioni, A. (1997) *The new golden rule*, London: Profile Books.

Etzioni, A. (1998) *The new golden rule: Community and morality in a democratic society*, New York, NY: Basic Books.

European Commissioner for Human Rights (2005) *Report of the European Commissioner for Human Rights on his visit to the UK*, Brussels: European Commission.

Farish, M. (2003) 'Disaster and decentralization: American cities and the Cold War', *Cultural Geographies*, vol 10, no 2, pp 125-48.

Farrington, D. (1992) 'Criminal career research in the United Kingdom', *British Journal of Criminology*, vol 32, no 4, pp 521-36.

Farrington, D. and Coid, J. (2003) *Early prevention of adult antisocial behaviour*, Cambridge: Cambridge University Press.

Feldman, L (2004) *Citizens without shelter: Homelessness, democracy, and political exclusion*, Ithaca, NY: Cornell University Press.

Field, F. (2003) *Neighbours from hell: The politics of behaviour*, London: Politico's.

Fine, B. (2001) *Social capital versus social theory*, London: Routledge.

Flint, J. (2002) 'Social housing agencies and the governance of anti-social behaviour', *Housing Studies*, vol 17, no 4, pp 619-37.

Flint, J. (2003) 'Housing and ethopolitics: constructing identities of active consumption and responsible community', *Economy and Society*, vol 32, no 3, pp 611-29.

Flint, J. (ed) (2006) *Housing, urban governance and anti-social behaviour*, Bristol: The Policy Press.

Flint, J. and Kearns, A. (2005) *Evaluation study of Reidvale Housing Association Community Policing Initiative: Final Report*, Glasgow: Reidvale Housing Association.

Florida, R. (2004) *Cities and the creative class*, New York, NY: Routledge.

Flusty, S. (1994) 'Building paranoia: the proliferation of interdictory space and the erosion of spatial justice', *Los Angeles Forum for Architecture and Urban Design*, no 11.

Fooks, G. and Pantazis, C. (1999) 'The criminalisation of homelessness, begging and street living', in P. Kennett and A. Marsh (eds) *Homelessness: Exploring the new terrain*, Bristol: The Policy Press, pp 123-59.

Ford, C. (2005) 'Conference good for North, says Labour', *Sunday Sun* (http://icnewcastle.icnetwork.co.uk/sundaysun/news/tm_method=full%26objectid=15162012%26siteid=50081-name_page.html, 6 February).

Foucault, M. (1991) 'Governmentality', in G. Burchell, C. Gordon and P. Miller (eds) *The Foucault effect: Studies in governmentality*, Hemel Hempstead: Harvester Wheatsheaf.

Fox, S. (1996) 'Beyond *War Plan UK*: civil defence in the 1980s', *Subterranea Britannica* (www.subbrit.org.uk/rsg/features/beyond/, 1/01/07).

Furedi, F. (2005) *Politics of fear: Beyond left and right*, London: Continuum Press.

Fyfe, N. and Bannister, J. (1996) 'City watching: CCTV surveillance in public spaces', *Area*, no 28, pp 37-46.

Fyfe, N., Bannister, J. and Kearns, A. (2006) '(In)civility and the city', *Urban Studies*, vol 43, nos 5/6, pp 853-61.

Gamble, A (1988) *The free economy and the strong state: The politics of Thatcherism*, London: Macmillan.

Garafalo, J. and Laub, J. (1978) 'The fear of crime: broadening our perspective', *Victimology*, no 3, pp 242-53.

Garland, D. (1996) 'The limits of the sovereign state: strategies of crime control in contemporary society', *British Journal of Criminology*, vol 36, no 4, pp 445-71.

Garland, D. (2000) 'The cultures of high crime societies: some preconditions of recent "law and order" policies', *British Journal of Criminology*, vol 40, pp 347-75.

Garland, D. (2001) *The culture of control*, New York, NY: Oxford University Press.

Garland, D. (2002) 'Of crimes and criminals: the development of criminology in Britain', in M. Maguire, R. Morgan and R. Reiner (eds) *The Oxford handbook of criminology* (3rd edn), Oxford: Oxford University Press.

Gilling, D. (2001) 'Community safety and social policy', *European Journal on Criminal Policy and Research*, vol 9, no 4, pp 381-400.

Gilling, D. and Barton, A. (1997) 'Crime prevention and community safety: a new home for social policy?', *Critical Social Policy*, no 17, pp 63-83.

GLA (Greater London Authority) (2002) *SDS technical report six – Late-night London: Planning and managing the late-night economy*, London: GLA.

GLA (2005) *The London anti-social behaviour strategy 2005-2008*, London: GLA.

Glassner, B. (1999) *The culture of fear*, New York, NY: Basic Books.

Glennerster, H., Lupton, R., Noden, P. and Power, A. (1998) *Poverty, social exclusion and neighbourhood: Studying the area bases of social exclusion*, CASEpaper 22, London: Centre for Analysis of Social Exclusion, London School of Economics and Political Science.

Godschalk, D. (2003) 'Urban hazard mitigation: creating resilient cities', *Natural Hazards Review*, vol 4, no 3, pp 136-43.

Gold, B. (2004) *CCTV and policing: Public area surveillance and policy practices in Britain*, Oxford: Oxford University Press.

Gold, J.R. and Revill, G. (2000) 'Landscapes of defence', *Landscape Research*, vol 24, no 3, pp 229-39.

Gold, R. (1970) 'Urban violence and contemporary defensive cities', *Journal of the American Institute of Planning*, no 36, pp 146-59.

Goldson, B. (2002) 'New punitiveness: the politics of child incarceration', in J. Muncie, G. Hughes and E. McLaughlin (eds) *Youth justice: Critical readings*, London: Sage Publications, pp 386-410.

Gomien, D., David, H. and Leo, Z. (1996) *Law and practise of the European Convention on Human Rights and the European Social Charter*, Germany: Council of Europe.

Goodhart, D. (2006) 'National anxieties', *Prospect*, June, pp 30-5.

Gordon, D. and Pantazis, C. (eds) (1997) *Breadline Britain in the 1990s*, Aldershot: Ashgate.

Graham, S. (2002) 'September 11th and the "War on Terrorism": one year on', in 'Special collection: reflections on cities' [special issue], *International Journal of Urban and Regional Research*, vol 26, no 3, pp 589-90.

Graham, S. (2006) '"Homeland insecurities": Katrina and the politics of "security" in metropolitan America', *Space and Culture*, vol 9, no 3, pp 63-7.

Graham, S. and Marvin, S. (2001) *Splintering urbanism: Networked infrastructures, technological mobilities and urban condition*, London: Routledge.

Green, H., McGinnity, A., Meltzer, H., Ford, T. and Goodman, R. (2005) *Mental health in children and young people in Great Britain*, Office for National Statistics, Basingstoke: Palgrave Macmillan.

Grier, A. and Thomas, T. (2003) '"A war for civilisation as we know it": some observations on tackling anti-social behaviour', *Youth & Policy*, no 82, Winter, pp 1-15.

Hale, S. (2004) 'The communitarian "philosophy" of New Labour', in S. Hale, W. Leggett and L. Martell (eds) *The Third Way and beyond: Criticisms, futures and alternatives*, Manchester: Manchester University Press.

Hall, P. (1992) *Urban and regional planning* (3rd edn), London: Routledge.

Hall, P. (1997) 'Regeneration policies for peripheral housing estates: inward- and outward-looking approaches', *Urban Studies*, vol 34, nos 5/6, pp 873-90.

Hall, P. (1998) *Cities and civilisation*, London: Whitefield & Nicholson.

Hall, S. and Winlow, S. (2004) 'Barbarians at the gate: crime and violence in the breakdown of the pseudo-pacification process', in J. Ferrell, K. Hayward, W. Morrison and M. Presdee (eds) *Cultural criminology unleashed*, London: Glasshouse Press.

Hall, S. and Winlow, S. (2005) 'Anti-nirvana: crime, culture and instrumentalism in the age of insecurity', *Crime Media Culture*, vol 1, no 1, pp 31-48.

Hall, T. and Hubbard, P.J. (1998) 'Mapping the entrepreneurial city', in T.R. Hall and P.J. Hubbard (eds) *The entrepreneurial city: Geographies of politics, regime and representation*, Chichester: John Wiley.

Hall, T. and Miles, M. (2003) *City futures*, London: Routledge.

Hallsworth, S. (2002) 'Representations and realities in local crime prevention: some lessons from London and lessons for criminology', in G. Hughes and A. Edwards (eds) *Crime control and community: The new politics of public safety*, Cullompton: Willan Publishing.

Hancock, L. (2001) *Community, crime and disorder: Safety and regeneration in urban neighbourhoods*, Basingstoke: Palgrave.

Hancock, L. (2003) 'Urban regeneration and crime reduction: contradictions and dilemmas', in R. Matthews and J. Young (eds) *The new politics of crime and punishment*, Cullompton: Willan Publishing.

Hancock, L. (2006) 'Urban regeneration, young people, crime and criminalisation', in B. Goldson and J. Muncie (eds) *Youth crime and justice*, London: Sage Publications.

Hancock, L. and Matthews, R. (2001) 'Crime, community safety and toleration', in R. Matthews and J. Pitts (eds) *Crime, disorder and community safety*, London: Routledge.

Hansard (1999) HC vol 336, col 263, 27 July, London: The Stationery Office.

Hansard (2001) HC vol 366, col 696, 9 April, London: The Stationery Office.

Harcourt, B.E. (2001) *Illusion of order: The false promise of broken windows policing*, Cambridge, MA: Harvard University Press.

Harradine, S., Kodz, J., Lernetti, F. and Jones, B. (2004) *Defining and measuring anti-social behaviour*, Home Office Development and Practice Report 26, London: Home Office.

Harrigan, J. and Martin, P. (2002) 'Terrorism and the resilience of cities', *FRBNY Economic Policy Review*, vol 8, no 2, pp 97-116.

Hastings, A. (1997) *The construction of nationalism, ethnicity, religion and nation*, Cambridge: Cambridge University Press.

Hastings, A. (2003) 'Strategic, multi-level neighbourhood regeneration: an outward looking approach at last?', in R. Imrie and M. Raco (eds) *Urban renaissance? New Labour, community and urban policy*, Bristol: The Policy Press.

Hastings, A. and Dean, J. (2003) 'Challenging images: tackling stigma through estate regeneration', *Policy & Politics*, vol 31, no 2, pp 171-84.

Haubirch, D. (2006) 'The foreign v the domestic after September 11th: the methodology of political analysis revisited', *Policy*, vol 26, no 2, pp 84-92.

Haylett, C. (2001a) 'Illegitimate subjects? Abject whites, neoliberal modernisation and middle-class multi-culturalism', *Environment and Planning D: Society and Space*, no 19, pp 351-70.

Haylett, C. (2001b) 'Modernization, welfare and "third way" politics: limits to theorizing in "thirds"?', *Transactions of the Institute of British Geographers*, NS vol 26, no 1, pp 43-56.

Haylett, C. (2003) 'Culture, class and urban policy: reconsidering equality', *Antipode*, vol 35, no 1, pp 55-73.

Hayward, K. (2002) 'The vilification and pleasures of youthful transgression', in J. Muncie, G. Hughes and E. McLaughlin (eds) *Youth justice: Critical readings*, London: Sage Publications.

Hayward, K. (2004) *City limits: Crime, consumer culture and the urban experience*, London: The Glasshouse Press.

Helms, G. (forthcoming) *Towards safe city centres? Remaking the spaces of an old-industrial city*, Aldershot: Ashgate.

Hennessey, P. (2005) 'Blair's baby ASBOs', *Daily Telegraph* (www.telegraph.co.uk/news/main.jhtml?xml=/news/2005/10/09/nasbo09.xml, 09/10/05).

Henstra, D., Kovacs, P., McBean, G. and Sweeting, R. (2004) 'Disaster resilient cities', Background paper, Institute for Catastrophic Loss Reduction, Infrastructure Canada (www.infrastructure.gc.ca/research-recherche/result/studies-rapports/rs11_e.shtml, 01/01/07).

Herbert, S. (2005) 'The trapdoor of community', *Annals of Association of American Geographers*, vol 95, no 4, pp 850-65.

Herbert, S. (2006) *Citizens, cops, and power: Recognizing the limits of community*, Chicago, IL: University of Chicago Press.

Hermer, J. (forthcoming) *Policing compassion: Begging, law and power in public spaces*, Oxford: Hart.

Hermer, J. and Mosher, J. (eds) (2002) *Disorderly people: Law and the politics of exclusion in Ontario*, Halifax: Fernwood Publishing.

Hetherington, P. (2005) 'Peripheral vision', *The Guardian*, 28 September.

Hill, D. (1994) *Citizens and cities: Urban policy in the 1990s*, Hemel Hempstead: Harvester Wheatsheaf.

HMIC (Her Majesty's Inspectorate of Constabulary) (2002) *Open all hours*, London: Home Office.

HMIC (2003) *Narrowing the gap: Police visibility and public reassurance: Managing public expectation and demand*, Edinburgh: Scottish Executive.

HMSO (2002a) *Police Reform Act 2002*, London: The Stationery Office.

HMSO (2002b) *Police Reform Bill*, London: The Stationery Office.

Hobbs, D., Hadfield, P., Lister, S. and Winlow, S. (2003) *Bouncers: Violence and governance in the night-time economy*, Oxford: Oxford University press.

Hobbs, D., Lister, S., Hadfield, P., Winlow, S. and Hall, S. (2000) 'Receiving shadows: governance and liminality in the night-time economy', *British Journal of Sociology*, vol 51, no 4 (December), pp 701-17.

Holden, A. and Iveson, K. (2003) 'Designs on the urban: New Labour's urban renaissance and the spaces of citizenship', *City*, vol 7, no 1, pp 57-72.

Home Office (2001) *Community cohesion: A report of the Independent Review chaired by Ted Cantle*, London: Home Office.

Home Office (2003) *Respect and responsibility – Taking a stand against anti-social behaviour*, Cm 5778, White Paper, London: The Stationery Office.

Home Office (2004a) 'Communities boosted by more than 1,500 extra community support officers', Home Office Press Release, 24 November.

Home Office (2004b) *Confident communities in a secure Britain: The Home Office strategic plan 2004-2008*, London: Home Office.

Home Office (2004c) *Building communities, beating crime: A better police service for the 21st century*, White Paper, London: The Stationery Office.

Home Office (2004d) *Building communities, beating crime: A better police service in the 21st century*, London: Home Office

Home Office (2004e) 'From neighbourhood policing to national security: ensuring the safety and protection of our communities', Home Office Press Release, 29 September.

Home Office (2005a) *Neighbourhood policing: Your police, your community, our commitment*, London: Home Office.

Home Office (2005b) *Consultation paper on standard powers for community support officers and a framework for the future development of powers*, London: Home Office.

Home Office (2005c) *Community support officers strength as at 30 June 2005 by Basic Command Unit*, London: Home Office.

Home Office (2005d) *Emerging findings and good practice from the community support officer evaluation*, London: Home Office.

Home Office (2005e) *Powers that may be designated on community support officers by a chief officer of police*, London: Home Office.

Home Office (2005f) *Guidance on publicising Anti-Social Behaviour Orders*, London: Home Office.

Home Office (2006a) *Respect Action Plan*, London: The Stationery Office.

Home Office (2006b) *The National Reassurance Policing Programme: A ten-site evaluation*, Findings 273, London: Home Office.

Home Office (2006c) *A coordinated prostitution policy and a summary of responses to Paying the Price*, London: The Stationery Office.

Hope, T. (1995) 'Community crime prevention', in M. Tonry and D.P. Farrington (eds) *Building a safer society: Strategic approaches to crime prevention, crime and justice: Volume 19*, Chicago, IL: Chicago University Press.

Hope, T. (1998) 'Community safety, crime and disorder', in A. Marlow and J. Pitts (eds) *Planning safer communities*, Lyme Regis: Russell House Publishing.

Hope, T. (1999) 'Privatopia on trial? Property guardianship in the suburbs', *Crime Prevention Studies*, no 10, pp 15-45.

Hope, T. (2000) 'Inequality and the clubbing of private security', in T. Hope and R. Sparks (eds) *Crime, risk and inequality*, London: Routledge, pp 83-106.

Hope, T. (2001a) 'Community, crime prevention in Britain: a strategic overview', *Criminal Justice*, vol 1, no 4, pp 421-39.

Hope, T. (2001b) 'Crime victimisation and inequality', in R. Matthews and J. Pitts (eds) *Crime, disorder and community safety*, London: Routledge.

Hopkins-Burke, R. (2004) 'Introduction', in R. Hopkins-Burke (ed) *Hard cop, soft cop: Dilemmas and debates in contemporary policing*, Cullompton: Willan Publishing, pp 1-22.

Hornby, M. (2006) '100 city jobs lost to India', *Liverpool Echo*, 13 January.

Hoskins, G. and Tallon, A. (2004) 'Promoting the "urban idyll": policies for city centre living', in C. Johnstone and M. Whitehead (eds) *New horizons in British urban policy: Perspectives on New Labour's urban renaissance*, Aldershot: Ashgate.

Hounslow Council (2004) 'Emergency planning' (www.hounslow.gov.uk/index/advice_and_benefits/emergency_planning.htm, 01/01/07).

House of Commons (2000) *Terrorism Act 2000*, London: The Stationery Office.

House of Commons (2001) *Anti-Terrorism, Crime and Security Act 2001*, London: The Stationery Office.

House of Commons (2004) *The Civil Contingencies Bill*, London: The Stationery Office.

House of Commons and ODPM (Office of the Deputy Prime Minister) (2003) *The evening economy and the urban renaissance: Twelfth report of session 2002-03*, London: The Stationery Office.

Hubbard, P. (1999) *Sex and the city: Geographies of prostitution in the urban West*, Chichester: Ashgate.

Hubbard, P. (2004) 'Revenge and injustice in the revanchist city: uncovering masculinist agendas', *Antipode*, vol 36, no 4, pp 665-86.

Huber, P.W. and Mills, M.P. (2002) 'How technology will defeat terrorism', *City Journal*, vol 12, no 1 (www.city-journal.org/html/12_1_how_tech.html, 01/01/07).

Hughes, G. (1998) *Understanding crime prevention: Social control, risk and late modernity*, Buckingham: Open University Press.

Hughes, G. (2002) 'Crime and disorder reduction partnerships: the future of community safety', in G. Hughes, E. McLaughlin and J. Muncie (eds) *Crime prevention and community safety: New directions*, London: Sage Publications.

Hughes, G. (2004) 'The community governance of crime, justice and safety: challenges and lesson-drawing', *British Journal of Community Justice*, vol 2, no 3, pp 7-20.

Hughes, G. (2006) 'Standing at the crossroads: community safety partnerships', *Criminal Justice Matters*, no 63, spring, pp 18-19.

Hughes, G. and Edwards, A. (eds) (2002) *Crime control and community: The new politics of public safety*, Cullompton: Willan Publishing.

Hughes, G. and McLaughlin, E. (2002) '"Together we'll crack it": partnership and the governance of crime prevention', in C. Glendinning, M. Powell and K. Rummery (eds) *Partnerships, New Labour and the governance of welfare*, Bristol: The Policy Press, pp. 149-66.

Hughes, G. and Mooney, G. (1998) 'Community', in G. Hughes (ed) *Imagining welfare futures*, London: Routledge, pp 55-102.

Hunt, T. (2005) *Building Jerusalem: The rise and fall of the Victorian city*, London: Phoenix Press.

Imrie, R. and Raco, M. (2003) 'Community and the changing nature of urban policy', in R. Imrie and M. Raco (eds) *Urban renaissance? New Labour, community and urban policy*, Bristol: The Policy Press, pp 3-36.

Imrie, R. and Thomas, H. (1995) 'Urban policy processes and the politics of urban regeneration', *International Journal of Urban and Regional Research*, no 19, pp 479-94.

Innes, M. (2004) 'Reinventing tradition? Reassurance, neighbourhood security and policing', *Criminal Justice*, vol 4, no 2, pp 151-71.

Innes, M. (2005) 'Why "soft" policing is hard: on the curious development of reassurance policing, how it became neighbourhood policing and what this signifies about the politics of police reform', *Journal of Community and Applied Social Psychology*, no 15, pp 156-9.

Innes, M. and Fielding, N. (2002) 'From community to communicative policing: "signal crimes" and the problem of public reassurance', *Sociological Research Online*, vol 7, no 2 (http://socresonline.org.uk/7/2/innes.html, 20/10/06).

Innes, M., Hayden, S., Lowe, T., Mackenzie, H., Roberts, C. and Twyman, L. (2004) *Signal crimes and reassurance policing*, Guildford: University of Surrey.

IPPR (Institute for Public Policy Research) (2000) *Housing united: The final report of the IPPR Forum on the Future of Social Housing*, London: IPPR.

IPPR (2006) *City people: City centre living in the UK*, London: IPPR.

Jacobs, J. (1984) *The death and life of great American cities* (2nd edn), London: Peregrine.

Jacobs, J. (1997) *The death and life of the great American cities*, New York, NY: Random House.

Jacobson, J., Millie, A. and Hough, M. (forthcoming) *Tackling anti-social behaviour: A critical review*, London: Institute for Criminal Policy Research, King's College London.

James, A. and James, A. (2001) 'Tightening the net: children, community and control', *British Journal of Sociology*, vol 52, no 2, pp 211-28.

James, Z. (2006) 'Policing space: managing new travellers in England', *The British Journal of Criminology*, no 46, pp 470-85.

Jeffs, T. (1997) 'Changing their ways: youth work and underclass theory', in R. MacDonald (ed) *Youth, the underclass and social exclusion*, London: Routledge, pp 153-66.

Jeffs, T. and Smith, M. (1996) 'Getting the dirtbags off the streets: curfews and other solutions to juvenile crime', *Youth and Policy*, no 52, pp 1-13.

Jessop, B. (1995) 'Towards a Schumpeterian workfare regime in Britain? Reflections on regulation, governance and welfare state', *Environment and Planning A*, no 27, pp 1613-26.

Johnson, M. (2006) 'Warning bells sound for prosperity on Merseyside', *The Daily Post*, 25 January.

Johnston, L. (2005) 'From "community" to "neighbourhood" policing: police community support officers and the "police extended family" in London', *Journal of Community and Applied Social Psychology*, no 15, pp 241-54.

Johnston, L. (2006) 'Diversifying police recruitment? The deployment of police community support officers in London', *The Howard Journal*, vol 45, no 4, pp 388-402.

Johnstone, C. (2004) 'Crime, disorder and the urban renaissance', in C. Johnstone and M. Whitehead (eds) *New horizons in British urban policy: Perspectives on New Labour's urban renaissance*, Aldershot: Ashgate.

Johnstone, C. and McWilliams, C. (2005) 'Urban policy and the city in the "new" Scotland', in G. Mooney and G. Scott (eds) *Exploring social policy in the 'new' Scotland*, Bristol: The Policy Press, pp 157-76.

Johnstone, C. and Whitehead, M. (eds) (2004) *New horizons in British urban policy: Perspectives on New Labour's urban renaissance*, Aldershot: Ashgate.

Jones, C. and Novak, T. (1999) *Poverty, welfare and the disciplinary state*, London: Routledge.

Jones, P. and Wilks-Heeg, S. (2004) 'Capitalising culture: Liverpool 2008', *Local Economy*, vol 19, no 4, pp 341-60.

Jones, T. and Newburn, T. (2001) *Widening access: Improving police relations with hard to reach groups*, Police Research Series Paper 138, London: Home Office.

Katz, C. (2001) 'Hiding the target: social reproduction in the privatized urban environment', in C. Minca (ed) *Postmodern geography: Theory and praxis*, Oxford: Blackwell, pp 93-110.

Kearns, A. and Turok, I. (2003) *Sustainable communities: Dimensions and challenges*, Liverpool: ESRC/ODPM Urban and Neighbourhood Studies Research Network.

Keith, M. (2005) *After the cosmopolitan? Multiculturalism and the future of racism*, London: Routledge.

Kelling, G.L. (1998) 'The evolution of broken windows', in M. Weatheritt (ed) *Zero tolerance policing: What does it mean and is it right for policing in Britain?*, London: Police Foundation.

Kelling, G.L. and Coles, M. (1998) *Fixing broken windows: Restoring order and reducing crime in our communities*, London: Martin Kessler Books.

Kerkin, K. (2003) 'Re-placing difference: planning and street sex work in a gentrifying area', *Urban Policy and Research*, vol 21, no 2, pp 137-49.

LaGrange, R., Ferraro, K. and Supancic, M. (1992) 'Perceived risk and fear of crime: role of social and physical incivilities', *Journal of Research in Crime and Delinquency*, vol 29, no 3, pp 311-34.

Lakoff, G. (2004) *Don't think of an elephant, know your value and frame the debate*, White River Junction, VT: Chelsea Green Publishing Co.

Lakoff, G. and Johnson, M. (1980) *Metaphors we live by*, Chicago, IL: University of Chicago Press.

Larsen, E.N. (1992) 'The politics of prostitution control: interest group politics in four Canadian cities', *International Journal of Urban and Regional Studies*, no 16, pp 169-87.

Law, A. and Mooney, G. (2006a) 'The maladies of social capital 1: the missing "capital" in theories of social capital', *Critique*, no 39, August, pp 127-43.

Law, A. and Mooney. G. (2006b) 'The maladies of social capital 2: resisting neo-liberal conformism', *Critique*, no 40, December, pp 253-68.

Law, A. and Mooney, G. (forthcoming) 'The maladies of social capital', *Critique*.

Laycock, G. (2005) 'Crime, science and evaluation', *Criminal Justice Matters*, no 62, winter, pp 10-11.

Lea, J. and Young, J. (1993) *What is to be done about law and order?* (2nd edn), London: Pluto Press.

Lee, P. and Nevin, B. (2003) 'Changing demand for housing: restructuring markets and public policy frameworks', *Housing Studies*, vol 18, no. 1, pp 65-86.

Lees, L. (2003a) 'The ambivalence of diversity and the politics of urban renaissance: the case of youth in downtown Portland, Maine', *International Journal of Urban and Regional Research*, no 27, pp 613-34.

Lees, L. (2003b) 'Visions of "urban renaissance": the Urban Task Force Report and the *urban White Paper*', in R. Imrie and M. Raco (eds) *Urban renaissance? New Labour, community and urban policy*, Bristol: The Policy Press.

Levitas, R. (1998) *The inclusive society? Social exclusion and New Labour*, Basingstoke: Macmillan.

Levitas, R. (2005) *The inclusive society?* (2nd edn), Oxford: Blackwell.

Lianos, M. and Douglas, M. (2000) 'Dangerization and the end of deviance: the institutional environment', *British Journal of Criminology*, no 40, pp 261-78.

Licensing Act 2003, England and Wales. London: The Stationery Office.

Lister, D. (1997) 'Beggars "ruining Edinburgh"', *The Independent*, p 3, 12 August.

Liverpool City Council (2005) *Licensing policy statement*, Liverpool: Liverpool City Council.

Loader, I. (2000) 'Plural policing and democratic governance', *Social and Legal Studies*, vol 9, no 3, pp 323-45.

LGA (Local Government Association) (2003a) *Emergency planning: A survey of top tier local authorities*, London: LGA Publications.

LGA (2003b) *Emergency planning for districts: A survey of district local authorities*, London: LGA Publications.

Lucus, K., Walker, G., Eames, M., Fay, H. and Poustie, M. (2004) *Environment and social justice: Rapid research and evidence review*, Final report, 8 December, London: Policy Studies Institute.

MacLeod, G. (2002) 'From urban entrepreneurialism to a revanchist city? On the spatial injustices of Glasgow's renaissance', *Antipode*, vol 34, no 3, pp 602-24.

MacLeod, G. and Ward, K. (2002) 'Spaces of utopia and dystopia: landscaping the contemporary city', *Geografiska Annaler: Series B, Human Geography*, vol 84, nos 3/4, pp 153-70.

McBeth, J. (1997) 'Capital's beggars needy or greedy?', *The Scotsman*, p 22, 23 June.

McLaughlin, E. (2002) '"Same bed, different dreams": postmodern reflections on crime prevention and community safety', in G. Hughes and A. Edwards (eds) *Crime control and community*, Cullompton: Willan Publishing.

McLaughlin, E. (2005) 'Forcing the issue: New Labour, new localism and the democratic renewal of police accountability', *The Howard Journal*, vol 44, no 5, pp 473-89.

Marcuse, P (1989) '"Dual city": a muddy metaphor for a quartered city', *International Journal of Urban and Regional Research*, vol 13, pp 697-707.

Marcuse, P. (2002) 'Urban form and globalization after September 11th: the view from New York', *International Journal of Urban and Regional Research*, vol 26, no 3, pp 596-606.

Marsh, A. (2004) 'The inexorable rise of the rational consumer? The Blair Government and the reshaping of social housing', *European Journal of Housing Policy*, vol 4, no 2, pp 185-207.

Matthews, R. (1992) 'Replacing broken windows: crime, incivilities and urban change', in R. Matthews and J. Young (eds) *Issues in realist criminology*, London: Sage Publications.

Matthews, R. (2003) 'Enforcing respect and reducing responsibility: a response to the White Paper on anti-social behaviour', *Community Safety Journal*, vol 2, no 4, pp 5-8.

Matthews, R. and Pitts, J. (eds) (2001) *Crime, disorder and community safety: A new agenda?*, London: Routledge.

May, T., Edmunds, M. and Hough, M. with Harvey, C. (1999) *Street business: The links between sex and drug markets*, Police Research Paper 118, London: Policing and Reducing Crime Unit, Home Office.

Meen, G., Gibb, K., Goody, J., McGrath, T. and Mackinnon, J. (2005) *Economic segregation in Britain: Causes, consequences and policy*, Bristol: The Policy Press.

Mersey Partnership (2005) 'Merseyside economic review 2005, summary' (http://merseyside.org.uk/, 01/01/07).

Merton, R. K. (1938) 'Social structure and anomie', *American Sociological Review*, no 3, pp 672-82.

Millie, A. and Herrington, V. (2005) 'Bridging the gap: understanding reassurance policing', *Howard Journal of Criminal Justice*, vol 44, no 1, pp 41-56.

Millie, A., Jacobson, J., Hough, M. and Paraskevopoulou, A. (2005) *Anti-social behaviour in London: Setting the context for the London anti-social behaviour strategy*, London: Greater London Authority.

Millie, A., Jacobson, J., McDonald, E. and Hough, M. (2005) *Anti-social behaviour strategies: Finding a balance*, Bristol/York: Joseph Rowntree Foundation/The Policy Press.

Mills, E.S. (2002) 'Terrorism and US real estate', *Journal of Urban Economics*, no 51, pp 198-204.

Mitchell, D. (1997) 'The annihilation of space by law: the roots and implications of anti-homeless laws in the United States', *Antipode*, vol 29, no 3, pp 303-35.

Mitchell, D. (2005) 'The SUV model of citizenship: floating bubbles, buffer zones, and the rise of the "purely atomic" individual', *Political Geography*, no 24, pp 77-100.

Monaghan, L. (2002) 'Regulating "unruly" bodies: work tasks, conflict and violence in Britain's night-time economy', *The British Journal of Sociology*, vol 53, no 3, pp 403-29.

Monaghan, L. (2004) 'Doorwork and legal risk: observations from an embodied ethnography', *Social and Legal Studies*, vol 13, no 4, pp 453-80.

Mooney, G. (1999) 'Urban "disorders"', in S. Pile, C. Brook and G. Mooney (eds) *Unruly cities?*, London: Routledge, pp 53-89.

Mooney, G. (2004) 'Cultural policy and urban transformation? Critical reflections on Glasgow, European City of Culture 1990', *Local Economy*, vol 19, no 4, pp 327-40.

Mooney, G. and Danson, M. (1997) 'Beyond "culture city": Glasgow as a "dual city"', in N. Jewson and S. MacGregor (eds) *Transforming cities*, London: Routledge, pp 73-87.

Moore, R. (2006) 'Can we save Oxford Street?', *Evening Standard*, p 13, 10 March.

Morrison, Z. (2003) 'Cultural justice and addressing "social exclusion": a case study of a Single Regeneration Budget project in Blackbird Leys, Oxford', in R. Imrie and M. Raco (eds) *Urban renaissance? New Labour, community and urban policy*, Bristol: The Policy Press, pp 139-61.

Muncie, J. (2003) *Youth and crime*, London: Sage Publications.

Murakami Wood, D. and Graham, S. (2006) 'Permeable boundaries in the software-sorted society: surveillance and the differentiation of mobility', in M. Sheller and J. Urry (eds) *Mobile technologies of the city*. London/New York: Routledge, pp 177-91.

Murray, C. (1990) *The emerging British underclass*, London: Institute of Economic Affairs.

Napo (2005) *Anti-Social Behaviour Orders: Analysis of the first six years – A briefing note for the launch of ASBO Concern, 7 April 2006*, London: ASBO Concern.

Neill, W.J.V., Fitzsimons, D.S. and Murtagh, B. (1995) *Reimaging the pariah city: Urban development in Belfast and Detroit*, Aldershot: Avebury.

Newburn, T (2001) 'The commodification of policing: security networks in the late modern city', *Urban Studies*, vol 38, nos 5-6, pp 829-48.

Newman, O. (1972a) *Defensible space: Crime prevention through urban design*, New York, NY: Macmillan.

Newman, O. (1972b) *Defensible space: People and design in the violent city*, London: Architectural Press.

NGI (NewcastleGateshead Initiative) (2005) 'Creative conferencing' (www.visitnewcastlegateshead.com/, 01/12/05).

Nicholas, S., Povey, D., Walker, A. and Kershaw, C. (2005) *Crime in England and Wales: 2004/2005*, London: Home Office.

Norris, C. and Armstrong, G. (1999) *The maximum surveillance society: The rise of CCTV*, Oxford: Berg.

Norris, C. and McCahill, M. (2006) 'CCTV: beyond penal modernism?', *The British Journal of Criminology*, no 46, pp 97-118.

Norris, C., McCahill, M. and Wood, D. (2004) 'Editorial: the growth of CCTV – a global perspective on the international diffusion of video surveillance in publicly accessible space', *Surveillance & Society*, vol 2, nos 2/3, pp 110-35 (www.surveillance-and-society.org/articles2(2)/editorial.pdf).

NRU (Neighbourhood Renewal Unit) (2002) *Factsheet 5: Neighbourhood wardens and street wardens*, London: ODPM.

NRU (2004) *Wardens' factsheet: Guidance for warden schemes on working with community support officers*, London: ODPM.

O'Malley, C. and Waiton, S. (2005) *Who's antisocial? New Labour and the politics of antisocial behaviour*, Occasional Paper no 2, London: Institute of Ideas.

O'Malley, P. (2000) 'Uncertain subjects: risks, liberalism and contract', *Economy and Society*, vol 29, no 4, pp 460-84.

OPDM (Office of the Deputy Prime Minister) (2000) *Our towns and cities: The future: Delivering an urban renaissance*, Presented to Parliament by the Deputy Prime Minister and Secretary of State for the Environment, Transport and the Regions by Command of Her Majesty, November, London: The Stationery Office.

ODPM (2002) *Living places: Cleaner, safer, greener*, London: ODPM.

ODPM (2003) *Sustainable communities: Building for the future*, London: The Stationery Office.

ODPM (2004a) *Planning policy statement 1: Delivering sustainable development*, London: The Stationery Office.

ODPM (2004b) *Civil resilience* (www.odpm.gov.uk/stellent/groups/ odpm_civilres/documents/sectionhomepage/odpm_civilres_page. hcsp, 01/10/05, page no longer available).

ODPM (2004c) *Safer places: The planning system and crime prevention*, London: The Stationery Office (www.communities.gov.uk/pub/724/ SaferPlacesThePlanningSystemandCrimePrevention_id1144724. pdf).

ODPM (2005a) *Sustainable communities: People, places and prosperity*, London: The Stationery Office.

ODPM (2005b) *State of the English cities*, London: ODPM.

ODPM (2005c) *Defining sustainable communities*, London: The Stationery Office.

ODPM (2005d) *The Mixed Communities Initiative: What is it?*, London: The Stationery Office.

ODPM (2005e) *Factsheet 3: How to guides on cleaner, safer, greener, spaces*, London: The Stationery Office.

ODPM (2005f) *The government's response to the ODPM Select Committee's eighth report on empty homes and low demand pathfinders*, London: UK Parliament.

ODPM (2005g) *Planning policy statement 1: Delivering sustainable development*, London: ODPM.

ODPM (2005h) *Citizen engagement and public services: Why neighbourhoods matter*, London: ODPM.

ODPM and Home Office (2004) *Safer places: The planning system and crime prevention*, London: The Stationery Office.

ODPM and Home Office (2005) *Safer and Stronger Communities Fund*, London: The Stationery Office.

Parenti, C. (1999) *Lockdown America*, London: Verso.

Parkinson, M., Champion, T., Evans, R., Simmie, J., Turok, I., Crookston, M. et al (2006) *State of the cities: A research study*, London: ODPM.

Paskell, C.A. and Power, A. (2005) *'The future's changed': Local impacts of housing, environment and regeneration policy since 1997*, CASEreport 29, London: Centre for Analysis of Social Exclusion, London School of Economics and Political Science.

Pawley, M. (1998) *Terminal architecture*, London: Reaktion.

PCRC (Privy Counsellor Review Committee) (2003) *Anti-Terrorism, Crime and Security Act 2001 Review Report*, London: The Stationery Office.

Pearson G. (1983) *Hooligan, a history of respectable fears*, London: Macmillan.

Peck, J. (2003) 'Geography and public policy: mapping the penal state', *Progress in Human Geography*, vol 27, no 2, pp 222-32.

Peck, J. (2005) 'Struggling with the creative class', *International Journal of Urban and Regional Research*, no 29, pp 740-70.

Peck, J. and Tickell, A. (2002) 'Neoliberalizing space', *Antipode*, vol 34, no 3, pp 380-404.

Pelling, M. (2003) *The vulnerability of cities: Natural disasters and social resilience*, London: Earthscan.

Phillips, M. (1998) 'Slums are not the problem: people are', *The Sunday Times*, 20 September.

Pinder, D. (2005) *Visions of the city: Utopianism, power and politics in twentieth-century urbanism*, Edinburgh: Edinburgh University Press; New York: Routledge.

Pitcher, J., Campbell, R., Hubbard, P., O'Neill, M. and Scoular, J. (2006) *Living and working in areas of street sex work: From conflict to coexistence*, Bristol: The Policy Press.

Podolefsky, A. and Dubow, F. (1981) *Strategies for community crime prevention: Collective responses to crime in urban America*, Springfield, IL: Charles C. Thomas.

Police Federation (2004) 'The Police Federation believes:...', *Police Federation News*, Issue 22 (November), p 3.

Police magazine (2005) 'Centre stage: interview with Sir Ian Blair', *Police: The Voice of the Service*, April, pp 12-15.

Poyner, B. (1983) *Design against CRIME: Beyond defensible space*, London: Butterworths.

Prime Minister's Questions (2006) *Hansard*, vol 447, part 170, col 1315.

PSUCD (Police Standards Unit and Crime Directorate) (2004) *Violent crime: Tackling violent crime in the night-time economy*, London: Home Office Communications Directorate.

Purdue, D. (2001) 'Neighbourhood governance: leadership, trust and social capital', *Urban Studies*, vol 38, no 12, pp 2211-24.

Putnam, R. (2001) *Bowling alone: The collapse and revival of American community*, New York, NY: Simon & Schuster.

Raco, M. (2003) 'Remaking place and securitising space: urban regeneration and the strategies, tactics and practices of policing in the UK', *Urban Studies*, vol 40, no 9, pp 1869-87.

Raco, M. (2005) 'Sustainable development, rolled-out neo-liberalism and sustainable communities', *Antipode*, no 37, pp 324-46.

Raco, M. (in press) 'Spatial policy, sustainability and state re-structuring: a re-assessment of sustainable community-building in England', in R. Krueger and D. Gibbs (eds) *Sustainable capitalism or capital sustainabilities?*, New York, NY: Guilford Press.

Raco, M. and Imrie, R. (2000) 'Governmentality and rights and responsibilities in urban policy', *Environment and Planning A*, no 32, pp 2187-204.

Reiner, R. (2000) *The politics of the police* (3rd edn), Oxford: Oxford University Press.

Reiner, R., Livingstone, S. and Allen, J. (2001) 'Casino culture: media, and crime in a winner–loser society', in K. Stenson and R.S. Sullivan (eds) *Crime, risk and justice: The politics of crime control in liberal democracies*, Cullompton: Willan Publishing.

Ritzer, G. (2000) *Modern sociological theory* (5th edn), London: McGraw-Hill.

Roberts, M. (2004) *Good practice in managing the evening and late night economy: A literature review from an environmental perspective*, London: Office of the Deputy Prime Minister.

Roberts, M. and Eldridge, A. (2005a) *Survey of corporate operators and national providers: Management of the evening and late night economies*, London: The Civic Trust (www.civictrust.org.uk/evening/EE%20 Operators%20Survey%20web.pdf, 10/03/06).

Roberts, M. and Eldridge, A. (2005b) *Management of the evening and late night economies: survey of corporate operators and national providers and survey of local managers in five selected 'hot spots'*, London: The Civic Trust (www.civictrust.org.uk/evening/Executive%20summary.pdf, 10/03/06).

Robson, G. and Butler, T. (2004) *London calling: The middle classes and the remaking of inner London*, Oxford: Berg.

Rogers, P. and Coaffee, J. (2005) 'Moral panics and urban renaissance: policy, tactics and youth in public space', *City*, vol 9, no 3, pp 321-40.

Rusk, J (2006a) 'Panhandling ban, free speech clash in Ontario appeal', *Globe and Mail*, p A 12, 28 February.

Rusk, J. (2006b) 'Safe Streets Act stifles free speech, court told', *Globe and Mail*, p A 10, 1 March.

Safir, H. and Whitman, E. (2003) *Security: Policing your homeland, your city, yourself*, New York, NY: Thomas Dunne Books.

Sagar, T. (2004) 'Street watch concept and practice: civilian participation in street prostitution control', *British Journal of Criminology*, vol 45, no 1, pp 98-112.

Sampson, R.J. and Grove, B. (1989) 'Community structure and crime', *American Journal of Sociology*, no 94, pp 774-802.

Sampson, R.J. and Raudenbush, S.W. (1999) 'Systematic social observation of public spaces: a new look at disorder in urban neighbourhoods', *American Journal of Sociology*, vol 105, no 3, pp 603-51.

Sampson, R.J., Raudenbush, S.W. and Earls, F. (1997) 'Neighbourhoods and violent crime: a multilevel study of collective efficacy', *Science*, no 277, pp 918-24.

Sanchez, L. (2004) 'The global e-rotic subject, the ban and prostitute free-zone', *Environment and Planning D – Society and Space*, vol 22, no 6, pp 861-83.

Savage, M., Bagnall, G. and Longhurst, B. (2005) *Globalisation and belonging*, London: Sage Publications.

Scarman, L. (1981) *Report into Brixton riots*, London: HMSO.

Schaefer, S. (1998) 'The 4,000 estates that shame Britain', *The Independent*, 16 September.

Scottish Executive (2003) *Tackling anti-social behaviour: An audit of Scottish local authority practice 2001-2002*, Edinburgh: Scottish Executive.

Scottish Executive (2006) *People and place: Regeneration policy statement*, Edinburgh: The Stationery Office.

Scoular, J. and O'Neill, M. (2006) 'Regulating prostitution: social inclusion, responsibilisation and the politics of prostitution reform', Draft paper [copy available from authors].

Sellin, T. (1938) *Culture, conflict and crime*, New York, NY: Social Science Research Council.

SEU (Social Exclusion Unit) (1998) *Bringing Britain together: A national strategy for neighbourhood renewal*, London: The Stationery Office.

SEU (1999) *Report of Policy Action Team 7: Unpopular housing*, London: Cabinet Office.

SEU (2000a) *National strategy for neighbourhood renewal: A framework for consultation*, London: Cabinet Office/SEU.

SEU (2000b) *Report of Policy Action Team 8: Anti-social behaviour*, London: SEU.

SEU (2001a) *A new commitment to neighbourhood renewal: National strategy action plan*, London: SEU, Cabinet Office.

SEU (2001b) *A new commitment to neighbourhood renewal: A national strategy action plan* (www.cabinet-office.gov.uk/seu/2001/Action%20Plan/contents.htm, 01/01/07).

Shaw, C.R. and McKay, H.D. (1942) *Juvenile delinquency and urban areas*, Chicago, IL: University of Chicago Press.

Shaw, K. (2004) *Liveability in NDC areas: Findings from six case studies – New Deal for Communities national evaluation, Research report 21*, Sheffield: CRESR.

Sheller, M. and Urry, J. (2006) 'The new mobilities paradigm', *Environment and Planning A*, no 38, pp 207-26.

Shilling, J. (2006) 'Two's company, three's antisocial?', *The Times*, p 8, 3 August.

Short, E. and Ditton, J. (1998) 'Seen and now heard: talking to the targets of open street CCTV', *British Journal of Criminology*, vol 38, no 3, pp 404-28.

Sibley, D. (1995) *Geographies of exclusion*, London: Routledge.

Simmons, J. and colleagues (2002) *Crime in England and Wales: 2001/2002*, London: Home Office.

Simon, J. (1997) 'Governing through crime', in G. Fisher and L. Friedman (eds) *The crime conundrum: Essays on criminal justice*, Boulder, CO & New York, NY: Westview Press, pp 171-90.

Singer, L. (2004) *Community support officer (detention power) pilot: Evaluation results*, London: Home Office.

Skeggs, B. (2005) 'The making of class and gender through visualising moral subject formation', *Sociology*, vol 39, no 5, pp 965-82.

Skogan, W.G. (1986) 'Fear of crime and neighbourhood change', in A.J. Reiss and M. Tonry (eds) *Communities and crime*, Chicago, IL: University of Chicago Press.

Skogan, W.G. (1988) 'Community organizations and crime', in M. Tonry and N. Morris (eds) *Crime and justice: A review of research: Volume 10*, Chicago, IL: University of Chicago Press.

Skogan, W.G. (1990) *Disorder and decline: Crime and the spiral of decay in American Neighbourhoods*, New York, NY: Free Press.

Slotterdijk, P. (1998) *Critique of cynical reason*, London: Verso.

Smith, C. (2006) 'UK visitor number slump after London bombings', *The Scotsman*, p 3, 21 February.

Smith, D. and Macnicol, J. (2001) 'Social insecurity and the informal economy', in R. Edwards and J. Glover (eds) *Risk and citizenship*, London: Routledge, pp 142-56.

Smith, N. (1996) *The new urban frontier: Gentrification and the revanchist city*, London: Routledge.

Smith, N. (1998) 'Giuliani time: the revanchist 1990s', *Social Text*, no 57, pp 1-20.

Smith, N. (2002) 'New globalism, new urbanism: gentrification as global urban strategy', *Antipode*, no 34, pp 427-49.

Smith, R. (2005) 'Lockdown!', *The Journal*, 28 January (Newcastle UK) (http://icnewcastle.icnetwork.co.uk/0100news/thejournal/tm_met hod=full%26objectid=15126087%26siteid=50081-name_page.html, 09/01/07).

Smithson, H. (2005) *Effectiveness of a dispersal order to reduce anti-social behaviour amongst young people: A case study approach in East Manchester*, London: Office of the Deputy Prime Minister.

Soja, E. (2000) *Postmetropolis: Critical studies of cities and regions*, Oxford: Blackwell.

Sorkin, M (1992) *Variations on a theme park: The new American city and the end of public space*, New York, NY: Hill and Wang.

Squires, P. (2006) 'New Labour and the politics of antisocial behaviour', *Critical Social Policy*, vol 26, no 1, pp 144-68.

Squires, P. and Stephen, D. (2005) 'Rethinking ASBOs', *Critical Social Policy*, vol 25, no 4, pp 517-28.

Squires, P. and Stephen, D. (2006) *Rougher justice: Anti-social behaviour and young people*, Cullompton: Willan Publishing.

SQW and Partners (2005) *Neighbourhood Management Programme: National evaluation annual review 2003/04*, London: ODPM.

Stedman-Jones, G. (1971) *Outcast London: A study in the relationships between classes in Victorian society*, Harmondsworth: Penguin Books; Oxford: Oxford University Press.

Stenson, K. (1991) 'Making sense of crime control', in K. Stenson and D. Cowell (eds) *The politics of crime control*, London: Sage Publications.

Stenson, K. (1998) 'Beyond histories of the present', *Economy and Society*, vol 29, no 4, pp 333-52.

Stenson, K. (2000a) 'Crime control, social policy and liberalism', in G. Lewis, S. Gewirtz and J. Clarke (eds) *Rethinking social policy*, London: Sage Publications.

Stenson, K. (2000b) 'Someday our prince will come: zero-tolerance policing and liberal government', in T. Hope and R. Sparks (eds) *Crime, risk and insecurity*, London: Routledge.

Stenson, K. (2001a) 'The new politics of crime control', in K. Stenson and R. R. Sullivan (eds) *Crime, risk and justice: The politics of crime control in liberal democracies*, Cullompton: Willan Publishing.

Stenson, K. (2001b) 'Reconstructing the government of crime', in G. Wickham and G. Pavlich (eds) *Rethinking law, society and governance: Foucault's Bequest*, Oxford: Hart, pp 93-108.

Stenson, K. (2005) 'Sovereignty, biopolitics and the local government of crime in Britain', *Theoretical Criminology*, vol 9, no 3, pp 265-87.

Stenson, K. and Edwards, A. (2001) 'Crime control and liberal government: the "third way" and the return to the local', in K. Stenson and R.R. Sullivan (eds) *Crime, risk and justice: The politics of crime control in liberal democracies*, Cullompton: Willan Publishing.

Stenson, K. and Edwards, A. (2003) 'Crime control and local governance: the struggle for sovereignty in advanced liberal polities', *Contemporary Politics*, vol 9, no 2, pp 203-18.

Stenson, K. and Edwards, A. (2004) 'Policy transfer in local crime control: beyond naïve emulation', in T. Newburn and R. Sparks (eds) *Criminal justice and political cultures: National and international dimensions of crime control*, Cullompton: Willan Publishing.

Stenson, K. and Watt, P. (1999) 'Crime, risk and governance in a southern English village', in G. Dingwall and S. Moody (eds) *Crime and conflict in the countryside*, Cardiff: University of Wales Press.

Swanstrom, T. (2002) 'Are fear and urbanism at war?', *Urban Affairs Review*, vol 38, no 1, pp 135-40.

Talen, E. (1999) 'Sense of community and neighbourhood form: an assessment of the social doctrine of the new urbanism', *Urban Studies*, vol 36, no 8, pp 1361-79.

Talen, E. (2005) *New urbanism and American planning: The conflict of cultures*, London: Routledge.

Taylor, M. (2000) 'Communities in the lead: power, organisational capacity and social capital', *Urban Studies*, no 37, pp 1019-35.

Taylor, R.B. (1999) *Crime, grime, fear, and decline: A longitudinal look*, National Institute of Justice Research in Brief, Washington, DC: National Institute of Justice.

Taylor, R.B. (2005) 'The incivilities or "broken windows" thesis', in L.E. Sullivan (ed) *Encyclopedia of law enforcement*, Thousand Oaks, CA: Sage Publications.

Tempest, M and Batty, D. (2004) 'Q & A: the Civil Contingencies Bill', *The Guardian* (http://society.guardian.co.uk/emergencyplanning/story/0,14501,1203817,00.html, 09/01/07).

Thompson, D. (2005) '£2.8 m', *The Journal* (Newcastle, UK), 29 January (http://icnewcastle.icnetwork.co.uk/0100news/thejournal/thejournal/tm_method=full%26objectid=15137751%26siteid=5008 1-name_page.html, 01/01/07).

Thrift, N. (2005) 'But malice afterthought: cities and the natural history of hatred', *Transactions of the British Institute of Geographers*, vol 30, no 2, pp 133-50.

Timmerman, P. (1981) *Vulnerability, resilience and the collapse of society: A review of models and possible climatic applications*, Toronto: Institute for Environmental Studies, University of Toronto.

Toynbee, P. (1998) 'The estate they're in', *The Guardian*, 15 September.

Toynbee, P. (2003) *Hard work: Life in low-pay Britain*, London: Bloomsbury.

Turok, I. (2004) 'Scottish urban policy: continuity, change and uncertainty post-devolution', in C. Johnstone and M. Whitehead (eds) *New horizons in British urban policy: Perspectives on New Labour's urban renaissance*, Aldershot: Ashgate.

Urban Parks Forum (2002) *Public parks assessment: A survey of local authority owned parks focussing on parks of historic interest*, Reading: Urban Parks Forum.

Urban Task Force (1999) *Towards an urban renaissance*, London: The Stationery Office; E & FN Spon.

Urban Task Force (2005) *Towards a strong urban renaissance*, London: Urban Task Force.

Urry, J. (2000) *Sociology beyond societies: Mobilities for the twenty-first century*, London: Routledge.

Vale, L. J. and Campanella, T. J. (2005) *The resilient city: How modern cities recover from disaster*, Oxford: Oxford University Press.

Vidler, A. (2001) 'The city transformed: designing defensible space', *New York Times*, online, 23 September.

Wacquant, L. (1999) *Prisons of poverty*, Minneapolis, MS: University of Minnesota Press.

Wacquant, L. (2001) 'The penalisation of poverty and the rise of neo-liberalism', *European Journal of Criminal Policy and Research*, no 9, pp 401-12.

Wacquant, L. (2006) *Punishing the poor: The new government of social insecurity*, Durham, NC: Duke University Press.

Walklate, S. and Evans, K. (1999) *Zero tolerance or community tolerance? Managing crime in high crime areas*, Aldershot: Ashgate.

Walsh, C. (2002) 'Curfews: no more hanging around', *Youth Justice*, vol 2, no 2, pp 70-81.

Ward, K. (2003) 'Entrepreneurial urbanism: state restructuring and civilizing "new" East Manchester', *Area*, vol 35, no 2, pp 116-27.

Warren, R. (2002) 'Situating the city and September 11th: military urban doctrine, "pop–up" armies and spatial chess', *International Journal of Urban and Regional Research*, vol 26, no 3, pp 614-19.

Watt, P. (2003) 'Urban marginality and labour market restructuring: local authority tenants and employment in an inner London borough', *Urban Studies*, vol 40, no 9, pp 1769-89.

Watt, P. and Jacobs, K. (2000) 'Discourses of social exclusion – an analysis of *Bringing Britain together: A national strategy for neighbourhood renewal*', *Housing, Theory and Society*, vol 17, no 1, pp 14-26.

Webster, W.R. (2004) 'The diffusion, regulation and governance of closed-circuit television in the UK', *Surveillance & Society*, vol 2, nos 2/3, pp 230-50 (www.surveillance-and-society.org/articles2(2)/diffusion.pdf, 09/01/07).

Whitehead, M. (2004) 'The urban neighbourhood and the moral geographies of British urban policy', in C. Johnstone and M. Whitehead (eds) *New horizons in British urban policy*, Aldershot: Ashgate, pp 59-73.

Whitehead, M. and Johnstone, C. (eds) (2001) *New horizons in British urban policy: Perspectives on New Labour's urban renaissance*, Aldershot: Ashgate.

Wiles, P. and Pease, K. (2000) 'Crime prevention and community safety: Tweedledum and Tweedledee?', in S. Ballintyne, K. Pease and V. McLaren (eds) *Secure foundations: Key issues in crime prevention, crime reduction and community safety*, London: Institute for Public Policy Research.

Wilkins, L. (1991) *Punishment, and crime and market forces*, Aldershot: Dartmouth.

Williams, C.A. (2003) 'Police surveillance and the emergence of CCTV in the 1960s', in M. Gill (ed) *CCTV*, Leicester: Perpetuity Press.

Williams, R.J. (2004) *The anxious city: English urbanism in the late twentieth century*, London: Routledge.

Willis, S. (2006) 'Guantanamo's symbolic economy', *New Left Review*, no 39, pp 123-31.

Wilson, J.Q. (1975) *Thinking about crime*, New York, NY: Basic Books.

Wilson, J.Q. and Kelling, G.L. (1982) 'Broken windows: the police and neighbourhood safety', *The Atlantic Monthly*, March, vol 249, no 3, pp 29-38.

Wilson, R. and Wylie, D. (1992) *The dispossessed*, London: Picador.

Wilson, W.J. (1987) *The truly disadvantaged*, Chicago, IL: University of Chicago Press.

Wood, M. (2004) *Perceptions and experiences of anti-social behaviour: Findings from the 2003/2004 British Crime Survey*, Home Office Online Report 49/04, London: Home Office.

Woolley, H. (2006) 'Freedom of the city: contemporary issues and policy influences on children and young people's use of public open space in England', *Children's Geographies*, vol 4, no 1, pp 45-59.

YJB (Youth Justice Board) (2005) *Anti-Social Behaviour Orders: An assessment of current management information systems and the scale of Anti-social Behaviour Order breaches resulting in custody*, London: YJB for England and Wales.

Young, J. (1999) *The exclusive society: Social exclusion, crime and difference in late modernity*, London: Sage Publications.

Young, J. (2001) 'Identity, community and social exclusion', in R. Matthews and J. Pitts (eds) *Crime, disorder and community safety: A new agenda*, London: Routledge.

Zedner, L. (2006) 'Policing before and after the police: the historical antecedents of contemporary crime control', *The British Journal of Criminology*, no 46, pp 78-96.

Zukin, S. (1995) *The culture of cities*, Oxford: Blackwell.

Index